I0730698

PROCEEDINGS

OF THE

National Rivers and Harbors Congress

ELEVENTH CONVENTION
WASHINGTON, D. C.
DECEMBER 9, 10 and 11, 1914

Published Under Authority of the Board of Directors by

S. A. THOMPSON, Secretary-Treasurer

824 Colorado Building, Washington, D. C.

Douglas A. Brown, Official Reporter

Cincinnati, Ohio

PRESS OF W. F. ROBERTS CO.
WASHINGTON, D. C.

FOREWORD

THE 1914 Convention of the NATIONAL RIVERS AND HARBORS CONGRESS—a full report of the proceedings of which will be found in the following pages—was the eleventh convention held by the organization since its formation in 1901, and the tenth since its reorganization in 1906.

The first convention was called after a Rivers and Harbors Bill had been talked to death in the closing hours of a short session of Congress   The eleventh convention was held after a filibuster in the Senate had compelled the substitution of a lump-sum appropriation of $20,000,000 for a carefully prepared and thoroughly meritorious bill carrying a total of more than $53,000,000.

The Convention of 1914 was held during a time of serious business depression due to the war in Europe. Added to this was the fact that the railroads of the country, without exception and for the first time, refused any reduction of rates, although low rates were granted to scores of other gatherings, many of which were smaller in size and less in importance than our annual convention   It is both significant and gratifying that even under such conditions nearly one thousand delegates were present, coming from 37 States, the District of Columbia and Canada, and representing 246 cities and 138 commercial organizations.

Whenever the people of the United States shall realize that the complete development of all our resources and the attainment of the highest possible prosperity can be secured only through the improvement and utilization of our waterways and harbors. there is no question that the needed appropriations will be forthcoming. It is the work of this organization to create an intelligent, forceful, result-compelling public opinion on the waterway question through the presentation of facts and of arguments based thereon. It is believed that the present volume will be found a worthy contribution to that end.

NATIONAL RIVERS AND HARBORS CONGRESS,

JOSEPH E RANSDELL, *President*

S A. THOMPSON, *Secretary*

NATIONAL

RIVERS AND HARBORS CONGRESS

OFFICERS 1914-1915

PRESIDENT

JOSEPH E RANSDELL..Lake Providence, La , Washington, D C.

SECRETARY-TREASURER

S. A. THOMPSON..824 Colorado Building, Washington, D C.

SERGEANT-AT-ARMS

JOHN I MARTIN ... . St. Louis, Mo.

DIRECTORS

*Honorary for Life.. .. .. J F ELLISON, Cincinnati, Ohio

North Atlantic Seaboard—

OLIN J. STEPHENS .. . .New York City
WILLIAM C. SPROUL ....Chester, Pa
THEODORE JUSTICE ....Philadelphia, Pa
E W DOUGLAS .. . .Troy, N. Y.
WILLARD THOMPSON . ...Baltimore, Md
FRANK FESSENDEN CRANE .. . ... Quincy, Mass.
A V HAMBURG ... .Newark, N J
CHARLES R. MILLER .. .. Wilmington, Del
ROLLIN S WOODRUFF .. . . New Haven, Conn
GEORGE L WHITFORD .... Warner, N H
GEORGE F. WASHBURN ... . Boston, Mass

Hudson, Champlain and Genesee Valleys District—

    Lewis Nixon ... .New York City
    F W Joslin . . ..Troy, N Y
    John R. Myers......... .. ...Rouses Point, N Y.
    Edward N McKinney ....Albany, N. Y
    James T Hutchings ....Rochester, N Y

South Atlantic Seaboard—

    Walter Clark . . . .Raleigh, N. C.
    Albert Schulteis* .... .Washington, D. C
    John C Freeman .. .. Richmond, Va.
    D U Fletcher .. ..Jacksonville, Fla
    F. Horton Colcock . ... Columbia, S. C.
    L. R Aiken .. .. Brunswick, Ga
    Howell M Miller .... .Washington, Va.
    John T Davis .. .. .Columbus, Ga
    Reid Whitford ... . Charleston, S. C.

Gulf Seaboard—

    Martin Behrman .. .. New Orleans, La
    W. W. Brandon ... .Tuscaloosa, Ala.
    Thomas P Hale. ... . Gulfport, Miss
    J. W. Worthington . .. . .Sheffield, Ala
    T. Cheney Lawless . . . Garden City, La.
    J S Cullinan... . ...Houston, Texas
    Frank P Holland . ...Dallas, Texas
    Roy Miller . .. . Corpus Christi, Texas

Mississippi Valley District—

    W. K. Kavanaugh . . . . St Louis, Mo
    J. L. Messmore .... .St. Louis, Mo
    John A Fox . ...Memphis, Tenn
    Charles Scott . . . .Rosedale, Miss
    Thomas Wilkinson ... .Burlington, Iowa
    M J Roach . . . . .. Memphis, Tenn.
    J. W Cooper ....St Paul, Minn

---

*Succeeded M. I. Weller, Died February 2, 1915

W. G. STREETT . . . .   Lake Village. Ark
A. L SHAPLEIGH .... .St. Louis, Mo
W. F. DECKER ....Minneapolis, Minn.

Great Lakes District—

JAMES H. DAVIDSON ....Oskosh. Wis
HENRY W. HILL   ....Buffalo, N. Y.
T. EDWARD WILDER . . .. Chicago, Ill.
JULIUS H. BARNES ....Duluth. Minn
E L SOUTHWORTH .... .Toledo, Ohio
P W CULLINAN.....................Oswego, N Y.
PERRY A. RANDALL .. .. Ft Wayne, Ind
WILLIAM A MEESE ....Moline, Ill
A. G. WELLS ....DePere. Wis
J W. CASWELL . ... Huntington. Ind

Ohio Valley District—

ALBERT BETTINGER ....Cincinnati, Ohio
JOHN L. VANCE .. ..Columbus, Ohio
WILLIAM B. RODGERS ....Pittsburgh, Pa.
GEORGE PARSONS .. .. .Cairo, Ill.
PINKNEY VARBLE ....Louisville, Ky.
M. C GARBER ....Madison, Ind.
J. H ROHSENBERGER ....Evansville, Ind.
R F SOMERVILLE . . ..Dayton, Ohio
GEORGE M. VERITY ....Middletown, Ohio
C. D DOTSON . . . .Parkersburg, W Va

Tennessee and Cumberland Districts—

M T BRYAN . . .. Nashville, Tenn
J A. PATTEN ... .Chattanooga, Tenn.
E. C CAMP .. . .Knoxville, Tenn

Arkansas Valley District—

GEORGE SENGEL . . . .Ft Smith, Ark
R T. DANIEL . . .. Tulsa. Okla
W M KAVANAUGH .. ..Little Rock, Ark.

Missouri Valley District—

W. T Bland . . . . .Kansas City, Mo.
I. P. Baker . . . . Bismarck, N D
Harry L George . . . . St. Joseph, Mo.
W B. Wait . . . . Chamberlain, S D.

Pacific Coast District—

A H Devers . . . . .Portland, Ore.
Joseph R Knowland . . .Alameda, Calif
W. D. Lyman . . . .Walla Walla, Wash
R C. Beach . . . . Lewiston, Idaho
J. R. McLaughlin . . . . Seattle, Wash

Vice-Presidents

Alabama. . . . . Henry A Bradshaw, Florence
Arkansas. . . . . .O. N. Killough, Wynne
California . . . . .William D. Stephens, Los Angeles
Colorado . . . . . Brooks Irione, Colorado Springs
Connecticut. . . . . .Frank H. Johnston, New Britain
Delaware . . . . .William H. Heald, Wilmington
District of Columbia . . . William T Galliher, Washington
Florida . . . . W. L Straub, St Petersburg
Georgia . . . . .R. J. Davant, Savannah
Idaho . . . . Frank R Gooding, Gooding
Illinois. . . . . .M. F. Rittenhouse, Chicago
Indiana . . . . J. W. Gleichman, Evansville
Iowa. . . . . .Irving C. Norwood, Davenport
Kansas. . . . . .W R Childs, Kansas City
Kentucky. . . . . .Benjamin W. Lord, Danville
Louisiana. . . . . T. B Gilbert, Wisner
Maine . . . . Silas B Adams, Portland
Maryland. . . . . .Key Compton, Baltimore*
Massachusetts. . . . . .John J Martin, Boston
Michigan. . . . . .William Alden Smith, Grand Rapids
Minnesota. . . . . George V. B Hill, Minneapolis

---

*Succeeded Gen Wm D Gill, Died February 9, 1915

Mississippi. . . . . EARL BREWER, Jackson
Missouri . . . . W S. DICKEY, Kansas City
Montana . . . . F E STRANAHAN, Ft Benton
Nebraska . . . . THOMAS B. COLEMAN, Omaha
Nevada . .   . . FRANCIS G. NEWLANDS, Reno
New Jersey. . . . . FREDERICK W DONNELLY, Trenton
New Mexico . . . . W A. FLEMING JONES, Las Cruces
New York . . . . ROBERT J McFARLAND. Brooklyn
North Carolina. . . . . JOHN H. SMALL, Washington
North Dakota . . . . JOHN BURKE, Bismarck
Ohio. . . . . E. C GIBBS. Cincinnati
Oklahoma . . . . P. S MITCHELL, Muskogee
Oregon. . . . . J W BENNETT, Marshfield
Pennsylvania . . . . T J. KEENAN. Pittsburgh
Rhode Island . . . . PETER GOELET GERRY, Newport
South Carolina . . . . WILSON G. HARVEY. Charleston
South Dakota . . . . ABNER AYRES, Chamberlain
Tennessee . . . . C E BUEK, Chattanooga
Texas . . . . .GEORGE WAVERLY BRIGGS, Galveston
Vermont . . . . JAMES P. TAYLOR, Burlington
Virginia . .   . . R A DOBIE. Norfolk
Washington . . . . MILLER FREEMAN. Seattle
West Virginia. . . . . C R WILSON, Huntington
Wisconsin . . . . WILLIAM GEORGE BRUCE. Milwaukee
Travelers' Protective Association
                W. EDGAR JENKINS, Baltimore, Md
United Commercial Travelers of America
                C W HODSON. Portland. Oregon

PROCEEDINGS OF THE
ELEVENTH ANNUAL CONVENTION

NATIONAL RIVERS AND HARBORS CONGRESS

The Eleventh Convention of the NATIONAL RIVERS AND HARBORS CONGRESS was held in the Assembly Hall of The New Willard Hotel. Washington. D. C, on December 9, 10 and 11, 1914, under the presidency of Hon Jos E Ransdell, United States Senator from Louisiana   A report of the proceedings will be found in the following pages.

FIRST SESSION
Wednesday Morning, December 9

On calling the Convention to order President Ransdell said

PRESIDENT RANSDELL—I will ask the delegates to rise while Rev Charles F Steck, D.D, Pastor of Epiphany Lutheran Church, of this city, invokes the blessing of Almighty God upon the deliberations of this Convention

INVOCATION
By Rev. Charles F. Steck, D.D.

Almighty and everlasting God. Who art worthy to be had in reverence by all the children of men, we adore Thee as the Father of lights from Whom cometh every good and perfect gift. We gratefully acknowledge that we are the work of Thy hand, that all our outward advantages and enjoyments are the gifts of Thy Providence; and that all our consolation and peace flow from Thee.

We thank Thee that the lines have fallen for us in pleasant places and that ours is a goodly heritage   Thou hast done great things for us, whereof we are glad   Ours is a land in which Thy Name is honored and in which the light of Thy Gospel shines —a land which is the glory of all lands—the home of liberty, of plenty and of peace.

We thank Thee that Thou art easy to be entreated, and that Thou hast taught us that for the things we desire Thou wouldst be inquired of, to do them for us   Forgive us, then, our sins, personal and national, pardon our transgressions, and establish our goings.   Bless the President and his Cabinet, the Congress and all our rulers   Give them a spirit of understanding and might, a spirit of knowledge and the fear of the Lord.   May all our people come to acknowledge Thee as the Ruler of rulers, and may we ever dwell together in unity and in all godliness and honesty.   Bless all men with knowledge and wisdom, with faith and love, with peace and hope   Especially do we commend to Thee those nations who are now at war   Overrule the counsels which make for continued bloodshed, and out of the dreadful carnage, confusion and destruction which have marked these past weeks bring, by the exercise of Thy great might, an order and peace for which all the world shall be glad.

And now, O Lord, we pray Thee, command Thy blessings upon these, Thy servants, who have assembled here in the interests of a policy whose end is to advantage the people of this and of all lands   We thank Thee for those natural resources in which our country abounds, and we would that the minds of these men, so willing to give to this business both time and thought, may be more and more impressed with the fact that they are workers together with Thee when they unselfishly build upon those foundations which Thou hast laid   Give them wisdom in their deliberations, harmony in their conclusions, and a constantly increasing influence in all that which has to do with promoting sound prosperity. proper civic pride, and that righteousness which exalteth the nation.

Grant these blessings, and all others for which we should pray, for the sake of our Lord Jesus Christ.   Amen.

PRESIDENT RANSDELL—Ladies and gentlemen, the man who is to open our Convention needs no introduction to an American audience. It gives me the greatest pleasure to present our distinguished Secretary of State, Hon. William Jennings Bryan. (Applause.)

Opening Address—Hon. William Jennings Bryan
Secretary of State

MR. CHAIRMAN AND MEMBERS OF THE CONVENTION

I am on the program for an address of welcome, and an address of welcome is an address devoted to assuring you that we are glad to see you; and I suppose that after I have employed enough words to leave no doubt that we are glad to see you, I will have finished my duties so far as delivering an address of welcome is concerned.

I know of no place where an address of welcome can be delivered with more ease or with more sincerity than in the City of Washington, for here are assembled the representatives of this entire nation; here are gathered those who represent the executive, the legislative and the judicial departments of our National Government. And those who, like you, come from the various States can feel certain that when you arrive here you will receive a royal welcome, for you are the sovereigns of the nation calling in the Capital where your servants serve you   (Applause.)

Let me, therefore, as one of your servants, as one of your "hired men," give you emphatic assurance that those who draw salaries paid by you are glad to see you. We ask you to make yourselves at home in this city. which, more than any other city in the Union, belongs to you   (Applause.)

But I am not content to stop when I have finished the address of welcome   I am afraid you would be disappointed if I did not do more than the program leads you to expect me to do; you would be disappointed if I did not commend the purposes for which you meet; and I would be disappointed if I were not permitted to commend those purposes. (Applause.)

You represent a very ancient method of transportation; for transportation by water far antedates transportation by the modern method of the railway   If you spoke of being interested in waterways and said nothing more than that, some doubt might be left as to which kind of waterways you meant. the natural waterways or those railroads which have been made waterways by the infusion of a large amount of water (Laughter and applause), but when you are spoken of as friends of rivers and harbors, no doubt is left as to the particular kind of transportation in which you are interested. You are dealing with the waterways, so to speak, that God Himself gave; for if you are interested in the deepening of our harbors, it is that the boats may come into them and go out from them, the boats that traverse the trackless deep. And if you are interested in rivers and in canals, it is that you may increase the means of transportation; and you are wise in taking as your motto, "A policy and not a project." (Applause.)

It is much easier to define a policy than to define a project, for a policy rests upon a principle, and people comprehend a principle much more easily than they comprehend details of a project; and the principle is entirely free from the suspicion that sometimes rests upon a project; and you do well to put emphasis upon the policy, upon the principle. I know of no better wish that I can express for you than to make the policy so popular that it will not be necessary to take up questionable projects in order to secure the substantial things that are necessary. (Applause.)

You will find that every River and Harbor Bill is attacked, not because of the principle involved, not because of the policy which it embodies, but because of some project that is included in the bill; and I think that the reason why questionable projects are sometimes included in a bill, and thus bring odium upon the principle involved, is that there is so much lethargy among people who do not feel an immediate concern in a particular appropriation, that those who stand back of a great principle are compelled to reinforce themselves by bringing in those who do have an immediate interest in some local project.

I say I know of no better wish that I can express for you than that you shall be able to so emphasize the principle and that you shall be able to make so popular the policy, that people will support that which is necessary and that which is justified without stopping to ask whether an appropriation is included for their own immediate district. (Applause.)

To do this I think it is important that you present the real fundamental propositions which underlie transportation by water. It will need very little argument to convince the public of the necessity for appropriations that deepen harbors; for, unless we have harbors, it is impossible for us to give that encouragement to foreign commerce we all desire our country to give; unless we have harbors into which large ships can come and out of which large ships can go, it is impossible for us to live up to the possibilities of international commerce today But when we come to what might be called interior applications of this principle, the important thing, I think, is to show that transportation by water is cheaper than transportation by rail can possibly be. (Applause.)

Now the economic question, the question of necessary cost, is, after all, the final test; and if it can be shown that a railroad can be conducted more cheaply than it is conducted today; if it can be shown that a railroad can be built for less than it can be built today; and if proof can be furnished that merchandise can be carried by rail at lower cost than it is carried today, then the efforts of the people will be directed toward the securing of conditions that will enable the people of this country to exchange their products at that lowered cost.

But if statistics show that you can transport merchandise of a certain kind by water cheaper than it can be transported by rail, then you can rest assured that the public mind will ultimately turn toward water transportation because of the economy that it brings to the people. (Applause) I am in favor of the water wagon (Applause); and the boat is the original water wagon (Applause) But you cannot have a water wagon without water, and therefore we must develop our internal transportation to furnish a chance for the water wagon (Applause)

I am sorry that I am not to be permitted to hear the distinguished representative from China (referring to Mr. Kai fu Shah, who was present upon the stage) I am sorry that my time is so limited that I shall not be able to listen to his presentation of the subject as it presents itself in that great Kingdom of the Orient—no, not the Kingdom of the Orient—that great Republic now of the Orient (Applause.) We no longer speak of the "Middle Kingdom" now. It is the great Republic of the East (Applause.)

It has been a long time since people began to develop the advantages of the waterways I feel that we have much to learn in regard to the possibilities of water transportation in the United States; and I am here to say to you that I have such faith in the intelligence of the American people, such confidence in the final triumph of everything that is right, that, believing as I do that it is possible to transport certain kinds of freight by water cheaper than it ever will be possible to transport that kind of freight by rail, I have absolute confidence that this country will turn its attention toward the development of its waterways, and that finally there will be unanimous approval of those things that can be shown to contribute to this end. (Applause.)

Now that is all I care to include in my address of welcome I welcome you most sincerely. In so far as I can speak as a representative of the Administration, I welcome you in the name of the Administration (Applause); but, more than that, speaking for myself, as a citizen of a great nation, as a citizen interested in everything that concerns my nation's welfare, I bid you God-speed in creating sentiment in favor of the policy of improving our waterways, both those that connect us with the outside world, and those that contribute to the advancement of our domestic commerce.

I thank you. (Applause)

PRESIDENT RANSDELL—We are exceedingly fortunate in having on our program this morning a representative, and an able one, of the oldest civilization (Applause) and the youngest republic on earth. (Applause.)

Permit me to introduce Mr Kai fu Shah, Envoy Extraordinary and Minister Plenipotentiary from China to the United States. (Applause.)

THE WATERWAYS OF CHINA

Address—Mr. Kai fu Shah

Envoy Extraordinary and Minister Plenipotentiary of China

Mr Chairman, Ladies and Gentlemen

I appreciate highly the honor you have done me by inviting me to address this Congress. It is a great pleasure to me to be able to meet in this assembly men who have transformed desert wastes into cultivated fields and men who have made two blades grow where was one before

During my stay in this country I have learned, as well as seen, something of the wonders achieved by the genius and enterprise of American engineers Nothing seems impossible for them They have harnessed the mighty forces of Niagara; they have impounded vast volumes of water for the use of agriculture; they have put under control the floods of the Mississippi; and, as a crowning achievement, they have completed the Panama Canal. These are indeed victories of peace no less renowned than those of war (Applause)

For the conservancy of her natural resources, China has problems similar to those of the United States The United States has already solved some of the problems, while China is beginning to tackle them in good earnest This is specially the case with the improvement of rivers, harbors, canals and other waterways. China is very fortunate in having three systems of large rivers that form a network of waterways covering the whole country—namely, the Yellow River in the north, the Yangtze River in the center, and the West River in the south.

The most important river, of course, is the Yangtze This great river has its source in the tableland of Tibet, and flows from 3,000 to 4,000 miles into the Yellow Sea Ocean-going steamers can ascend the stream for 500 miles to Hankow; smaller steamers can go 500 miles farther to Ichang; and small boats can make their way 1,000 miles still farther to Chungking. The river is thus navigable for 2,000 miles from its mouth, and renders the nooks and corners of the country readily accessible

One of the sources of the Yangtze is the Min River, which flows between immense gorges in a north and south direction through the Province of Szechuen   This river was harnessed over two thousand years ago by a noted Chinese engineer and made to contribute to the prosperity of the Plain of Chengtu   This plain is situated near the center of the Province, 1,700 feet above the level of the sea, and rises gradually from southeast to northwest   It has an area of about 3,500 square miles, that is, a little smaller than the State of Connecticut.   The Min River enters this plateau from the northwest.   In times of flood it is a raging stream

What the Chinese engineer did was to make a deep cut through the gorge and allow the water to flow into the plain   This work was carried out so successfully that the whole Plain of Chengtu, which was undoubtedly the dried-up bottom of a mountain lake, was transformed into what has since become known as the Garden of China.   The irrigation works thus inaugurated have been maintained from year to year in good repair ever since.   In making the annual repairs the injunction left by the famous engineer has always been observed   It is "Dig the channels deep, and keep the banks low."   These words in large Chinese characters may now be seen everywhere engraved on the rocks.

The Chinese have, in the course of centuries, built a network of canals for irrigation and transportation purposes   The largest single canal is the Yun Ho, or, as it is commonly called, the Grand Canal   The Grand Canal is the work of many generations   The middle section was built about the 6th century B C.; the southern section during the year 605-617 A D ; and the northern section during the years 1280-1283 A.D.   This canal furnishes the means of transporting grain from the south to the north

I am glad to be able to confirm what Professor F. H King says in his book entitled "Farmers of Forty Centuries" about the canals in China.   On his trip from Shanghai to Nanking he made a record of the number of canals seen from the train close along the track, and he saw as many as 593 canals in a distance of 162 miles.   Again, in a district with an area of 176 by 160 miles, a portion of Chekiang and Kiangsu Provinces, he found as many as 2,700 canals, the total length of which he estimated at not less than 25,000 miles. He calculated that 40 canals across the United States from east to west and 60 from north to south might not equal in number of miles those in China (Applause.)

That China recognizes the importance of improving her waterways is shown by the establishment of the Bureau of River Conservancy The purpose of this Bureau is to investigate and deal with the irrigation and conservancy problems that are confronting the Government. The foremost problem which the Government has to deal with now is the conservancy of the Huai River This river traverses the Provinces of Honan, Anhui and Kiangsu In rainy seasons those regions are usually flooded because the waters cannot find an outlet to the sea Over 4,100 years ago the situation was very much worse than that of the present day. As the people were suffering from disastrous floods the Government sent a distinguished engineer to undertake the work of reclaiming the land He was at this work for 13 years and was so successful that he was afterwards called to the throne. This was Yu, who has been called "The Great" to this day by reason of this great achievement.

Steps have been taken by my Government to meet the present situation, and an arrangement has been made with the American Red Cross to undertake the work For its humanitarian work in China the American Red Cross deserves the goodwill and thanks of the Chinese people (Applause) And I take this opportunity to thank the President and the American Congress for designating such a distinguished engineer as Col William L. Sibert to go to China at the head of a Board of American Engineers last summer to see what could be done (Applause.) They have since returned to this country and submitted a report In the opinion of the Board the waters of the Huai River should be drained into the Yangtze Enough land will be reclaimed and improved to make this enterprise successful from a financial point of view. They estimate the undertaking to cost $30,-000,000, while the value of the benefits is put at $48,350,000 The work, in their opinion, can be completed in six years

China is a land that offers unlimited opportunities for American capital, and I hope that American capitalists will take advantage of every opportunity they now have.

I thank you, ladies and gentlemen, for your courtesy and attention. (Applause.)

PRESIDENT RANSDELL—Our program indicates that the next speaker was to have been Lieut.-Col William L Sibert, U S Engineer Corps, late member of the Panama Canal Commission, who was to have told us something of flood conditions in China Unfortunately Colonel Sibert can not be with us until tomorrow. It is a pleasure deferred, but not lost, as all of us will hear him tomorrow, when he will tell us of the flood problem on those great Chinese rivers to which the Minister has alluded

In the place of Colonel Sibert I have asked to address you this morning a gentleman who was present when the NATIONAL RIVERS AND HARBORS CONGRESS was born in 1901, and who has never missed attendance upon a single Convention since He is known, honored and loved by every waterway man in the United States, Hon Albert Bettinger, of Cincinnati, Ohio (Applause.)

Address—Hon. Albert Bettinger
Cincinnati, Ohio

MR. PRESIDENT, LADIES AND GENTLEMEN:

This organization had its beginning in 1901, in the City of Baltimore The purpose of its organization at that time was to register in a public and impressive manner a protest against the fact that a Rivers and Harbors Bill had been talked to death in the National Congress That purpose accomplished, the meeting adjourned

The Association was revived in January, 1906; the purpose of its revival being, as its prospectus stated, to establish in these United States a healthy public sentiment in favor of the improvement of waterways, and to lift legislation of that character out of the slough of "pork barrelism" into which it had at times drifted

Since that time this Association has held annual Conventions, except that in the first year of its revival, 1906, it held two Conventions   It has had the support of citizens from every corner of the country, every State in the Union participating in its deliberations.   Governors from nearly every State have accepted invitations to speak from this rostrum and to lend their words of support and inspiration to the acts of this Congress.

The political parties of the country without exception took note of the splendid work that this Association was doing, and endorsed its acts and its policies   In short, the commendation of its acts was unanimous.

Its influence was acknowledged by the Congress of the United States   Times without number members of both Houses appeared on this rostrum and gave us their words of encouragement, and acknowledged the great service which this Association was performing in bringing before the public in a favorable light the matter of river and harbor improvements

Not one word of adverse criticism was published or uttered in this wide land against the policy, against the slogan, against the principle, which this Association was advocating, until recently a Member of Congress, of the House of Representatives, took it upon himself to denounce this Association as a great lobbying scheme, and in every other way, by direct charge and innuendo, attributed to it a perniciousness of purpose and of action that could be applied only to the most unconscionable lobbyist.

There was no occasion created by that fact for us to take any note of it whatsoever; and there would not be now any occasion for taking any note of the effort that was made to have a Congressional committee appointed to investigate the actions of this Association, were it not for one fact, that is, that one of the most distinguished members of the Senate, the man who gave us more inspiration than any other for the organization of this Association, and for its conduct and for its activity, by letter commended and endorsed the course of this Member of Congress; and I refer to Senator Burton

It is not my purpose to criticize the Senator, or to say anything other than to bring to your notice his own words.   I am

going to ask you for a few moments to listen to the reading of a
number of extracts from his speeches, and then I am going to
ask you to hear a few extracts from speeches of other notable
men in this country—I want to add nothing of my own—in
praise or commendation of the acts of this Association

In 1906, when this Association held the first meeting after
its reorganization, Senator Burton said this to us:

> "I thank you most sincerely for this very kindly re-
> ception   It gives me sincere pleasure to look upon a
> convention of delegates representing, as I am in-
> formed, more than half of the States of the Union,
> gathered together to favor river and harbor improve-
> ments   I recall very vividly a similar gathering in a
> hall of Johns Hopkins University in October, 1901."

And then, after relating the circumstances that brought the
Association together, he proceeds, and this is what he said of
the policy

> "At the end of a preceding Congress a River and
> Harbor Bill had been talked to death.   That Conven-·
> tion pursued a course which commends itself, I think,
> to the judgment of every one who has considered the
> question of the best means of advocating legislation
> here at Washington   It was decided that no argu-
> ments should be heard on behalf of any specific project,
> but the object of the Convention was to give its sanc-
> tion and advocacy to the general subject of the im-
> provement of the rivers and harbors and waterways of
> the country.   It conferred a very substantial benefit
> It aided the Committee on Rivers and Harbors very
> materially in its work, and in the next Congress, at its
> first session, we passed and obtained the approval of a
> bill larger than the one which failed in March, 1901 "

In December of the same year we held another Convention, and then Mr Burton appeared before this body and said this

"It gives me the greatest encouragement to recognize the growth of the movement which is exemplified by this Congress The first Convention in 1901, in Baltimore, although an influential body, was small in number. The next meeting, less than a year ago in this room, though showing a considerable increase, did not compare with this. This gathering, so representative in its nature, including men in all walks of life, including all localities, shows that the people of the United States are alive to their advocacy of more liberal appropriations for rivers and harbors (Applause) * * * I remember five years ago that a bill which we had prepared very carefully was killed by obstructive tactics in one of our legislative bodies at the very closing hour of the session It gives me pleasure to recount, also, that the following session it passed a measure more thoroughly brought up to date than the one which was lost, and including some larger amounts * * * First, it is my earnest desire that this Convention should not make specific recommendations for any particular project in the United States. That does not mean that you are not going to be earnest on behalf of that which most concerns your own localities You would not be true to your cities and your States if you were not, but this is a National movement The spirit of this movement is that the United States will be benefited by more liberal river and harbor improvements, and if that sentiment prevails, we, the Congressmen and Senators, are but your servants; you, the voters, are the priests in the temple of government. If profane hands defile the altars of administration, it is because you stand idly by. You are our bosses—our governors. Now, then, it is desirable that you should express your opinion and lead the sentiment of the country in favor of the idea that

the transportation interests, as represented by improvement of the waterways, should receive the support of its people. When that idea becomes established, the Congress, upon which the responsibility of
legislation rests, can make provision for deserving improvements in the country   *   *   *   We have been
unable, with an average expenditure of twenty million dollars a year, to make that provision which we
would like to make for the country   We have been
doing the best we could.   *   *   *   I am thankful to
say that in this country of ours, more than in any
other country on the globe, the inland waterways and
harbors are free to an extent that obtains nowhere
else on the globe.   That is part of our national life.
*   *   *   I congratulate you upon this movement.
We certainly are interested in a cause which will help
this country of ours.   It is not merely the selfish
or the local interests of one locality, but it tends to the
upbuilding of our common country "

And so on for quantity.

In 1907 we have this:

"I congratulate the NATIONAL RIVERS AND HAR-
BORS CONGRESS   Rarely, if ever, has a gathering of this
kind assembled in larger numbers or with a more earnest purpose.   I congratulate the officers of this Congress, especially its President and its Secretary, for
their untiring and successful efforts.   *   *   *   I
commend this Congress for its broad policy.   Its fundamental platform has been, and I trust will continue,
that no special projects are to be advocated, but that
its delegates are to come together, as you are now
come together, from thirty-six States of the Union,
advocating a broad, general policy which shall be liberal to the whole country, but letting individual projects take care of themselves "

Now, then, so much for Mr. Burton to this Association—Senator Burton to this Association

Some of the provisions of the Rivers and Harbors Bill have been attacked. It has been stated that they have all of them, save one or two insignificant ones, been recommended by the Engineers; and the intimation has been thrown out time and again during the debates that the Engineers are not reliable in the information which they afford to the Congress of the United States, and that some better method must be devised by which the Congress may be instructed as to what projects deserve its attention   Let me read to you the report prepared by Mr. Burton, presumably because he was Chairman of the National Waterways Commission, upon that question

> "The Commission would advise that without careful and unbiased examination of proposed improvements no project should be adopted by Congress   Numerous propositions have been made for the creation of a Board of Public Works, or other bodies, which shall decide upon the feasibility and desirability of propositions for expenditures on rivers and harbors   The Commission is unwilling to recommend a change of this kind, and points to the fact that the past recommendations of the Engineer Corps have been carefully prepared and with a degree of expert knowledge and comprehension of the commercial needs of the country which could not well be supplied by any other body or organization   The advantages which attach to the Engineer Corps are that they are in the permanent service of the Government and are free from those influences which would inevitably be brought to bear upon them in civil life   Those engineers now engaged in the work are carefully trained in the planning and execution of these improvements, and have special qualifications for judging the feasibility and cost of proposed river and harbor projects. They also have a good general knowledge of the probable commercial results which would accrue, though on this

point the Commission would say that their opinions
have not been regarded as conclusive. In this connection the Commission would call attention to the
necessity for an increase in the number of the Engineer Corps " (Applause.)   ,

A more magnificent tribute could not have been uttered to
the reliability of the Engineer Corps, nor could it have been given
by one more familiar with the subject than Mr Burton. (Applause)

Now I want to invite your attention and just approval to
what has been said by a few of the great men of this country
from this platform to this Association; and what has been said
causes us to ponder, and ask ourselves the question, "What has
caused the change in the attitude of the distinguished Senator?
Has this Association changed? Has it changed its policy, or
its methods, or its purposes—or has the Senator changed?"

President Roosevelt, in the Belasco Theatre, Washington.
on December 8, 1908, in speaking of this Association to the Conservation Congress, said

"A special word is due the NATIONAL RIVERS AND
HARBORS CONGRESS. It is the one organization that is
advocating a waterway policy and not a waterway
project, and is national in its scope, for it represents
practically all the friends of waterway improvement
in the United States The question of river and harbor improvements and the benefit that each will bring
to the producer and consumer has, through its work,
been favorably and prominently brought to the attention of the country Prominent commercial organizations and men of character and influence throughout
practically every section of the country are enlisted in
the cause it represents Its work being strictly
national, and in no sense local or sectional. merits
and should receive the support of our citizens "
(Applause)

President Taft, in addressing the Lakes to the Gulf Deep Waterway Association, in Chicago, on October 7, 1908, said this:

"Perhaps the greatest influence toward the framing of a broad, comprehensive, progressive policy of river and harbor improvements is being exercised by the National Rivers and Harbors Congress Its motto is 'A Policy, not a Project.' Through its work the question of waterway improvements has been most prominently and favorably brought before the public; and men of the highest character and influence throughout the country are enlisting in its cause It urges the appropriation of fifty millions of dollars per annum Such a policy has my hearty approval" (Applause)

The distinguished, and now lamented, Chairman of the Rivers and Harbors Committee, of the House, Hon D. S Alexander, in addressing this Congress, used these words·

"In the meantime a great sentiment has been aroused throughout the country in favor of river and harbor improvements Beginning four or five years ago, it has continued to increase, rapidly growing in strength, until this city, in the last three or four years, has witnessed the presence of a great Rivers and Harbors Congress, representing the friends of river and harbor improvements from nearly every State in the Union This has had a decidedly leavening effect and the Committee on Rivers and Harbors believes that the time is now ripe for returning to the old custom of an annual River and Harbor Bill." (Applause.)

Hon Stephen M Sparkman, before he became Chairman of the Rivers and Harbors Committee, in an interview published in 1910, said:

"As much depends on the National Rivers and Harbors Congress, which meets in Washington, December 7-9th in national convention, as on the United

> States Congress, whether there will be a River and
> Harbor Bill this session The hands of the Federal
> Congress must be supported by this great body of
> waterway enthusiasts, otherwise we may be defeated
> in our plans."

In April, 1911, after he had become Chairman of that important committee, Mr Sparkman, in speaking of the propaganda inaugurated, said this:

> "The campaign of education which this great na-
> tional organization has been carrying on has been of
> vast benefit in creating public sentiment looking to the
> needs of the whole country along the line of making
> our rivers work and thereby assisting in the solution
> of the great problem of transportation." (Applause)

Coming now to a few of the Senators of the United States—
in a speech to this Convention, or to this body in 1907. Senator
Francis C. Newlands, United States Senator from Nevada.
Vice-Chairman of the Inland Waterways Commission, said:

> "It gives me great pleasure to be present at this
> Convention, for I know how important the meetings
> of this organization have been in forming public opin-
> ion The real legislative bodies of the country are
> composed of gatherings of this kind, meetings of men
> not engaged in politics, with a view to conference re-
> garding the general good Such bodies form public
> opinion The Congress of the United States records
> public opinion This RIVERS AND HARBORS CONGRESS
> has taken the initiative. The Congress of the United
> States rarely takes the initiative Men connected with
> such organizations as this lead; Congress usually
> follows " (Applause)

Now I fear that I am taking more time than I ought to, but
I want to read from an address by a distinguished man who

never has spoken without commanding the greatest possible respect. I refer to Senator Elihu Root (Applause), who appeared here as a special representative of the Administration, of which he was so conspicuous a part, and he said this

> "It is a great pleasure for me to extend to you a welcome from the National Administration upon your entrance to the duties which you have before you in the National Capital It is both a pleasure and a duty to express to this Congress the sincere appreciation and hearty sympathy of the National Administration in the great interests which you are seeking to subserve. The contribution of the National Government to the improvement of rivers and harbors in the United States has been a subject of much misunderstanding and of much unmerited criticism, deprecation and derision."

And it seems that we have not even now outlived that period.

> "Now it is time that something should be done, something sufficiently distinct and positive, compelling attention, making thought and consideration and correct understanding necessary among the people of the United States, so that they may come to a realization that the river and harbor improvement of the United States is no mere bartering of opportunities by politicians, but is a great matter of public policy * * * We have come to a point where the railroads of the country are unable to perform that function which is necessary to continued progress in the increase of our national weath Conditions are such that there is no human possibility that railroads can keep pace with the necessities of our natural production for the transportation of our products, and the one avenue that is open for us to keep up our progress is the avenue of water transportation." (Applause)

I have many more citations to which I might call your attention, but these will suffice to show to you that we have had the recognition and encouragement of the best statesmen of the land. They show that we have followed the direction of these great public men, we have taken their advice, we have worked under their inspiration; and we have not swerved a hair's breadth from the original motto of this Association, "A Policy and Not a Project" (Applause); and the purpose of these remarks is not in discouragement, but to inspire you to renewed action along precisely the same lines on which you have been working for the past ten years. (Applause.) Your policy is sound, and your record is absolutely clean. (Applause.)

Talk about an investigation! A telephone message to the Secretary of this Association will open every book and page of its history to any honest inquirer. (Applause)

The acts of this Association are an open book. The Association is composed of men who have no axes to grind; who come here in the interest of the public to accomplish the further development of the commerce of the United States by the utilization of the greatest natural asset which this country has, its unimproved rivers and harbors. (Applause.)

SECRETARY THOMPSON—Delegates from each State are requested to get together and select from their number a member for the Committee on Nominations and a member for the Committee on Resolutions, and also to elect, either from their number or from the citizenship of their State, some one to act as Vice-President for the State during the ensuing year

For the information of some who are, perhaps, here for the first time, I would say that the Directors are nominated by the Committee on Nominations, but any State delegation, or any delegate, so far as that is concerned, has the right to submit nominations for any office in the organization from the President down to the Committees, with the exception of the Vice-Presidents for the States, whose selection rests entirely in the hands of the delegates from each State

President Ransdell then delivered his Annual Report and Address as follows:

ANNUAL REPORT AND ADDRESS
Hon. Joseph E. Ransdell, U. S. Senator, Louisiana
President National Rivers and Harbors Congress

Ladies and Gentlemen, Delegates to this Convention:

In accordance with custom the President of the Association is expected to make an Annual Report I wish now to endeavor to do that briefly, and to tell you something about what we have tried to do since our last Convention

It is needless for me to remind you that we have had a strenuous year That term expresses the situation mildly. Many things have conspired to that end. In the first place, although a Rivers and Harbors Bill passed the House of Representatives fairly early in the spring, the Senate Commerce Committee was so absorbed by many things, the absence of its Chairman, and the enforced attendance of its Acting Chairman on another great committee of the Senate, that it was very late before a report could be made upon the Rivers and Harbors Bill.

About the time that report came out the Administration's proposed legislation in regard to trusts absorbed the attention of Congress, and it was quite late in the year before active consideration of the Rivers and Harbors Bill was taken up. Then, much, very much, to our sorrow and misfortune, the great war in Europe broke out, which necessitated several pieces of emergency legislation All of you know that emergency legislation has precedence in legislative bodies. Not only that, but there was a great cry for economy It was found necessary by Congress to levy a war revenue bill with the purpose of raising about a hundred million dollars, on account of the estimated deficit in the national revenues because of the falling off in importations from foreign lands

We all know how unpopular a special tax is, we all know how popular the cry of economy is. Under those circumstances there was delay, delay, delay—enforced delay in the consideration of the Rivers and Harbors Bill, and many cries of economy

The question was asked, "Why should we spend fifty-three million dollars on river and harbor projects, many of which are questionable, when we are obliged to raise a hundred million dollars of special tax, a tax which will be burdensome?"

Unfortunately, these delays and these cries for economy finally prevailed to the extent of reducing the Rivers and Harbors Bill from about fifty-three million dollars to a lump sum appropriation of twenty millions.

Many of you may believe that there is some merit in the claim of our opponents that to their vigorous opposition is due the small Rivers and Harbors Bill Let me say to you, friends, that the Rivers and Harbors Bill presented to the Senate of the United States and to the Commerce Committee would not have been changed, in my judgment, in any material particular had it not been for the outbreak of the European War (Applause.) It was not the result of the criticism of those men who fought the measure, but it was the unfortunate situation brought about by the greatest war in all history which affected terribly, and is still affecting very greatly, this Republic of ours

The opponents of river and harbor legislation have been very busy during the past twelve months, more so than ever before I hardly know to what fact or facts to attribute that serious opposition, though I may make a shrewd guess, and possibly most of you will agree with me, that it is due, in part at least, to Section 11 of the Panama Canal Act, which provides that on and after July 1. 1914, no railroad company shall own, lease, operate or control in any way, fashion or form whatsoever, any waterway which competes with said railroad (Applause) Heretofore, as you all know, the National Government improved the waterways, and the railroads manipulated them in a great many instances for their own use and benefit and in their own manner Subsequent to July 1, 1914, a railroad made itself liable to criminal prosecution if it carried out its former methods of manipulating waterways in its own way That fact may be responsible for some of the opposition which has grown up throughout the land toward our waterways.

As was stated by a previous speaker, the charge has been made that this Association has a lobby. Now I do not intend to say much about that   Do any of you conceive yourselves to be lobbyists?   I do not believe it   This Association was born in 1901 in the City of Baltimore, and at that convention a great protest was uttered against the action of members of the United States Senate in talking the Rivers and Harbors Bill to death, in March, 1901   This organization was revived and put on its present business basis in January, 1906, when a great convention was held in the old Arlington Hotel in this city.   Another one was held in December of that year, and annually thereafter we have held conventions in this city.

Who have attended those conventions?   Who have constituted our membership?   The very best men, the livest men, the most vigorous men, of practically every State in this Union, certainly of every State which is at all interested in waterways or their improvement.

Has there been anything concealed or underhanded about our efforts?   Certainly not   Everything has been open and above-board   And what have we attempted to do?   We have tried in every legitimate way to educate the American public to understand, to know, and to believe that water transportation is cheaper than transportation by rail; that if we improve the waterways the people are going to get the benefit of having their freights carried at less rates; that they are going to get freights moved in many instances when the railroads are too congested to move them.   We have tried to create an intelligent, forceful public opinion in favor of the proper improvement of every worthy watercourse in this land, whether that watercourse be in the East, or in the South, the North, or the West

We have never allowed the question of politics to enter this organization; we have never allowed the word "sectionalism" to enter into our deliberations or to be considered by this organization   (Applause.)

We have never under any circumstances advocated any particular project, no matter how worthy that project might be. We have stood for a broad constructive, far-reaching policy of waterway improvement, limited solely to the projects that are worthy and the projects that have received the approval of the Engineer Corps of the Army. (Applause)

We have carried on this educational campaign through lecturers and speakers who have literally gone from the Atlantic to the Pacific and from the Great Lakes to the Gulf, talking in every State in this Union; talking to individuals where they could not get bodies of men to listen to them, talking to Boards of Trade and other commercial bodies, to conventions—whereever they could get half a dozen American citizens together These lecturers, these field secretaries, and your national officers, have gone throughout the land preaching everywhere the gospel of improved waterways as cheapeners of freight rates and facilitators of freight movements

We have had a great Publicity Bureau conducted in the City of Washington. Our special representative of that Bureau made it his business in and out of season to confer with men prominent in the affairs of the nation, and with prominent men who visit here occasionally; with members of Congress, and others. to get their views on this important subject; and in every instance those views were given to every reporter in the City of Washington, and were mailed out to thousands of newspapers throughout the country We did everything possible to place before the American reading public the opinions of the leaders of thought on this important topic. and, as stated by Mr Bettinger, our books are open to any man Our present Secretary-Treasurer, Mr Thompson, has sent out literally hundreds of thousands of pieces of literature this year to people throughout the land He has done everything he could to enlighten 'the people and to answer inquiries whenever they were made, and no one has ever been denied any information asked for, not only on the general topic, but in regard to the workings of the organization, for we have nothing secret from any one.

One feature of the opposition to the bill this year grievously wounded me, and I believe it did every member of the organization I refer to the charge that the last Rivers and Harbors Bill was framed on political and sectional lines, that the South was in the saddle. I deny the charge, and defy any man to prove it. (Applause.) For eight years I was a member of the Rivers and Harbors Committee in the House of Representatives when the Republican party was in power: and it was our

proud boast that all thought of "politics" and "sectionalism" was left behind when we entered the walls of that committee room (Applause) Never under any circumstances during those eight years did I hear the words "politics" or "sectionalism" in those committee rooms. Our sole test, the acid test to which we sub-
mitted every project was, "Is it worthy? Will it benefit the people of the United States? Has it the approval of the Engineer Corps of the Army? Is it going to do good?" And whether it was in the North, in the East, in the South, or in the West, if it stood those tests we appropriated for it if we were able to do so; though, of course, you understand we could not appropriate for everything in every bill That was during my eight years as a member of the minority.

Then for four years I have served on the Rivers and Harbors Committee of the House and on the Commerce Committee of the Senate as a member of the majority party, the party now in power, and I can say just as truthfully that during the last four years we as scrupulously avoided politics and sectionalism as we did during the previous Administrations. (Applause.) We required the same test of merit

It is most unfortunate that those charges were made. Let me remind you, friends, that when the great twenty-foot project through the lakes was adopted over twenty years ago, the Chairman of the Rivers and Harbors Committee was a citizen of the Southland, Newton C. Blanchard, of Louisiana. At that time, owing to the horrors of the Civil War and the reconstruction period, development had hardly begun in the South There were very few of our waterways ready to be improved, and the leader in those days in the waterway movement, and the man who worked out that magnificent project of twenty feet on the Great Lakes, again I repeat, was a southerner! (Applause)

A man from the Great Lakes, Theodore Burton, of Ohio, was Chairman of the Rivers and Harbors Committee when the great work at the mouth of the Mississippi River and at the port of Galveston was put under way. We had no politics then

Later on another man from the Great Lakes and the North, D. L Alexander, of New York, was Chairman when for the first time Congress placed the lower Mississippi and the Ohio on a business-like plan for proper and wise improvement of those great streams (Applause.) Mr. Alexander did not ask whether the Mississippi was in New York, whether it was in the North, or in the South. He asked only, "Is it worthy?" And he led in having it placed on a business basis, and in having the great Ohio, which bounds the country between the North and the South, also put on a business basis

These accusations, friends, are unworthy of their authors, and I appeal to every member of this Association to decry them, and to put them down, in God's name We have troubles enough with waterway appropriations without falling out among ourselves and fighting over sectionalism and political issues "In union there is strength," and if the waterways people pull together with the union that we had in the past I earnestly believe we will have strength enough to secure the improvement of all worthy waterways; but if we play into the hands of our enemies and get to fighting each other we will not secure the improvement of anything, and we had better disband (Applause.)

It is very unfortunate that there should be so much misconception about this pending river and harbor legislation, and this cry of "pork barrel"; that there is so much destructive criticism and so little constructive statesmanship urged in lieu thereof (Applause) We have all read about that twenty-five dollar cow that kicked over the lamp which set fire to the city of Chicago and destroyed a great city No one would pretend to intimate that the cow could rebuild the city. It is very easy to criticise a great system of legislation like the River and Harbor Bill, and we have had some pretty lively criticism, but none of those critics have ever suggested a better method Can they suggest something better? Is there a better method? I do not know, and I do not pretend to say Everything earthly is faulty We are all making mistakes all the time; and if those gentlemen who so glibly criticise present methods will tell us of a better method, I, as one member of the American Congress, will be glad to adopt such suggestions, provided they suggest something that is really better

But we would be very foolish to abandon the method which has been followed from the very birth of the Republic to this

good day, and under which we have expended nearly $800,000,-
000 00 on the improvement of the rivers and harbors of this, the
greatest nation in all the world, and which has resulted in wonderful benefits to all the people of the Republic, unless sure of
the wisdom of the change   Let us stick to our present method
until we get something better   (Applause.)

I do not pretend to say that there were no mistakes in the
last Rivers and Harbors Bill   Perhaps there were. If there were
I did not know them, and I am pretty familiar with the measure.
I can say to you, as one who took an active part in working it
out, that there was no log-rolling by any one, so far as I know;
that there was no lobbying by this Association in favor of it:
and that in framing this bill we followed the advice of the Engineer Corps of the Army

Let us reason about that quietly as business men   This is a
big country   Not only do we have to improve the rivers and '
harbors in the continental United States, but we have to go into
Alaska, we have to improve the harbors in Hawaii, in Porto
Rico; and of course, the Panama Canal is our greatest project
This is an enormous country   How is it possible physically for
the members of the Rivers and Harbors Committee of the House
and the members of the Commerce Committee of the Senate to
know of their own knowledge, by personal inspection and examination, all the facts in regard to these many projects? You realize
that that would be a physical impossibility   We must of necessity
take somebody else's advice in working out the plans, and that
advice is furnished by the Engineer Corps of the Army, which is
as near independent as any body of men can be   That Corps
is selected from the honor men of West Point, and the men who
go to West Point are appointed literally from every congressional
district in the Union.   The West Point men are as well distributed geographically as the men of any institution in the
world (for every member of Congress, whether senator or representative, has a chance to appoint some one from his respective
state or congressional district to West Point, and the honor men
of West Point are selected to make up the Engineer Corps of
the Army   These honor men are the ones who reach the highest
rank in the Engineer Corps.

Now let us see how a project originates. It is a simple thing, yet I doubt if it is understood Let us assume that the people of my state of Louisiana are desirous of getting the Ouachita River improved. The local people, mind you, want the Ouachita River improved and they appeal to their representative to have it done. He introduces a bill asking that it be surveyed and a report or showing made to Congress so that it may make the necessary appropriation. Then the Chief of Engineers orders the local engineer, situated at Vicksburg, to make an examination and survey of that project The local engineer does not start in with big plans and spend a lot of money on it, but his first step is to go in person to the Ouachita River and examine it for four hundred miles from Camden to its mouth, go over it in person, in skiffs or otherwise, go over every bit of that river, find out all he can about it, and ascertain whether it is worth improving. He then makes a written report to his division engineer located at New Orleans. If it looks good to the division engineer, it becomes the duty of that official to submit that preliminary report to the Board of Engineers for Rivers and Harbors, a body composed of seven men, located in this city. The Board of Engineers for Rivers and Harbors read the report carefully, investigate it, and if they find that it is proper and wise to have a survey made, they recommend it Then the Chief of Engineers in turn approves it and orders the local engineer to make the survey. Mind you, all these steps are taken on the preliminary survey Having run the gauntlet of the preliminary survey, the local engineer then puts his force in the field In that particular case he spent ten or twelve years making the survey. It was done before I came to Congress. (Applause) I refer to it simply as an illustration. He spent ten or twelve years making the survey. The survey went through the same process, first the local engineer, then the division engineer, then the Board of Engineers for Rivers and Harbors, and finally the Chief of Engineers, and not until the Chief of Engineers or the Board of Engineers for Rivers and Harbors reported favorably upon that project was it ever given legislative status

In other words, unless a project, after this accurate and full survey, receives the approval of the Board of Engineers for Rivers and Harbors, or the Chief of Engineers, Congress will not make appropriations for it   There were two exceptional cases in the last bill—the exception always proves the rule—where appropriations were made for two very small projects, carrying about one hundred thousand dollars, without this approval, but in both of those instances Congress made an independent and careful investigation of those projects by examining a number of competent witnesses

Let us see how conservative the engineers are   Do they follow the lead of the local people? Do they follow the advice of the local congressman and the local senator? Oh, no, friends, out of a list of 400 surveys submitted to the Engineer Corps, they disapproved and recommended against 260. (Applause.) They favored only 140 out of 400; and mind you, friends, each one of those 400 had back of it a senator or a representative, as well as the local community; but this great, conservative, independent band of men, these government engineers with no local interest to serve. these engineers who serve for life, who have only one thought—the discharge of their proper duties—who, when they retire, do so on a pension sufficient to support them in comfort in their old age, these engineers who are rarely ever located at one place longer than three years, so that they cannot become local in their opinions and sympathies, this great Engineer Corps. let me repeat, turned down 260 out of 400 surveys, approving only 140; and unless Congress goes back on its rule, only 140 of those 400 projects will have legislative status   Appropriations for only two out of the rejected 260 were made by Congress

Now suppose some member of Congress goes to the Rivers and Harbors Committee and says, "Mr Chairman, I want an appropriation for Podunk Creek" The Chairman says, "All right, let's see what the report of the Engineer says." The report is brought to him by the clerk. and he sees that a survey was made of the Creek and there was an unfavorable report The Chairman smiles sweetly and says, "Mr. Member, I am very sorry, but the Engineer Corps reports unfavorably as to the improvement of Podunk Creek. Mr Clerk, call the next case"; and that ends it   Can there be a more conservative and proper system than that? Do you know of anything human that is safer than that? How many scandals have you ever heard of connected with the Engineer Corps? When large sums of money pass through the hands of men, unfortunately sometimes some of it sticks there. These engineers have spent about $800,000,-000.00 on waterways, and there never has been a charge brought that any one of them, except Captain Carter, at Savannah, ever allowed any of the money to stick to his fingers—and some people even believe that Captain Carter was not guilty. (Applause) Is there a record of efficiency anywhere in the United States equal to that of the Engineer Corps? Can our great judicial system show such a record? There have been many impeachments of the judiciary. A great many judges have been recalled by the votes of their constituents, and we have had several of them impeached and turned out of office; yet there has been only one scandal against the whole Engineer Corps Let me repeat as a practical proposition, that it is only when the Engineer Corps has reported in favor of a project that it has any standing at all before the houses of Congress Now some of you who have tried to get measures approved by this Engineer Corps know what you have been up against I know I have. (Applause.)

Some people have been advocating that we change our method and have a great commission, or put all the money in the hands of the Engineer Corps and have them spend it where they think best. Now while no man thinks more highly than I do of the Engineer Corps, for I concede that they have splendidly performed their duties, yet I believe Congress also has a function to perform, and I think they perform it equally well. (Applause) In regard to a commission, I do not think commissions are extraordinarily popular in this republic of ours We had one big commission a few years ago known as the—well, they didn't call it a commission, it was the Irrigation Service, Reclamation Service—but it was practically a commission created by act of Congress in 1902. Under that act the Secretary of the Interior was authorized to expend the proceeds of the sales of public lands in the thirteen arid land states and the three arid land territories in reclamation, and with the big lump sum so derived the Secretary of the Interior could do as he pleased in irrigation projects, subject only to the limitation that he must spend at least fifty-one per cent of the money derived from the sale of the land in any state or territory within its borders, otherwise he could do as he pleased The work has gone on very well and I do not know that it is subject to any criticism whatsoever. I am not going to criticise it. I have viewed it as a magnificent piece of constructive legislation During twelve years of operation the Reclamation Service has spent $103,000,000, has irrigated 1,291,000 acres of land, and has under process of improvement 1,680,000 acres additional But the law was changed last August and the Secretary of the Interior must now get the consent of Congress before he can make any further expenditures on irrigation projects He has to tell Congress what he wishes to do with the irrigation funds, and he has to report to Congress just as the Chief of Engineers does with regard to the waterway projects, and Congress, if it sees fit, approves, and if it does not see fit, it does not approve So, after twelve years of operation, the law has been changed, and Congress has resumed the legislative functions which it surrendered in 1902

In regard to waterway improvements, this Association has always stood, and still stands, for the continuing contract system Individually I have talked time and time again, and shall continue to talk, in favor of placing a project when once adopted under a continuing contract, so that it may be regularly carried through and finished (Applause) just as we did in Panama Why, before the first Panama Canal Act we had the experience of De Lesseps, the great French engineer, and his Company We had the mistakes which they made to guide us We had the reports of three great engineering commissions appointed to survey and study all possible routes across the Isthmus Every investigation was made that could be made. Debates in Congress were held for years and years on the subject All political parties declared in favor of the improvement, there was not a public man in the nation who dared raise his voice in opposition to the Isthmian Canal. All that preceded our adoption of the Panama Canal Act, in 1902, which specifically directed that the route of the Canal across the Isthmus should be at Panama; not at Nicaraugua, as some wanted, not at Darien, as some desired, but at Panama. This Act specifically said that we were to have a lock canal instead of a tide-level canal. The Act gave the dimensions of the Canal and stated what it was to cost; and then having passed upon all these legislative features, we said to the President of the United States, "Mr. President, go ahead and build this canal under the plans we have outlined, and call on us for money and we will give it to you just as fast as you need it." That was wise legislation; that was business-like legislation.

When the Congress of the United States adopts a great project like that of the Ohio River, or the Hudson River, or the Port of Boston, or the mouth of the Columbia River, or the Port at Galveston, or the flood control on the lower Mississippi River, or any of our really great projects, we maintain that they should be placed under a continuing contract; and we would have the Engineer Corps authorized to go ahead and finish them just as fast as good business methods warrant. That is the method which this Association stands for. (Applause.)

That would be no surrender of legislative power or authority and discretion, because in every instance, let me remind you, before a project is adopted it would be preceded by a careful survey and report of the Engineer Corps such as I have described to you. After Congress is once committed to a project by adopting it, the proper thing is to let the Engineer Corps go on and finish it without putting it in the hands of some commission.

Ladies and gentlemen, do you believe that the American Congress is going to create a commission of seven to ten men, install them in some fine office building, give them a great corps of clerks, secretaries and traveling men, and then say, "Here is $60,000,000 a year for ten years; go ahead and conquer all the waterways in this land and improve them as you see fit. We will resign our functions to you entirely?" Do you think that would be wise? Do you think Congress is going to do it, or that Congress ought to do it? Would it not be better to adhere to the old method of having Congress first pass upon the merits of a project, and, having favorably passed upon it, then to improve it just as rapidly as possible? Unquestionably, in my opinion.

If you are going to surrender the legislative function in regard to the improvement of waterways, why not create a naval commission and tell them, "You members of the Navy Commission understand naval matters so much better than the 435 members of the House of Representatives and the 96 members of the Senate, that we will just give you $150,000,000 a year for ten years, and authorize you to build as many battleships as you wish, and as many ships of any kind as you wish; we will not pretend to exercise any functions, we will just turn it all over to you;" and then create another commission and say to them, "You are so much wiser than Congress, you have so much better means of obtaining information and learning about everything than Congress has, that we will give you $125,000,000 a year for ten years for the Army, and we will let you spend it as you see fit for the public defense."

Such steps would be so preposterous that a mere statement thereof carries their refutation, but they are not more so than a complete surrender of every function of Congress to a waterway commission I do not believe that Congress should ever surrender its functions in such matters. and I am quite sure it will never do so.

And now, let me close, my friends I know I have talked too long to you (A voice. "No!"), but I feel so warmly and so enthusiastically on this subject that I could not refrain.

I wish to again remind you that during the entire history of this organization, from its birth to the present moment. we have had one pole-star only, the improvement of the waterways of our country for the purpose of navigation (Applause) in order that transportation facilities should be increased and cheapened That has been our whole doctrine—navigation and transportation. There have been many attempts to have us turn aside from our course and follow false gods, but, thank Heaven, we have never done it so far, and we must not do it now

We must not be alarmed by the criticisms that have been made against us Why, if we were not criticised, I would feel badly over it, I would think we did not amount to anything (Applause) I remember well, when we first organized it was a very easy matter to get the biggest railroad presidents of the

United States to come and give us an address. They did it freely, because we did not amount to anything at that time, but I know for the past three or four years I have tried, and tried hard, to get some of those railroad presidents to come and give us a paper, but they will not do it any more. (Applause.) We amount to something now, and they know it. We are making the American people understand, as they have never understood before, that if the waterways are improved and the waterways are used, they are going to regulate and cheapen transportation not only among the communities where the charges are entirely too high (Applause), but everywhere. Let us stick to our program of a policy, and under no circumstances a project. Let us insist upon the same test that we have always called for, that no waterway shall receive an appropriation, no matter what the pressure back of it, unless it is really worthy, unless it has real merit back of it. If we do that, the American people are bound to respect us in the future as they have done in the past. (Applause.)

PRESIDENT RANSDELL—Bear in mind, ladies and gentlemen, that we are to meet at two o'clock this afternoon, and that we have a most interesting program. We have also an exceedingly interesting program tonight   We want you all to come this afternoon and tonight and bring your friends   Urge as many as you can to come to this Convention

At two o'clock we will meet again   The Convention stands in recess until that hour.

The Convention recessed accordingly.

SECOND SESSION
Wednesday Afternoon, December 9

The Convention met pursuant to recess, President Ransdell in the chair

President Ransdell—Please come to order, Gentlemen The Secretary has some announcements

Secretary Thompson—A telegram has been received from the Secretary of the Lawrence Chamber of Commerce announcing the coming of a delegation numbering fifty or more on a special train which will arrive this afternoon

It is important that every delegate should register, giving his name and home address We shall have literature to send you that will be of interest and it is also desirable that we know how many have actually been present If you have not already signed the cards in the registration room, please be sure to do so before leaving

The following letter has been received

City of New York

Office of the Mayor

December 8, 1914

Dear Sir·

I regret that I cannot accept the invitation to attend the Eleventh Annual Convention of the National Rivers and Harbors Congress, as my engagements here are such that it is impossible for me to do so. I had hoped that Commissioner Smith might be able to go in my place, but his letter to me of even date, which I enclose herewith, explains why he finds that he cannot attend.

It would appear, however, that my attendance at the Convention would do little, if any good During the last session of Congress, I went to Washington, together with the Dock Commissioner and a representative committee, and presented to the

House Committee on Rivers and Harbors the necessities of the port of New York, including the immediate and pressing need for the allowance of the new project for the deepening of the channel of the East River and the removal of the dangerous reefs and shoals, pointing out that the immediate removal of Coenties Reef is necessary in connection with the construction of the new East River subway tubes now under way. The House Committee reported this new project favorably, but the Senate threw all new projects out of the bill, and New York lost the approval of this project.

When I went to Washington at that time, and subsequently, I pointed out to the House Committee and to the President personally the enormous importance to the port of New York of the approval of this new project for the East River which is. in practical effect, merely an amendment of the project of 1868. I believe that I made it plain that the work is necessary in order to serve the ever increasing commerce of the port, and is also of the utmost importance to the National Government as a factor in the national defense, providing, as it would, an outlet to the East by way of the Sound for the Government's ships of war.

You gentlemen know so intimately the facts relating to the commerce of this port as compared with the commerce of the country, and the appropriations made to this port as compared with the appropriations made to other ports of the country, that I need hardly call them to your attention You know that the commerce of the port of New York represents upwards of fifty per cent of the foreign commerce of the country and that, nevertheless, the appropriations made to this port up to the present time have constituted less than two per cent of the total appropriations made for river and harbor improvements in the United States. That the port of New York has been starved in the past and grossly neglected by the National Government is indisputable, and known to all those who have taken the trouble to look into the facts

If it be the fixed determination of Congress to continue this policy towards the port of New York, nothing I can say, and nothing that the Dock Commissioner can say, would alter that determination   The facts were all fully presented to Congress and to the President during the session of the last Congress. The arguments then presented still remain in full force and effect, emphasized merely by the ever growing appreciation throughout the country of the necessity for developing our means of national defense, and all those works and port and harbor facilities that might contribute to it.

Very truly yours,

JOHN PUROY MITCHELL

HON JOSEPH E. RANSDELL,

President, Eleventh Annual Convention of the National Rivers and Harbors Congress, Washington, D C

The letter of Commissioner Smith is as follows:

NEW YORK, November 8, 1914.

TO THE HONORABLE THE MAYOR
JOHN PUROY MITCHELL

Sir·

It is with regret that I am unable to attend the Rivers and Harbors Congress in session on December 9th, at Washington, D C.

Were I able to be present in my capacity as a delegate from the State of New York, and as representative of New York City's Department having to do with waterways, I would say·

"That New York City, in its effort to make the great national gateway for maritime commerce on the Atlantic Coast the complete harbor it should be, can expect little or no aid from the National Congress, and any participation in movements or meetings for the furtherance of waterway improvements can only be considered as indicative of approbation of such movements without any hope of sharing in any benefit from National Congressional action taken on the strength of such movements or meetings"

You will recall that you have gone to considerable trouble and have taken valuable time to personally appear before the President, Committees of the House, and have used your individual argument with individuals identified with National Government, seriously and informatively requesting their aid to secure for New York Harbor in its National aspect, the needed improvements therein, and if the petitioning of the Chief Executive of the major commercial center of the Atlantic seaboard receives so little consideration, it would be quite hopeless for any one of less authority to exert themselves.

That New York City itself is spending large sums to develop the harbor as a part of the National defense and a secure haven in time of maritime disturbance; that the State has spent one hundred and eighty millions on a waterway that adds to the prosperity of many States, that fifty per cent of the entire import and export business of the United States passes here, is as nothing in the eyes of those in control of the means to have the needed work done.

We have a recent instance of twelve hundred embryo and matured citizens coming from an inland State on a visit of educational and enlightening purport to the East The thing they most wanted to see was the great harbor of New York and the ocean, and individual expression made indicated that the importance of the harbor as a National advantage was clearly in the mind of the whole number Yet representatives in Congress of these inland States are the ones who are ever ready to aid in prohibiting New York harbor from Government means for the improvements needed

We have done many things to demonstrate to the whole National Congress that New York is at all times ready and willing to give every encouragement to the development of other harbors, irrespective of their location. We believe all harbors should have consideration, and we are always at a complete loss to understand why New York is so continuously neglected in National consideration

Very respectfully yours,

R A C SMITH, Commissioner.

President Ransdell—Ladies and gentlemen, the first address of the afternoon will be delivered by one who has traveled perhaps a greater distance than any other delegate to attend this meeting At least very few have come so far, for he lives in the city of Portland, Oregon. This is not the first time that he has been at our conventions, for he has attended every one we have held He is one of the best friends of waterways and is a representative of that great organization, the United Commercial Travelers of America, which is perhaps more interested in the transportation problem and the cheapening of freights than any other organization in the country.

It gives me great pleasure to present Mr C W Hodson, of Portland, Oregon, Past Supreme Councillor of the United Commercial Travelers of America. (Applause.)

THE TRAVELING MAN'S VIEW
Address—C. W. Hodson, Portland, Oregon
Past Supreme Councillor, U. C. T. of A.

Mr Chairman, and Members of the Congress:

I come to speak to you today as the representative of over 75,000 of those live, wide-awake harbingers of prosperity who have associated themselves together under the name of the Order of United Commercial Travelers of America There is not a city of commercial importance anywhere throughout the length and breadth of the land which does not count some of our members amongst its citizens In their quest for business they seek out the remotest nooks and corners of the country, and reach out to the islands and lands beyond the seas.

These men have learned from experience that of the cost of distribution of the wares they sell, over sixty per cent is consumed by transportation alone. They have also learned that anything which tends toward a reduction of that distribution cost serves to promote a larger movement of their commodities, thus very materially benefiting them That is the reason for their interest in the great cause of waterway improvement

My life and business activities being ordered in the extreme Northwestern part of our country, in the section comprising the States of Oregon, Washington, Idaho, Montana and a portion of British Columbia, known as the Columbia River basin. it is of that great river and its tributaries I will speak particularly, knowing that the same principles apply and the same benefits will follow development in all other sections of the United States.

Whatever of criticism of individuals or policies I may utter will be my personal views, for which I will assume entire responsibility. The figures I will give you are accurate and authentic, having been gathered from official sources by an assistant to the Secretary of the Portland Chamber of Commerce, of which body I also have the honor to be a member.

Last year there cleared from the Columbia River 1507 ocean-going vessels carrying merchandise valued at $57,833,000, included in which was more than half of all the wheat exported from the Pacific Coast, Portland being the third largest shipper in the United States.

In the three Northwestern States most affected by Columbia River navigation the Federal Government owns in the National Forest Reserves three hundred billions of feet of commercial timber, of which one-half is located in the State of Oregon Last year the approximate average selling price for all timber sold by the Government out of these reserves was $2 50 per thousand feet; giving the same value to the total Government holdings now remaining in the three States, produces a grand total of $750,000,000 as the present worth of this Federal property. As all this is held under the Federal power, it is prevented from becoming a State asset from which tax revenue can be raised for improvement work. This ownership alone should impel the Government to improve the entire Columbia waterway, and particularly the bar at the mouth of the river. This enormous wealth retained by the Federal power should be ample warrant for the largest river and harbor expenditure, in proportion to present or prospective public use, ever made by Congress. The Government should also realize that improving the waterway is a simple business problem, because, as the market facilities are made better, the value of the Federal timber holdings increases As the authorities have retained in no other navigation district such stupendous wealth as the $750,000,000 named here, the Columbia could properly be given most extraordinary consideration.

But the Government has not been asked by the people of that district to supply all the funds for the improvement of the river. The City of Portland some years ago organized itself into a taxation district, and, by means of the powers conferred upon it by the State Legislature, has raised by direct tax and expended upon the improvement of the channel of the lower Columbia and Willamette Rivers, over and above the amounts supplied by the General Government, over $6,000,000 In addition, the cities of Astoria, Oregon, and Vancouver, Washington, have also organized similar taxation districts and, in proportion to their ability, have raised and expended large sums in permanent river improvement work. During the spring of this year, when the Government appropriations became exhausted, and work at the mouth of the river was about to be discontinued until the next appropriation should become available, the Port of Portland appropriated $475,000, and the Port of Astoria, $25,000— a half million all told—which was turned over to the Federal engineers for use in order that the work might not be delayed Point me to other such instances wherein local communities have even made an approach to such self-help; and by the way, may this action not presage the adoption of a new policy for regulating Governmental action in improving waterways—namely, that communities demanding Government aid shall show such faith in their enterprises that they are willing to embark their own capital in their improvement? There is food for thought in this suggestion, when we hear so much talk about and condemnation of the "pork-barrel" system now alleged to be in vogue, and which talk resulted so disastrously for the last Rivers and Harbors Bill.

But to return to my text and attempt to show why it is good business policy for the General Government to join hands with the residents of the Columbia basin in forwarding the improvement of that great stream

In Oregon there is a stand of over five hundred billions of feet of timber In Washington, Idaho, and that part of Montana draining to the Pacific, the total stand passes a thousand billions

of feet. All of this, except a limited amount in Southwestern
Oregon and a somewhat larger total in Northwestern Washington, is directly affected by the market facilities of the Columbia Idaho and Western Montana last year sent to the Pacific
seaboard about ten millions of feet of pine for export This is
but the beginning of an enormous movement which will naturally
take the course of the Columbia when the few remaining impedi-
ments to navigation are removed, of which the bar at the mouth
of the river is first Oregon and Washington now cut about
six billion feet of lumber a year. There is being consumed in
the territory tributary to New York and Philadelphia about
the same quantity of soft wood per year, supplied largely by
Southern yellow pine Oregon could easily cut four billion feet
more per year than now, to supply this market at far lower figures than yellow pine brings Our people want to reach that
market Great lumber carriers drawing 28 to 30 feet is their
immediate need They should have forty feet of water or
more on the bar by the time the Panama Canal is formally opened
to the commerce of the world Inability to reach this market in
the most economical carriers will entail a loss of millions annually, and result in British Columbia, with cheap foreign ships
and no tariff duties, gaining a foothold that will keep the Northwestern States out of the great Atlantic seaboard market for
many years to come

Government figures in wheat production last year credited
Idaho with fourteen million bushels, Oregon with twenty-one
million bushels, Washington with fifty-three million bushels,
Montana with nineteen million bushels, and Utah with six million
bushels This is eighty-eight million bushels for the three Northwestern States Owing to the desire of the railway companies to
get loading for empties from the Rocky Mountains westward,
rates are already made which will bring much of the Montana
and British Columbia grain to this seaboard. Assurance is given
by railway managers that Montana, all of Idaho, and perhaps
part of Utah will take the Western route When the Celilo Canal
is finished, the Columbia River will be the supreme regulating
power in the Northwestern rate field Products grown distantly

from it will get the benefit of the water-compelled rate as soon as they reach the navigation zone of the river

Every bushel of wheat—more than a hundred million last year—will be affected. Apply a water-compelled rate saving to this more than one hundred millions of bushels of wheat that would profit by going down the Columbia to the sea, and it is plainly seen that the return to the farmer and consumer is of immense importance   The present wheat rate between Umatilla and Portland, a distance of one hundred and eighty-six miles, is five times as great as between Chicago and New York, a distance of a thousand miles   All concede that wheat production in the Columbia basin will increase amazingly with cheaper transportation, cheaper lands, and application of dry farming methods, as well as from extended irrigation   Professor Shaw, the eminent Minnesota dry-farm expert, has said that Eastern Oregon alone, when cultivated on present known dry-farm principles, can be made to yield a hundred million bushels of wheat without destroying the proper balance with other crops

Apples are shipped from the Northwest to all parts of the world. Last year fifteen thousand carloads were marketed   Next year there will be thirty thousand carloads   Trees are already planted, which, if kept to maturity and properly fostered, will yield sixty to seventy thousand carloads a year   These trees will be kept if the product can be sold at a fair profit, but will be cut down and destroyed if the market does not open   The world market for Pacific Northwest fancy apples depends on the cost of delivery to the distant consumer   The railway and water haul to Europe, in ventilated cars and boats, without refrigeration, is now about seventy cents a box. Direct steamship service is needed to cut materially under this rate and to make the market what the present planted acreage demands   When the minimum cost of marketing is realized for the orchards of the three Northwestern States, the Columbia route becomes supreme.

Last year the production of wool in the Columbia basin was fifteen million pounds in Idaho; eighteen million pounds in Oregon: three million six hundred thousand pounds in Washington; thirty-one million one hundred seventy-five thousand pounds in Montana; eleven million five hundred fifty thousand pounds in

Utah These clips are all tributary to the Pacific through the Columbia River Efforts are now being made to have the growers drive their herds as far toward the navigable streams as possible before shearing. The full benefit, however, cannot be derived unless the Columbia is open to the sea for large carriers. The rail rate on wool from Portland to Boston is today $1 00. This rate grades up for a distance toward the interior to $1.66. It is certain that a rate of forty cents will be made on wool from Portland to Boston through the Panama Canal, if the large vessels can be accommodated conveniently. The same sort of showing can be made for hay, potatoes, dairy products, livestock and all the other great natural resources of that wonderland .

In this Columbia basin are over two hundred fifty-five thousand square miles of territory. In all New York, New Hampshire, Massachusetts, Connecticut, Rhode Island, New Jersey, Pennsylvania, Delaware, Maryland, Virginia, North Carolina, and South Carolina, there are but two hundred fifty-four thousand square miles. This basin, dependent for its full hopes upon the port of the Columbia, is truly an empire, yet it has barely been touched. In Oregon alone about four million acres of land are actually cultivated, whereas there are about twenty million acres pronounced tillable, but not cultivated The percentage in Idaho is equally great, and somewhat less in Washington. Only by making these lands profitable to the farmer can the cultivator be drawn there To make them profitable the lowest possible charge for transportation must be had. All know that the Columbia is the line affording this, which must be accepted and developed .

On the Columbia and its tributaries there are about two thousand miles which could be navigated by freight-carrying craft. If those portions could all be connected in one straight line they would form a continuous channel from Astoria on the Pacific to Chicago and the Great Lakes in the Middle West, a distance of two-thirds the entire width of the American continent At present only about thirteen hundred miles of these streams are navigable for limited reaches because of inland barriers When the Celilo Canal is finished, the first great step in water competition to the very heart of the Columbia basin

is taken. Every year thereafter will see the continuous reach
of navigable water lengthened from the sea. It is this line of
improvement which will give favorable transportation rates to
the farmers settling the now vacant lands of the great Northwest
and make swift and sure agricultural development possible.

In thus enumerating some of the possible benefits to be derived by the improvement of the Columbia River, I am taking no
account of the hydro-electric energy which that stream and its
tributaries afford. In the State of Oregon alone estimates show
that three and one-quarter million horse power can be developed,
while in the three States of Oregon, Washington, and Idaho, and
that part of Montana tributary to the Pacific, the grand total will
reach twelve million horse power. This energy, as a rule, may
be utilized at very low cost. When low transportation charges
on the Pacific are to be had from the mouth of the Columbia,
this stupendous asset will be brought nearer realization for
material gain.

Much of the opposition to waterway improvement (in fact
almost all of it) is attributed nowadays to railway and other
corporate influence. Assume this to be true. Is there reason
for it? Are the people of this country in position to point the
finger of accusation at these great corporations without experiencing any twinge of conscience?

About ten years ago there was a great public awakening to
what railroad operators and corporate manipulators had been
and were doing Investigation revealed a scandalous condition
of affairs, contributed to in no small degree by the fact that the
people generally were so busy attending to their own personal affairs as to have no time for looking after the welfare of the public Like all the rest of us, these operators and manipulators
were attending strictly to their own personal affairs, and it was
suddenly discovered that the work had been so well done that
the entire business of the country was practically under the domi-
nation and control of a few. Immediately a cry went up for
deliverance, destruction and revenge. Within the twinkling of
an eye there arose throughout the land scores of leaders and
would-be leaders, who sought to guide the "dear people" out of
their slough of despond, among them being those conscientiously

bent on correcting abuses and providing means of safely and sanely placing the business affairs of the nation on an honest, sound, rational basis. There were, too, hordes of others—crack brained theorists, demagogues, shysters, mountebanks—who saw in the disturbed conditions opportunity for self-aggrandizement, personal gain and political preferment. The limit of their ambition was the sky overhead and the ends of the earth around them, and ranged from serving three terms or more as President of the United States to election as constables of obscure precincts. The people's emotions and fears were played upon to such an extent that for a time it seemed as though reason had been dethroned in the pursuit of vengeance The National Congress, State Legislatures, Boards of County Commissioners, City Councils, and even petty town officials, all joined in the cry of "crucify" and vied with each other in going to extremes The whole nation embarked on a wild, misguided legislative debauch.

What has been the result? Credit destroyed; transportation companies verging on bankruptcy, the business man unable to determine how or whether he can continue his calling without becoming the subject of criminal prosecution Punitive legislation has reached the point where the revenues of our great railway systems have been reduced almost to the point of confiscation of the properties; demands of employees for increases in pay and shortening of hours of service; increased cost of equipment made necessary by reason of similar demands on manufacturers and on top of all that, a regulation downward by National and State Commissions of rates for carrying service, have served to bring our great transportation systems to the brink of financial ruin Commercial enterprises throughout the land lie gasping for breath at the feet of the political yeggman, and yet none in official position seek to stay the hand of the destroyer Well may we cry in anguish, "How long, O Lord, how long?"

We have all more or less joined in the hue and cry, and applauded the efforts of our so-called, self-styled leaders To the extent that we have so participated in these shameless proceedings during the past ten years, directly or by non-attention, are we responsible for the conditions confronting us today, and to that extent should we honestly be willing to shoulder our share of the responsibility In these enthusiastic, but misguided efforts, we have all contributed in a measure to arousing feelings of resentment on the part of the owners and operators of these great corporations Being intensely human, it was but natural that they should feel impelled to retaliate in kind, striking out in the dark, blindly, it is true, hitting friend and foe alike, in the hope of staying the hand of the executioner and saving at least a portion of their trusts from impending disaster They have been grievously and criminally wrong in the past. They admit it, and are now at the bench of repentance promising reforms for the future, hedged about by a web of legal enactments which makes it next to impossible for them to do other than as they promise to do They have been our greatest consumers, but their purchasing powers have about struck bottom

In the face of this condition, would it not be well for us to seriously reflect? Shall we continue further as we have been going, or shall we act the part of sane, thinking men, and give business of all kinds, big and little, an opportunity to straighten up, throw back its shoulders and take a good, long, deep breath of relief, or shall we, in our insane quest for further vengeance, destroy ourselves as well as those we pursue? Would it not be wise to pause and consider?

It is axiomatic that introduction of waterway transportation on a competitive basis reduces rates; but it is none the less true that it increases volume to such an extent as to more than overcome apparent losses by reason of such reduction.

Desire for monopoly is a human attribute, and finds lodgment in the breast of the steamboat owner and business man, as well as the railroad operator. Neither has any advantage of the other on that score That being true, what is the proper course for us to follow? Is it not to pursue our way, demanding and asserting our legitimate right to waterway improvement and conceding the same privilege to others, and seeing to it that we are both accorded fair treatment? After all, who are the final arbiters of the question of these rights? The people. How can we secure our hearing and have our day in the great court of public opinion? By education; by showing the justice of our cause—not seeking to tear down the other fellow, but endeavoring to build up ourselves What the people want, that will they have The ballot box is always determinative; and should there temporarily strut across the stage some self-appointed arbiter of our destinies. seeking his own personal aggrandizement by playing upon our emotions and prejudices, we need but take stock of ourselves and plant our feet squarely on the solid ground of good common sense. walk up to the polls and exercise our franchise in a sane manner, and retire him and his kind to justly merited obscurity This has been done; it can and will be done again

It is true that some of the railroads are in opposition to our waterway plans, but to a large extent they have been driven to take the position they have We are advised, however, so if they now succeed in their plans of crippling our enterprises, we alone are to blame But, in saying this I do not advocate embarking on a campaign of reprisal Let us demand and see that we get what we are justly entitled to I hold no brief for the railroads, nor do I wish to be considered an apologist for them and their shortcomings; but because they have most grievously wronged in the past does not warrant us in going wrong now I leave this thought with you.

There is still another influence at work in opposition to the plans of this Congress, and that is from cities located inland from tidewater and away from navigable streams and lakes An example of this menace is reflected in an editorial extract from a newspaper published in an inland city, which I secured on my trip eastward to attend this meeting Its editor was enumerating a list of what he considered some of the difficulties confronting the present Administration. and among other things was the following:

"Appropriations for harbors and rivers will be another sore spot. The lobby for inflated appropriations for these objects was defeated at the last session of Congress. but it is undaunted by defeat and will return to the charge upon the Treasury more determinedly than ever. Its activities in time of prosperity are pernicious, and in times like these, when the nation needs every dollar, its illegitimate demands should receive no countenance."

I might say for your information that the above-mentioned city has four transcontinental railways running through it, is located five hundred miles from the closest tidewater, yet is demanding through rates equal to those enjoyed by cities located where the Almighty made it possible for ocean carriers to discharge their cargoes. The opposition to river and harbor improvement by the Federal Government from this class of cities must not be underestimated Nothing but education will overcome their prejudices. The general public must be taught that the welfare of one is the concern of all, and that if the public as a whole is to prosper, the individual communities composing that public must be prosperous Our mission, therefore, is constructive education; to improve worthy waterways; develop the country; retire the long-haired, wild-eyed demagogical agitators and shysters; return to safe, sane and conservative commercial methods, and give all kinds of business a rest and a chance to recuperate.

To this end command the services of over seventy-five thousand of my co-workers in the Grand Army of Commercial Traveling Men (Applause.)

President Ransdell—Ladies and gentlemen, I now desire to present a gentleman who needs no introduction. He has spoken all over this country at waterway congresses and has been one of the greatest champions that the waterways ever had, or ever will have. He is going to tell us something about the so-called "pork barrel."

This gentleman is the Honorable J. Hampton Moore, M C from Pennsylvania, and President of the Atlantic Deeper Waterways Association—an Association of which you have doubtless heard (Applause.)

THE PORK BARREL

Address—J. Hampton Moore, M. C., Pennsylvania
President Atlantic Deeper Waterways Association

MR PRESIDENT, LADIES AND GENTLEMEN

The topic assigned to me was not of my own choice It was selected for me. It would have pleased me much if our distinguished President of the NATIONAL RIVERS AND HARBORS CONGRESS, the Senator from Louisiana, had taken this topic to himself He is a Member of the Senate of the United States, while I am only a Member of the House; and they know much more about "pork" in the Senate than we do in the House (Laughter) There is another reason why I should like to have had the Senator respond to this subject He comes from a farming community down on a plantation in Louisiana, while I come from a great city, Philadelphia, which we regard as the second port of the United States (Applause), and the "pork barrel" is distinctly an agricultural product (Laughter) We have no use for it in urban life, it belongs to the farm How the Senator would define the term I do not know, neither can I tell how the magazine writers acquired their knowledge of it. They are perched up yonder in the eighteenth stories of their skyscrapers in New York, most of them, and as their hands are not calloused from toil upon the dredge or from work along the canal, it is difficult to determine where they get their sensational information about rivers and harbors

I hold no brief for them, nor for the lexicographers of the railroads, who also seem to be intensely familiar with the "pork barrel" when it suits their purposes. In this I do not refer to "the big men" of the railroads, only to those little brains who think they are doing something big for the railroads when they oppose waterways (Applause)

DEFINITION OF THE "PORK BARREL"

I can give a commonplace definition of the term, however, what the boy on the street understands it to mean, and it is this A "pork barrel" is not what you get for your own river and harbor, but what the other fellow gets·for his (Laughter and applause) You never hear of "pork barrel" when things are coming your way; you always hear of it, and only hear of it, when things are going the other fellow's way Even at that, if there is evil in it, I would not want to defend it.

There are many men of many minds in this country of 100,000,000 people, and they are represented in the Senate and in the House of Representatives at Washington If you who come in from various States of the Union think you will find here one homogeneous mass of public opinion you are very greatly mistaken, because in the Senate there are 96 ways of thinking upon a public question and in the House there are more than 400. It takes a pretty clever leader to get us together upon one line of thought, and therefore we may not all agree upon all the matters affecting our transportation affairs, nor upon the size or effect of our appropriations.

Reform and Reformers

And besides what we have here in Washington in the way of Representatives, there are many other men of many minds in this country who have their influence upon Congress and Congressmen, and some of them have turned reformers. It is odd how some of us can swing around from our known and natural methods of life to become reformers Only this morning I was discussing this anomaly with a delegate from Virginia, who gave me a new thought on reformers. He said "the two greatest reformers in the world are poverty and old age " (Laughter and applause) It seems easy for men to reform when they have got enough for themselves, or when some other fellow begins to get something There are reformers who have a purpose in preaching reform Some of them have noble aspirations but others may be "Greeks bearing gifts " We have observed all of these varieties in the waterways movement

(At this point Mr. Moore made some humorous references to James J. Hill, Andrew Carnegie, and Theodore E Burton, of Ohio, and their interest in peace, war, and waterways) He continued:

These reformers are entitled to our consideration. But even they do not complete the picture. There are others who believe in "principle," to the extent that they would not even accept public office. (Laughter.) In one of the leading addresses this morning, that of the distinguished Secretary of State, it was said that the people generally stuck to principles and that they would not be bothered with the details of projects. The reference, of course, was to the motto, "A policy and not a project." That is an excellent idea, Mr. President, but we need not deceive ourselves; few men come here to talk "policy" who do not have in mind a project for which they intend to stand. It is like coming to talk "principles" and then asking for an office We all believe in the "policy," but most of us likewise believe in our "projects."

I am one who believes in a "project." If there be any of you who do not believe in a "project." it would be interesting to have you rise and tell whether I am mistaken in my judgment of human nature How many of you are not interested in some project in your own vicinity that you would like to see advanced? I pause that you may think it over I see no one rise

Appropriations Should Not Be Sectional

Call it "pork barrel" if you please I shall stand by the Delaware River and its improvement so long as I am honored by the people of Pennsylvania as one of their Representatives in Congress. (Applause) That great river works for the whole country and properly improved is capable of greater work. Call the great Atlantic coastal project "pork barrel," but I will stand for it so long as the people of the Atlantic Coast insist by convention and resolution that it is needful to commerce and the progress and safety of the country (Applause) That project means big business and the saving of life and property Call your great Mississippi River 9-foot channel project "pork barrel," Mr. President, and you would be seemingly untrue to the people of Louisiana, to the people of the Mississippi Valley whom you represent Call the Columbia River and the Snake

River "pork barrel," then the gentlemen who sit here as representatives of the commercial forces at that corner of the United States would .be answerable to the people back home. Mr President, we are expected to look after our projects, not in a sectional spirit but for the welfare of the entire country.

The "policy" defined here, and for which we are presumed to unite, is the securing for the approved projects of all the States of an annual appropriation bill of not less than $50,-000,000 This Convention, as I understand it, is for the purpose of helping that each may have a square deal and equal rights in the apportionment of appropriations for the improvement of our respective sections of the country. (Applause.) We should not be dejected because, perchance, some Member of Congress invites criticism striving to obtain recognition for his own locality, nor because some editor whose magazine is enjoying second-class postage at the expense of the people of the United States discovers in the cry of "pork barrel" a convenient medium for increasing his circulation Nor should these great public works be made the sport of statesmen brought to the bar of repentance by "poverty or old age," or those disciples of reform who, seeing all evil in others, live on in the hope that their sanctified countenances may some day adorn the pages of the "pork barrel" magazines (Applause)

A Transformation on the Trinity

We have said there are "many men of many minds" in the Congress Among them are the discoverers of the "pork barrel " In the last session of Congress they made much of the Trinity River in Texas. I ought not to say much about it, because I have criticized the Trinity project myself when comparing it with other and more important streams, but in 1909 the distinguished Representative from Ohio, Mr. Burton, a member of my own political party, who made an enviable reputation as chairman of the Rivers and Harbors Committee, said that the Trinity River in Texas was good enough for him He was then preaching the doctrine of peace. He said there were great commercial possibilities ahead of the Trinity, and that it ought to be improved to the extent of hundreds of thousands of dollars which he authorized to go into a bill (Applause) At the last session. only a few months ago, when the coastal States—and all others. in fact, except one or two of the inland States that have no rivers—were waiting with bated breath to know their fate, the same distinguished Representative—now become a Senator. though the change of title does not of necessity imply a real reform (laughter)—thumped and pounded the Trinity River and other items in the Rivers and Harbors Bill until all the projects, regardless of their importance, went down with the measure

Like our friend. Mr. Carnegie, who easily evoluted. from a maker of war materials to an apostle of peace, Mr Burton departed from his advocacy of the Trinity River improvement to become its bitter opponent upon the floor of the Senate. (Laughter and applause.) I like the Senator for his many excellent qualities of statesmanship, and it may be that he is right about some of the individual projects which he picked out of the last Rivers and Harbors Bill But the Senator is human, like the rest of us. and some of his earlier contributions to the literature of waterways may have put a few of us to a disadvantage in attempting to follow his footsteps. I trust the distinguished and able Senator from Ohio is doing some good I am not sure he is but, just between us waterway men and women, I would venture to say that if anyone were looking forward to presidential honors. a clever campaign manager would think it fine capital if the dear. good people of the Middle West could be made to believe that you "pork barrel" devils in Oregon, Louisiana, Maryland, and Florida, in your efforts to obtain competitive transportation to the country's markets, were ctually looting the honest farmers who are suffering because they cannot now get sufficient prices for their products——(Applause drowning the close of the sentence)

ARMY APPROPRIATIONS COMPARED

Let us say something about this "pork barrel" business in the aggregate. I am not pleading for an unjust cause. nor for an unworthy stream Much of my waterways information and much of my instruction comes from those who defeated the Rivers and Harbors Bill in the last session of Congress. I have taken the trouble to have the figures collated with regard to certain other branches of the Government of the United States for the last 40 years—literally. 39 years—but we will call it 40 years. Let us see what they are Since 1875, we have appropriated—and these gentlemen who are arguing for peace on sea and land, and who object to the opening of our coastal canals, voted for these measures as they came along—we appropriated for the Army of the United States, in these 40 years, approximately $2,000,000,000; they voted for it and there was no "pork barrel" in it nor scandal attached to it, and you and they should remember that while the Army is a protective arm of the Government service it is not a productive arm of the Government service. Somebody must work to maintain the Army of the United States; it is not the Army itself that raises revenue and gets the money to maintain the Army The Army is our creature. and while we are glad to support it, we must work elsewhere than in the Army to raise money for the cost of war (Applause.) But in 40 years we have raised this approximately $2 000,000,000 to support the Army of the United States, which, though small it is, we are proud to call our own   (Applause)

Navy Department and Pensions

During this same period of 40 years. due very largely to the lesson we learned in the Spanish-American War, we have appropriated for the support of the Navy of the United States more than $2,000,000,000; and proud as we are of it as a protective arm of the Government, the Navy is not a productive arm, it does not delve in mines; it does not work in the mills or on the farms It is supported by those who work in the mines, by those who work in the mills, and by those who work upon the farms; yet we dedicated more than $2,000,000,000 of our money to the maintenance of the Navy of the United States in the last 40 years There was no "pork barrel" attached to that (Applause)

I hesitate to make another comparison, yet I think I will.
We are a grateful Nation, the most grateful of all the nations
upon the face of the globe, for during the last 40 years, the
period of which I am now speaking, we have appropriated from
the men who worked in the mines, and the men who worked in
the mills, and the men who plowed the seas, and the men who
worked upon the farms—we have taken from them and given
to the old soldiers of this country who sustained the Union in
1861-1864 more than $4,500,000,000 (Applause.) We have
sustained them We have kept the old soldiers We have been
faithful to them, as they were to us. We have stood by them,
and we have paid our debt to this enormous extent, equal to
the entire amount that we have appropriated to both the Army
and Navy of the United States during the last 40 years. There
was no "pork barrel" there. (Applause.)   .

WHERE THE REVENUE COMES FROM

Now, where did we get this money? We got it out of business. We got it out of labor We got it out of commerce. We
got it out of that intercourse between men which we call trade;
and with this intercourse, with this intercommunication between
the active spirits of the laboring and the industrial and the
manufacturing and the commercial world we have maintained
these old soldiers and we have kept this Army and Navy going
We have looked out for every other branch of the Government
service to the tune of a billion dollars every session of Congress. One-third of all the revenue of the Government used in
order to meet these enormous bills comes in at the ports along
the coast of this country. It comes in through these harbors
which the Government is supposed to maintain. We collect it
at the customhouses. Another one-third comes from the internal revenue laid upon the labor and commerce of the people.
We are taxing them very heavily now in every direction We
are not taxing the Army and Navy and the pensioners; we are
taxing labor, commerce, and trade, and the burden is borne
largely by those who deal in that intangible commodity known
as transportation

SQUARE DEAL FOR WATERWAYS

If it were not for what you do for transportation, most of us would still be living in the old thatched log houses, digging our own potatoes and cooking our own meals. It is transportation that has brought together you men from Maine to California, from the Lakes to the Gulf, it is transportation that has given you the facilities of life and happiness of which the world did not dream a hundred years ago (Applause.) Do you give the railroads credit for all of this? They are entitled to much of the credit, but not to all, although, in a practical sense, they do most of it   Relatively up to a year or two ago they carried eight or nine hundred million tons of the commerce of the country, and the boats on the rivers and on the lakes carried 100,000,000 tons But as to the cost of it—and this is why we ask a square deal for waterways—you can carry a cargo of clay from over yonder in France, 3,000 miles away, and land it at the port of New York by boat cheaper than you can deliver it from New York to the city of Trenton, N J., 58 miles away, by rail. The farmer has had to pay, according to figures furnished by the Director of the Census a couple of years ago, 1 6 cents more to carry a bushel of wheat 9 miles from his farm to the railroad than it could be carried 3,000 miles from New York to Liverpool   And what has this burden bearer of the country, this waterway carrier, this commerce maker of the country, this labor dispenser of the country, supporting all these other great arms of the Government, protective and otherwise, what has it received from the Government of the United States in the last 40 years for the improvement of rivers and harbors? Six hundred and ninety-three million dollars all told   Compare that with what went to the Army and the Navy, compare it with what went to the dear old soldiers of this country. Yet this great burden bearer, the greatest burden bearer of them all, except the railroad, received the least at the hands of the Government and must stand the greatest amount of abuse.   It is an outrage which the waterways men of this country ought to resent. (Applause)

Ladies and gentlemen, the president tells me I have talked five minutes overtime. I have not started, but I am going to quit in the five minutes he gives me I shall respect the Chair (Many voices, "Go on! Go on!")

No "NEW PROJECTS"—ECONOMY

Well, then, let me talk a minute about something that is very dear to many of us. We are told that the coming Rivers and Harbors Bill is not to carry any new projects That was the scheme upon which the filibuster succeeded in the last session of Congress—no new projects—economy! Economy on useful works, while we have been spending more money on other things this Congress than we ever did in other years in the history of this Nation!

Who is it that says we shall not spend money to open up the streams of this country? Is it the President? If it is, he should be frank and let the country know, but I do not want to believe it is the President Is it the Secretary of State, who spoke to us this morning? He is an advocate of peace, and I do not blame him for that; but does he want us to be unprepared upon our rivers and harbors to do business, or to meet an enemy in the event of war? If he is opposed to such improvement, which I would not like to believe, he should speak out for we ought to know where he stands on that question Is it the chairman of the Rivers and Harbors Committee, or the members of the Committee? I should not want to think so The truth is the people of this country want us to do business for the country, and they would not excuse us if we were bottled up along the coast in event of war So those who oppose these improvements ought to speak in order that the people here can take the word home and let their communities know just what our Representatives stand for in Washington

IMPORTANCE OF ATLANTIC COASTAL WATERWAYS

We have asked for the opening of certain coast canals. It is important that we should connect up the God-given waterways of the Atlantic Coast. It is not a new suggestion The demand has been before Congress since the days of Washington and Monroe. We have been put off until our patience is sorely tried. Why? Some wise old men of both parties have told us we had no right to ask for such improvement when we had the great bosom of the Atlantic Ocean to come and go on. Why, gentlemen, you have come to this Convention in the midst of one of the frequent storms that rage along our coast

If you look at the newspapers, today, you will find reports of wreckage and devastation that has gone unchecked There has been loss of life and property. It is but one of many similar visitations. In 10 years we have lost more than 2,200 lives on the Atlantic Coast, because we must take the risk of the open sea. What we have asked for in particular is a cut of 13 miles from Delaware Bay to Chesapeake Bay. That would reduce an outside sailing of 325 miles, and give the Nation muchneeded communication between the navy yards and repair stations and the base of supplies for our naval vessels in the event of need. I refer to the Chesapeake & Delaware Canal, that neglected old waterway which, back in the days of the Civil War, when the railroads were incompetent, carried troops to Washington at Lincoln's call—the troops that saved the Capital (Applause.) I mean that old canal which, if it remains inadequate and under private ownership as it is, would, in the event of a foreign invasion find Washington in relatively the same position it was in during the War of 1812, when the British were in possession of the Capital and the President was obliged to seek a haven across the Potomac.

WATERWAYS FOR NATIONAL DEFENSE

I do not know whether you who come from the mountains back yonder where the streams are not burdened with commerce fully understand this question I do not believe you would feel secure even in your remoteness from the scene of activity, if an attack were made upon the coast. In such a case you would be called upon, and as loyal Americans you would promptly respond to the call, to defend the honor of the flag, but you would be ashamed to find that such canals as the Chesapeake & Delaware, capable of the greatest possible service, were unfitted for the passage of the smallest Government craft to carry .men or supplies. In a matter so vital should we wait until another country has sent its battleships to bottle up our ports? We need the inside passages now for business purposes; that's the essence of our agitation, but once we have them for business purposes we are always prepared for what may happen. What would Germany do without the Kiel Canal, its key to the ocean and the Baltic Sea? Oh, we could take a chapter from the history of those European countries now so unhappily engaged in war They have not neglected their waterways as we have It has cost them money to build their waterways and inland passages, but it seems to have been worth the price. It will cost us less to improve our waterways now than to wait until war obliges us to improve them Even now the naval vessels of the Government are unable to navigate such streams as the Hudson River One of them went aground at Albany only a few weeks ago because of the uncompleted works there; nor could they pass through the old Chesapeake and Delaware Canal even in times of peace; we have tried it to our dismay. If, then, in times of peace these costly craft of the Nation must take a dangerous outside route and be driven ashore, as they sometimes are, endangering the lives of the men and risking the property of the Government, is it not time we should insist that some of the enormous sums of money that go into other branches of the Government service shall be appropriated to the Government needs for the defense of the country? (Applause)

I wish I could go on   (Cries of "Go on !") I wanted to discuss the waste and loss incurred by the filibuster, but. the Chairman says my time is up   (Applause.)

SECRETARY THOMPSON announced the Members at Large appointed by the President, and also the names already handed in by Chairmen of State Delegations for Committees on Nominations and on Resolutions, and urged State Delegations that had not made selections for these committees to do so at once.

The full list of these committees, as later perfected and announced, follows:

Committee on Nominations

Appointed by President Ransdell, at Large—Olin J. Stephens, Chairman, New York; Thomas Wilkinson, Iowa; J. M. Reilly, New Jersey; C. W. Hodson, Oregon; Perry A. Randall, Indiana; C. S. E Holland, Texas; Theodore Justice, Pennsylvania; V. M. LeFebvre, Louisiana; F. Horton Colcock, South Carolina; F. W. Joslin, New York; M. T Bryan, Tennessee; John J Martin, Massachusetts; Robert Somerville, Mississippi.

Selected by State Delegations—Alabama, Judge J. J Mitchell, Florence; Arkansas, Harry E Cook, Lake Village, California, Hon. Charles F Curry, Sacramento; Connecticut, Charles H. Nichols, New Haven, Florida, John G Ruge, Apalachicola; Georgia, W J. Twiggs, Augusta; Illinois, L K. Sherman, Chicago; Indiana, Col D N Foster, Ft Wayne; Iowa, Capt. W. A. Blair, Davenport; Louisiana, R. L. Hill, Lake Providence; Maryland, Col. Jacob W Hook, Baltimore; Massachusetts, Ralph S Bauer, Lynn; Minnesota, W F Decker, Minneapolis; Mississippi, Walton Shields, Greenville; Missouri, William E Spratt, St Joseph; Nebraska, Robert H. Manley, Omaha; New Jersey, James M. Reilly, Newark; New York, Capt. Fred Russell, Queens, Ohio, Frank M Boggs, Portsmouth; Oregon, Henry H. Gilfry, Marshfield; Pennsylvania, Capt. Thomas Rees, Pittsburgh, Tennessee, John Stagmaier, Chattanooga; Texas, Adolph Boldt, Houston, West Virginia, A. W Werninger, Huntington; United Commercial Travelers of America, R. S Tucker, Troy, New York.

Committee on Resolutions

Appointed by President Ransdell, at Large—William B Rodgers, Chairman, Pennsylvania, J S. Cullinan, Texas; S. C. Mead, New York, J R McLaughlin, Washington: W T. Bland, Missouri; Albert Bettinger, Ohio; J. W Worthington, Alabama; Frank Fessenden Crane, Massachusetts; J F Ellison, Ohio; T Edward Wilder, Illinois; O. N Killough, Arkansas, E. J. Hamley, Louisiana, J. L Messmore, Missouri.

Selected by State Delegations—Alabama, W B Oliver, Tuscaloosa; Arkansas, Hon James R Yerger, Lake Village; California, Hon. Charles W. Bell, Pasadena; Connecticut, Mayor T. C. Murphy, Norwich; Delaware, H. R. Burton, Lewes; Florida, John G Ruge, Apalachicola; Georgia, J. R. McCord, Atlanta; Illinois, A. W. Charles, Carmi; Indiana, J. H. Rohsenberger, Evansville; Iowa, A. C. Miller, Des Moines; Louisiana, Major F. M. Kerr, New Orleans; Maryland, Robert J. Beacham, Baltimore; Massachusetts, S. F. Sherman, Lawrence; Minnesota, J. W Cooper, St. Paul; Mississippi, J. J. Hayes, Vicksburg; Missouri, O V Wilson, Kansas City; Nebraska, John W Gamble, Omaha; New Jersey, Ernest H. Rowe, Jersey City; New York, Hon Peter G. Ten Eyck, Albany; Ohio, A. K Nippert, Cincinnati; Oregon, C. W. Hodson, Portland; Pennsylvania, George E Bartol, Philadelphia; South Carolina, F Horton Colcock, Columbia; Tennessee, Judge George T. Hughes, Columbia; Texas, Walter Gresham, Galveston; Virginia, T Edwin Baird, Norfolk, West Virginia, C. D Dotson, Parkersburg; United Commercial Travelers of America, C C Taylor, Greensboro, North Carolina.

PRESIDENT RANSDELL—Ladies and gentlemen, let me present a Member of the United States Senate who will occupy a position of very great power in framing the next Rivers and Harbors Bill—the Acting Chairman of the Committee on Commerce of the Senate; a gentleman who has always been a friend of waterways; who is not only a member of the United States Senate but President of the Mississippi-to-Atlantic Inland Waterway Association. One of the great streams in his State was singled out for special criticism by those who thought they had found a mare's nest in the recent River and Harbor Bill This gentleman has been asked to tell us something about the Oklawaha River, and he will now do so—Senator Fletcher, of Florida. (Applause.)

THE OKLAWAHA RIVER
Address—Senator Duncan U. Fletcher, Florida
President Mississippi-to-Atlantic Inland Waterway Association

Mr President and Gentlemen:

As I look into the faces of those assembled here my wonder increases that anyone, whether under the protection of his privilege on the floor of the House, or elsewhere, could seriously charge that you constitute a "powerful lobby," a gathering of "waterway euthusiasts," here to "press on the Federal Congress a $50,000,000 or $60,000,000 pork barrel for 1915."

For some six years I have attended the annual meetings of the National Rivers and Harbors Congress, and I have felt, as I mingled with its members from all portions of the country, that I was in, if not select, at least reputable society. In recent months, since your last meeting, I must tell you, though you may have read of it, that you have been publicly declared to be the "gratuitous makers" of "pork barrel" proposals for legislation and "the greatest lobby in all history"

I have felt honored in the past by an invitation to address the members of this Congress, whose intelligence impressed me; whose open, public discussion of the general policy they urged was not surpassed in display of force and ability by speakers upon that subject in any body anywhere (Applause); who, at their own expense and at great sacrifices, came here in response to a high sense of public duty, to render a public service in assembling and distributing information useful in determining governmental policy with reference to governmental properties and resources; and now I learn that you have all along been prompted by ulterior, unworthy motives, and that in very truth your "battle cry" is for "loot."

Before me are men who stand for the highest in citizenship in their communities, men of known patriotic impulses, who have done something for their country and fellows, to whom the question must now be put, "Are you prepared for an investigation into your purposes and conduct, as has been publicly proposed?" It has been my understanding that at each recurring December, from practically every State in the Union the select,

forward-moving, public-spirited citizen, representing the best in
his community, and that means the best in the Nation, has come
here to attend these meetings and offer his views on a subject
of vast importance to the whole country, and counsel and advise with his fellows from the Pacific to the Atlantic and from
the Lakes to the Gulf, in the hope that, aided somewhat by such
deliberations, and interchange of information and ideas, action
would be taken by those in authority to carry into effect the
measures considered to be sound and wise; and yet the country
is now informed, by speeches carried at the expense of the Government to remotest regions and by sympathizing newspapers,
that your organization "has injected into pork-barrel legislation of former years an element of cheek and phenomenal nerve
both astounding and wicked in its influence."

The Only Course

If there be a grain of truth in the reckless statements
made and published broadcast, reflecting on you, the only
course open to you, my friends, is to adjourn and, hat in hand,
hie yourselves, "unhonored and unsung," to the earliest train
for home Yes, there is one thing you should do before you
dissolve, and that is, adopt a memorial to the Congress of the
United States to the effect that since you have been *exposed,* it
would be useless for you to offer any suggestions or submit any
petition to it, discredited as you are, and you hereby efface yourselves individually and collectively and offer your most humble
apologies for ever having existed at all, and ask forgiveness
for your presumption in assembling once a year in Washington
and listening to addresses by Presidents of the United States,
and Cabinet Officials, Ambassadors and Ministers from Foreign
Countries, Representatives and Senators, and expert statesmen
and leaders in economic thought from various portions of the
country, as has been your custom, and particularly for the extreme "nerve" you displayed in communicating your resolutions to Congress, and now, having renounced all intention of
having anything more to say on the subject of rivers and harbors, and humbly begging pardon for what you have heretofore

said and done, pray to be spared an investigation   (Laughter and applause)

You ought to be ashamed of yourselves—or you ought not There's no half-way business about it. You ought to go home and stay there—or you ought to stand on your rights and let the people know you are here. You ought to surrender abjectly —or stand your ground and fight. To my mind the old stoics had a good working philosophy—"Don't jubilate, don't whine— fight!" (Applause)

You men who have something at stake in the land you live in, who know conditions in your respective communities, who desire to do what will promote the prosperity of your country, and the welfare of its people, do you realize that it has been published *ad libitum*, and so far as those who oppose the policy of improving and developing our waterways are concerned, can, they have blazoned it on the sky that your influence has been, and is, "wicked," that you are plunderers of the Treasury, ene- mies of society, a "menace" to honest and decent governmental action ? Apparently the attack on rivers and harbors legislation has been largely centered on you

If, in spite of this, you feel that you can safely proceed, taking the philosophic view that the man who, or the organization which, accomplishes anything worth while these days, must expect to be tongue-lashed and ink-spattered, then I should feel that it is in order to point out some excuses for your organization and justification for your work.

You have felt that the *principle* for which you stood was sound, because you had the highest authority for it   You have felt that the *policy* you desired to further was quite well estab- lished, because you had it supported by pledges which all politi- cal parties have been making to the people since 1856   You sup- posed you were justified in urging that the accepted principle and the assured policy with reference to the treatment of the harbors and navigable waterways of the country should be faith- fully written into law and diligently observed.

A Commission and Its Report

Some six years ago there was a stir for a commission to look into the matter of waterway improvements—probably urged by opponents of such improvements. As a result the National Waterways Commission, composed of twelve members of the Senate and House of Representatives, was created by Act of Congress, March 3, 1909. The duty imposed on it by statute was to investigate questions pertaining to water transportation and the improvement of waterways., and to make recommendations to Congress The Act provided that a preliminary report should be filed not later than January 1, 1910, and this was presented by Mr. Burton, Chairman of the Commission, January 24, 1910

The Commission was composed of Theodore E Burton, Chairman, Jacob H. Gallinger, Vice-Chairman, Samuel H. Pyles, William Alden Smith, F. M. Simmons, James P Clarke, and William Lorimer, from the Senate, and D S. Alexander, Frederick C. Stevens, Irving P. Wanger, Stephen M. Sparkman, and John A Moon, of the House of Representatives.

It will be seen that the present Chairman of the Commerce Committee of the Senate was a member of this Commission and that the present Chairman of the Rivers and Harbors Committee of the House was also a member of this Commission. Senatoi Burton, who vigorously opposed the last Rivers and Harbors Bill, and is reported to be opposed to the general plan and policy of rivers and harbors legislation as heretofore adopted and pursued, was the Chairman of that Commission It may be interesting to refer to some of the findings and conclusions reached and reported by that Commission

Senate Document No. 301, Sixty-first Congress, Second Session, is before me, and, on page 6, contains this language·

> "The most frequent argument for river transportation has been that for coarser freights over long distance water transportation afforded very great advantages. There can be little question of the general accuracy of this statement. A boat or barge floating

in the water is readily moved and at low speeds requires far less power than the movement of a railway car or other receptable for freight used on land. The general statement has been made and widely accepted that with an equal expenditure of power about five times as much freight can be handled by water as by rail. The expense of equipping a transportation line, at least so far as the boats are concerned, is but trivial in comparison with that of constructing a railway. River transportation again has a decided advantage in that the waters are free and any one having the requisite capital and ability can engage in the business. This tends to create competition and to prevent monopoly."

The Commission further reports, page 9:

"It has been repeatedly urged that rivers should be improved because of the tendency of such improvements to lower railroad rates. This tendency can not be denied. It is very manifest in every portion of the country where rivers have been improved."

The report says, page 10:

"It has been brought to our attention that in a number of instances railways have temporarily reduced rates and continued them upon a lower basis until competing water lines have been driven out of business. The Commission would recommend that in such cases, when a rate is once reduced by a railway it should not be permitted to raise the same unless, after a hearing by the Interstate Commerce Commission, or other competent body, it should be found that such proposed increase rests upon changed conditions other than the elimination or decrease of water competition."

That recommendation has been written into law.

The Commission further recommended as follows, page 10:

> "The transportation facilities of the country will, as
> we believe, be still further promoted by compelling
> joint rates and pro-rating agreements; also, by re-
> quiring through bills of lading and physical connection
> between rail and water agencies."

Congress has gone a considerable ways in carrying out this
recommendation

The Commission declares that the general policy of almost
all European countries has been toward the development and improvement of their waterways; presents tables to show the
marked increase of inland water-borne traffic, especially in Germany, but in all European countries except England, calls attention to the fact that this increase, with few exceptions, has taken
place on canals which are of shallow draft, the average depth
being about six feet; and adds that "the well-established policy
in this case is to secure co-operation between railways and waterways by official control of railway rates with a view to maintaining profitable traffic on the latter."

The Commission favors "the policy of making improvements
in vogue in the United States, to-wit, that policy under which the
General Government improves rivers, either by open channel
work or by the construction of locks and dams, charging no tolls
therefor, rendering navigation entirely free." Harbors are improved under the same policy, which has also been followed in
France since 1879. The Commission adds, "the liberal policy
heretofore pursued by the Government in this regard has greatly
benefited the public and has resulted in a great increase in wealth
to the country at large"

In view of certain recent utterances, particular attention is
called to this language in the report, on pages 15 and 16·

> "The Commission regards the present law, providing
> for preliminary steps before the adoption of projects
> for improvement, as well adapted to secure the best
> results. * * * Numerous propositions have been

made for the creation of a board of public works, or
other body, which shall decide upon the feasibility and
desirability of propositions for expenditures on rivers
and harbors. The Commission is unwilling to recommend a change of this kind, and points to the fact that
the past recommendations of the Engineer Corps have
been carefully prepared and with a degree of expert
knowledge and comprehension of the commercial needs
of the country which could not well be supplied by any
other body or organization."

Those gentlemen who most vigorously opposed the last Rivers and Harbors Bill, and who exchanged fulsome felicitations
and generous compliments with each other over the result, took
then, and have given notice they will continue to take, po-
sitions directly opposed to the report of this great Waterways Commission, which but recently ended its labors. The demand some of them now make for a "strong advisory board of
high-class men * * * to have supervision of all waterways,"
is visionary and absurd, and means simply the stopping of such
public works.

AN UNWARRANTED CHARGE

When it was pointed out that the last Rivers and Harbors
Bill, which certain newspapers, inspired or misguided, said was
a "steal," and these gentlemen boldly denounced as a "pork barrel" measure, contained some 330 items, all but two minor ones
of which had been approved by the Board of Engineers for
Rivers and Harbors and the Chief of Engineers, they began to
find fault with the present system and plan of procedure. They
can offer nothing as good, but they had to resort to this indi-
rect argument that the Board of Engineers are incompetent or
corrupt in order to save their faces on the charge of "pork barrel." If there was "pork" in the bill the Engineers had put it
there. There may be a difference of opinion whether the Country
has not more confidence in the Engineers than in those making
that unwarranted charge. (Applause.) I say "unwarranted"

deliberately, and I regret that time will only permit an illustration which will have to serve the purpose of a fuller demonstration.

It seems to have been inferred that, because the Honorable Chairman of the House Committee was from Florida, and Florida had a Senator on the Commerce Committee of the Senate, in a "rotten" measure containing "pork," a likely place to find it would be in the Florida items. The bill was searched, therefore, and two items were picked out as vulnerable, then indefensible, then positively bad, and finally they got to be land speculation schemes and pure graft. Those two items were Kissimmee River and Oklawaha River.

The Kissimmee River

It was charged and published throughout the country that the Kissimmee River was "dry eight months in the year" and ought to be insured against fire. The river never was dry a minute Think of dealing with a serious matter with that kind of levity and misrepresentation!

From the way slurs and insinuations have been uttered regarding this stream, you would infer that it is a small creek a few miles in length, serving no useful purpose, and you would also infer that the appropriation asked for amounts to hundreds of thousands of dollars On the contrary, the Kissimmee itself is 137 miles long, and flows through three good-sized lakes and empties into Lake Okechobee. which is itself about 40 miles across, and from which a boat can pass to the Gulf of Mexico on one side or to the Atlantic Ocean on the other. Together with Lake Okechobee and the Caloosahatchee River. it affords a valuable waterway 309 miles in length from the Gulf of Mexico to the city of Kissimmee. and furnishes the only means of communication. other than roads. between some 3,000 square miles of territory along the river and the nearest point touched by a railroad I would like to know if it is reasonable to call this a "creek " and belittle it as a stream of no consequence or importance?

The Engineer's report shows that the number of regular steamers in trade on it is five; that the commerce for the year

1912 amounted to 71,950 tons, consisting of fruit, fish, fertilizer, feed, groceries, general merchandise, naval stores, logs, lumber, vegetables and wood; and that the value of this commerce was $2,935,000, being an increase of more than 700 per cent in three years. Few streams in the country can make such a showing.

On account of low water navigation on the Kissimmee has been practical for only seven or eight months in the year. It is now proposed to make a channel 30 to 60 feet wide and three feet deep at ordinary low water. The Engineer estimates that with a channel useful the year round there will be a further increase in the commerce of 100 per cent. After what I have said about the river, its length, its connection with great lakes, and with the Atlantic Ocean and the Gulf of Mexico, you will be surprised to know that the appropriation asked for to complete the project is only $47,000. To what desperation are the opponents of waterways driven when they resort to criticisms of this kind!

The Oklawaha River

The first appropriation for the Oklawaha was made in 1891— twenty-three years ago. It is no newly discovered stream, nor is it any "River of Doubt," but it has just been discovered to be a "pork" proposition. As a result of work already done there is a channel six feet deep for 32 miles above its mouth in the St. Johns River, a practical channel four feet deep at ordinary low water to Silver Springs Run, and thence a channel three feet deep at low water to Leesburg on Lake Griffin, 94 miles from the mouth.

The improvement proposed means the joining of Lakes Griffin, Harris, Eustis, and Dora, and a connection with the Atlantic Ocean through the St. Johns River. The commerce consists of logs, general merchandise, naval stores, and fruit, amounting in 1912 to 102.647 tons, valued at $1,179,466. The Engineer's report shows that two steamers and five power boats ply the river the entire year carrying passengers and general freight, and that there are more than 75 launches engaged in towing lighters and rafts and in general traffic.

The proposed improvement would give water transportation from a productive and beautiful section of Florida to Jacksonville, the distributing point where railroads and ships compete for business There is no more meritorious project, no improvement more needed anywhere in the country than this one The report of the Board of Engineers was made after a visit to the locality, during which public hearings were held and a thorough examination was made of all the conditions

Is it possible that people will be prejudiced against this most worthy project because some man in Wisconsin, or Iowa, or Connecticut, who was never within a thousand miles of it and knows practically nothing about it, chooses to call the stream "a creek" and the project a "land speculation scheme?" Neither the Oklawaha River nor the Kissimmee River project is in the interest of real estate speculation, nor is any drainage or reclamation scheme involved. The reports will show that the project is for navigation purposes alone If either benefits private parties in the way of furnishing transportation for products, as it should and would do, that is only incidental to the improvement

Show me a project which, when completed, will not increase land values, will not increase productive acreage, and will not add to creation and distribution, and I will be able to point to a project which should not have been undertaken at all, a project where waste takes the place of conservation Show me a project, the completion of which means increase in land values, increase in productive acreage, a rich addition to creation and distribution, and I will point to a project which it would be a shortsighted policy to overlook, and a most criminal neglect to ignore. (Applause.)

Just a word more about the Oklawaha On the lakes which I have named are a number of flourishing towns and settlements, the commerce of which is now handled entirely by rail What water competition would mean is clearly shown by the fact that while Leesburg and Sanford are practically the same distance from Jacksonville. the freight rates from the former are practically twice as much from the latter. Sanford. of course has the benefit of water transportation on the St Johns River The Engineers state that the towns which would be benefited by this improvement have a commerce amounting to over 400,000 tons annually. and a conservative estimate of the saving that would result from the improvement, on a basis of only 200,000 tons, would be about $600,000 annually. The estimated cost of the improvement is $733,000.

Here is a project in which the annual saving is nearly as great as the total cost of construction, and yet a project like that, which has been approved by the District Engineer, by the Board of Engineers after a personal inspection of the locality, by the Chief of Engineers and by committees of both Houses of Congress, has been pictured before the world as a "pork barrel" proposition.

The worst of it is, my friends, that we may look for a repetition of this absurd performance because the same people are determined to defeat any legislation intended to accomplish the improvement of our waterways. Not only that, but the friends of the policy and the principle advocated by the National Rivers and Harbors Congress will be denounced as lobbyists and the supporters of the next bill framed on the lines heretofore followed will be denounced as "pork barrel" grafters. There can be but one purpose back of that course   Whether we guess the purpose or not, we know the effect aimed at, and there can be no doubt as to what the consequences are intended to be

The "Sectional" Bogy

It will be argued, again, as it has already been, that the bill is "sectional," in that it provides for more items in the South than in any other section   This is an unworthy criticism, but it may be answered by the simple statement that of the 28,000 miles of navigable rivers in the whole country, 25,000 miles are in the South. If rivers are to be improved you must go where they are to do the work (Laughter and applause); but while the items are more numerous for the South, the greater amount of appropriations goes to the North and East.

Economy

The last Rivers and Harbors Bill, as reported to the Senate, carried in cash apropriations and contract authorizations a total of $53,683,000, but later the Commerce Committee reported a substitute carrying a total of about $35,000,000 Even this latter amount was criticized as too large It is worthy of note that from 1899 to 1907, inclusive—during which time the distinguished Senator from Ohio, who was the chief critic of the recent bill, was Chairman of the Rivers and Harbors Committee—the cash appropriations were $110,898,891, and the contract authorizations were $127,009,365, a total of $238,808,356. The bill of 1905 called for over $65,000,000, and that of 1907 for over $87,000,000.

It is generally supposed that the country has grown and that its need for transportation facilities has increased along with our industries, production and consumption Yet, the cry of "economy" and the alarm about taxes were used to defeat a measure calling for only $35,000,000. The argument that financial depression and decrease of revenues compel us to provide practically only for the maintenance of work already completed is unsound Of all times, the time to carry on a needful public work is when there is a call for the employment of labor and a necessity for circulation of money, both of which results, together with the stimulation of industry and commerce, are accomplished by the prosecution of public improvements

It is economy in the highest sense to take care of these public properties, the Nation's properties, at just such times as we are now experiencing It is extravagance and waste to starve home development in order to exploit national prestige It is not extravagant, under any conditions, for the Government to expend five per cent of its revenues annually in improving its own property and developing its own resources. "Economy lies always in wise expenditures " (Applause)

President Ransdell—I now wish to introduce a gentleman who presided over one of the greatest States of this Nation as its chief executive for eight years During his incumbency as Governor a vast amount of beneficial legislation was enacted, much of it in favor of waterways Among other things a twenty-million-dollar bond issue was voted to assist in waterway improvement.

This gentleman has been here before. He is known and honored by all the friends of waterways. It gives me pleasure to present ex-Governor Deneen, of Illinois (Applause.)

ILLINOIS AND THE WATERWAYS OF THE MIDDLE WEST

Address—Hon. Charles S. Deneen
Late Governor of Illinois

Mr. Chairman, Ladies and Gentlemen:

I appreciate very much this complimentary introduction, and shall try and show my high appreciation of it by saying what I have to say in the time allotted to me

I have been requested by those who are concerned in the waterway movement in my State to speak to the subject of "Illinois and the Waterways of the Middle West." Illinois has been interested in the waterway movement from the very beginning Our interest arises out of our very fortunate situation. The lowest elevation in our State is about 300 feet, the highest about 1,000 feet, above the level of the sea Because of that fact half the waters of the country gravitate to our shores; the Ohio River, gathering its waters from Western New York and passing our State to the Gulf, the Tennessee and the Cumberland, gathering their waters from Northern Alabama and discharging them against our State; the Missouri River, gathering its waters from Montana and draining that vast area from Kansas to Northwestern Canada, discharges its waters against our State; and the Mississippi River passes by our State for five hundred miles Furthermore, the water-shed between the St Lawrence system and the Mississippi system is located not only in our State but in our metropolis; and the greatest trunk line of waterways in the world, extending 3.300 miles from the Gulf of St. Lawrence via the St Lawrence River, the Great Lakes, the Chicago River, the Des Plaines River, the Illinois River, and the Mississippi River to the Gulf of Mexico, runs through the heart of our State—we are right in the center of it We are interested in both gulfs and both waterways

Because of that we are interested not only in a general policy of waterway improvement, but we are interested in more than one project. For instance, we are interested in the project referred to by Congressman Moore for a nine-foot channel between Pittsburgh and Cairo, and we are interested likewise in the project for expending twelve million dollars to make a six-foot channel from the mouth of the Missouri to Kansas City. (Applause.) We are interested likewise in the project to make a six-foot channel from Grafton to St. Paul We are interested in the improvement of navigation in the Cumberland and Tennessee Rivers. We are interested in the Erie Canal. We are interested in the Welland Canal and the Canadian system of canals. Because of our situation they all interest us. We are interested in the Panama Canal because we expect to have connection with it and to enlarge the trade of our State through the opportunities which it will afford, because not only are we in the very center of the waterways of the country, but we are interested also in railroad transportation.

We are situated at the Southwest corner of the Great Lakes Chicago is the nearest lake port to New Orleans It is also the meeting place of the trans-continental railroads Because of that we are interested in transportation by railroads and waterways We are the meeting place for both, where products are assembled and distributed throughout the country The minerals of Minnesota and Wisconsin meet the coal of Illinois on our borders In our State for years lumber was assembled; it was a great distributing point. We now are the point where they assemble the live stock and the minerals of the Middle West, and where they distribute those products We are at the point where the raw materials of the great Mississippi Valley are assembled and then sent forth as finished products which go to the uttermost parts of the earth.

. Because, therefore, of our situation and opportunities, we are interested in the development of waterways in Canada, in the United States, and in the Panama Canal From the very beginning the men who discovered our State and traveled over it became interested in the great waterway trunk line of the world, the St. Lawrence and the Mississippi, to which I have referred

I intend to trace very briefly the growth of that idea and the development of a great purpose with reference to both It began with the explorers who came to our State, Joliet and Marquette, away back in 1674, each of whom saw the enormous advantages of our situation which pointed to the feasibility of making connections there at Chicago

When our Northwest Territory was organized, the provision was inserted in the organic law making the streams connecting the Mississippi and the St Lawrence public highways Before our State was organized and while it was even yet a territory, the Treasurer of the United States, Hon. Albert Gallatin, advocated the development of the waterways to which I have referred When our State, as a Territory, asked to be admitted to the Union, our delegate asked that the Northern boundary might be extended and fixed sixty-one miles north of the then territorial boundary, for two purposes; first, that we might have a lake port on Lake Michigan; second, that the connecting link between the Mississippi River system and the St Lawrence system might not be prejudiced by a divided jurisdiction. It was done, so that our State boundary itself was fixed with that in view.

After our State was organized we asked Congress to make appropriations to make the connection referred to, and Congress aided the State by land grants, beginning in 1822 and running on until 1833, to build a canal through Illinois and Michigan connecting these two systems. Our State undertook the work and finished it in 1848 This was a very useful canal, not only to the State, but to the Middle West

In 1911 we found that the tolls that had been received in operating the canal had amounted to about $600,000, and the expenditures had amounted to about $250,000 In 1885 one Commissioner of the canal estimated that the canal had at that time saved in freight rates alone $180,000,000 (Applause) It had a small, narrow channel, and its locks permitted barges of only 200 tons burden to travel through them, whereas the railroads running along it carried about 1,700 tons of freight in a train

Then our people began to develop further the idea that had prevailed so long in our State; and our municipality of Chicago asked the State to permit it to build, not only the Sanitary District Channel, but a ship canal, the first great link between the Lakes and the Gulf. That permission was given in 1889, and the channel was completed within ten years thereafter. The municipality, which is practically Chicago, built a canal 160 feet wide at the bottom, with a minimum depth of 24 feet, and has expended upon it already $80,000,000, or contracted for such expenditure. It is not the longest canal, but it is one of the largest canals, if not the largest, in the world—certainly the largest within our own continent. Shortly after it was finished Congress appointed a Commission to make a survey for the working out of a proper channel to the Gulf, and the Commission chose St. Louis as one of the great units in its development The Commission stated that it would cost $31,000,000 to extend it from the Southern terminus of the Sanitary District ship canal to St. Louis. I give these figures because the statement was made some time ago as to the vast amount of money that would be required to dig a channel to New Orleans The figures were $31,000,000 from Chicago to St Louis, and $15,000,000 from Lockport down to La Salle.

Our State entered again upon the construction, or assisting in the construction, of this great channel and a commission was appointed by the State to study the collateral benefits that might accrue to Illinois and whether or not our State might make a contribution to that great work

Our Commission reported back, within two years, that the fall between Lockport and La Salle was 140 feet; that 100,000 E. H P could be created by the fall of the water going from the lake through the Chicago River and the channel; and that it could yield a revenue of about $2,500,000 a year for the State The General Assembly of our State submitted to the people an amendment to our Constitution which would authorize the General Assembly to appropriate and expend $20,000,000 for the purpose of digging a channel from Lockport on to Utica and La Salle. It was submitted to our people and widely discussed, and the majority in favor of it was about 450,000 votes, the largest vote recorded upon any issue ever submitted to the people of our State

We had had an unfortunate experience in the early history of our State in making appropriations for railroads and canals, and the Constitution of our State forbade making such appropriations. So the people passed upon this one measure to permit the General Assembly to expend $20,000,000 for that purpose.

Private initiative secured favorable locations upon the channel before the State could acquire it. In two different places large water power corporations fastened themselves upon the District. and litigation in our courts and division of sentiment in our General Assembly has prevented the final crystallization of the public sentiment of our State into decision as to the methods of expending the $20,000,000 which has been authorized; but the obstacles are being removed and the way being made clear for the expenditure of that money, and soon Illinois will have contributed, I hope, $100,000,000 to the communication between the Great Lakes and the Gulf of Mexico, through channels of the Chicago River, the Des Plaines River, the Illinois River and the Mississippi River   (Applause)

While I do not remember accurately, and will not so state, and will not attempt to convey an ambiguous impression, my recollection is that the contribution of Illinois is between one-third and one-quarter of the aggregate expense that will be required to develop the channel which has been outlined by the Commission, on to New Orleans   In any event, our State will have expended $80,000,000, and in providing for the additional expenditure of $20,000,000 will make a contribution equal to the advantages which will accrue to it as compared with the other States along the channel   Illinois, which led in this movement, has contributed this large amount because of the great advantages that will accrue to it

Our State has appointed another commission to ascertain the advantage to it of waterway transportation   I will not have time to refer to the reports made by them, but I will just mention one thing which has been published by our Board of Trade in a recent report   Taking the ten years ending in 1909, and comparing the difference in freight charges between rail transportation and water transportation on corn and wheat between Chicago and New York City, the difference amounted to $72,000,000

Our State is one that creates bulky products from its farms and from its mines, and it gathers to it such products from all parts of the West, and because of that it has a vital interest in cheap transportation. We want this in order to move our agricultural and manufactured products to market at the least possible cost, and to draw these products to us.

Furthermore, we realize that with the opening of the Panama Canal there will be a radical change in freight rates, and we fear that the change will affect our State. Because of this our people —and I believe I speak the sentiment of our whole people. since they have registered it very plainly by a majority vote of 450,000 in favor of a great waterway—feel an increasing interest in the development of the waterways of the interior of the continent and of the great terminal cities, and in the Erie Canal, the Gulf of St. Lawrence, the Gulf of Mexico and the Panama Canal itself

Our State has constantly supported such legislation and has constantly supported the great projects that have been passed upon by experts for waterway development in all parts of the country. Our relations are such with the West and with the Eastern coast that we feel that whatever affects any part of the country affects us, and we stand willing to support any fair and just appropriations for the development of waterways wherever they can be utilized to the best advantage in any part of our country or continent. (Applause)

President Ransdell. Ladies and gentlemen, we will now have an address from a gentleman who has been actually trying to navigate the very much neglected rivers of the interior He is a practical inventor and navigator. Permit me to introduce Mr. John H Bernhard, of New Orleans, La (Applause)

PRACTICAL NAVIGATION
Address—John H. Bernhard
New Orleans, La.

MR. CHAIRMAN, LADIES AND GENTLEMEN.

It is hardly necessary for me to say that we are here to voice our desire for the improvement of inland and territorial waters and harbors of the United States We do not desire to see these waters improved for the bare pleasure of knowing that the channels are deepened, straightened or widened, or the harbors protected, but we desire to see the waters improved so that they may become valuable channels of commerce We want to see the potential value of our waterways become an interest-yielding value If it is ridiculous to talk about the potential value of land and leave the place idle, barren, failing to give us annually its portion of crops; it is equally ridiculous to talk about the potential value of our inland and territorial waters and be content to see them idle

That our inland waters are idle, we cannot better show than through the mighty Mississippi River, this Father of Waters, on whose banks one may sit for hours and never see a boat pass; for all the profits the tremendous potential value this river yielded us last year and years before, we would be the richer did we wish it from the face of the earth, could we effectively do so This great river, with a minimum depth (for over 1,300 miles) of eight feet, twice that of the Rhine, with its branches reaching thirty-two States of the Union, with tributaries like the Ohio, Missouri, Cumberland, Tennessee. Illinois, Red, and many others, its valleys covering a territory measured in millions of square miles, protected in the east by the Appalachian, in the west by the Rocky Mountains, producing two-thirds of our national wealth, three-fourths of our foreign exports, populated with nearly fifty million denizens, this Mississippi River's total freight movement, including that of all its tributaries, hardly reached the two million ton mark last year—a negligible part of our entire freight movement

St. Louis, the heart of this valley, not far from where the Missouri and Illinois join the Mississippi, received and sent last year 57,000,000 tons of freight, 211,000 tons of which were moved by water. Rotterdam, on the smaller Rhine, received and sent last year 30,000,000 tons of freight, 600,000 tons of which were moved by rail. (Applause.)

That the non-use of these streams is a great economic crime might be proven with the following few statements Nowhere in the entire history of the world can one point to a city of over 300,000 inhabitants that is not on a navigable waterway It costs four times more to move freight in the United States by rail than it costs to move it by water. It costs in Europe six times more, owing to the cheaper cost of water, and the greater cost of rail, transportation. In our fight for improvement of rivers, bays, sounds, canals, lakes, harbors, bayous—yes, even creeks— we are leading a fight for economic liberty.

REBATING WATER CITIES AGAINST INLAND CITIES

I speak of our endeavors as a fight, because we have, strange as it may seem, opponents, who fight us with the old approved weapon of rebates—rebates against water competition While rebates are forbidden by State or Federal statutes, railroads grant them quite as much today as at any time in the past, the only distinction being that formerly they were granted to individuals surreptitiously, and now they are granted to cities and towns openly; the former became illegal, the latter is legalized These rebates arise from the unjust practice of railroads in basing rates to river points on water carrier competition

The railroads say they must be allowed to meet the competition of the boats, otherwise the boats will take their business between river points The Interstate Commerce Commission admits this claim, and allows the railroads to haul freight at a loss to river points, and then recoup themselves for this loss by exorbitant charges to off-river points From these facts, one of two things must be true; either the railroads lose money on all hauls to river points, or they get excessive returns on hauls to off-river points, plainly a rebate case, robbing Peter to pay Paul The river towns are having their freight hauled at the expense of the off-river towns, and pay for this privilege with the loss of still lower rates by boats, and the public loses all around, but keeps on talking about the potential value of the streams, penalizing itself annually to the extent of $700,000,000 in favor of foreign countries Railroads are often strengthened in their attitude by the river towns, who do not realize that, even to them, the value of the river is nil if idle, and that they should bring traffic upon the river instead of looking upon the river as justification of the statement, "We have the God-given advantage of being on a navigable waterway and we demand the natural benefit inherent in this location We could get cheap rates by boats if they were operated, therefore, we insist on the same low rates by rail."

RAIL VERSUS WATER RATES

Examples of actually existing rates will be illuminating First-class freight is shipped from New Orleans to Memphis, a distance of 396 miles, for $9 per ton, or 22.7 mill per ton mile. To ship the same commodities from New Orleans to Amite, La , a distance of 68 miles, costs $10 40 per ton, or 152 mills per ton mile. The citizens of Amite pay more than six and a half times as much per ton mile for their freight charges as do the more fortunately situated residents of Memphis Suppose the Government should charge Amite people 13 cents a letter for postage, but those in Memphis only 2 cents.

To ship a barrel of flour from New Orleans to Amite costs 34 cents, or 5 mills per barrel-mile; to ship one from New Orleans to Memphis costs 25 cents, or 0 63 mill per barrel-mile. The cost to the consumer in Amite is eight times as much for carrying a barrel of flour one mile as it is to the consumer in Memphis. First-class freight from New Orleans to Memphis, 396 miles, is 45 cents per hundred; from New Orleans to Opelika, Ala , 386 miles, it is 99 cents per hundred—more than twice as much for a shorter distance to the off-river point

These are rates from one city to a town that can be reached by water compared with rates from the same city to a town that can only be reached by rail.

The following table will illustrate the "ratewalls" that hinder the freight movement to the river:

	Distance from Birmingham		
	418 miles to New Orleans.	56 miles to Tuscaloosa	Ratio, Per Cent.
Sugar	$ 3 40	$4.80	140
Coffee	7.00	3 00	43
Rice	5.00	3 90	78
Molasses	4.40	1 80	41
Dried Fruit	11 00	1 60	14½
Peas and Beans .	11 00	1 50	13½
Hay	3.60	1.40	39
Grain	3.60	1.40	39
Flour	4.40	1 60	36½
Coal	1.25	.80	64
Coke	1.75	80	46
Wire and Nails	3.20	2 00	62½
Pig Iron	3.00	1 00	33⅓
Steel Rails . . .	3.00	1.50	50
Cast Iron Pipe . . .	3.00	1 50	50
Machinery	5.40	3.90	72

Thus, although the distance from Birmingham to Tuscaloosa is about one-eighth of the distance from Birmingham to New Orleans, the average freight rate is about one-half that to New Orleans, but Tuscaloosa lies on a navigable water from which New Orleans, Mobile, or other cities may be reached.

UPSTREAM VERSUS DOWNSTREAM RATES

Let me as third example show the variations in rates over the same distance, over the same road, by just one example where hundreds could be given   Flour moves from St Paul to New Orleans for $5 50 per ton for domestic use; from New Orleans to St Paul, same routing $9 80   But one is downstream and the higher rates are upstream. "No," says the railroad, "it is because the natural movement of flour is from St Paul to New

Orleans " I say the latter is true because the rates forbid any other movement, but great would be the tonnage of finer winter flour that would move upstream were the rates not prohibitive. At any rate why should there be any difference in rates over the same distance and railroad? Did not the Congress rule long ago that rates to all shippers should, under same conditions, be equal regardless of the tonnage shipped by the individual shipper? Why is this not equally true for one community against another? Had this flour been moved by water (and was this flour meant for export) it would have more cheaply been loaded from barge to ship than it otherwise could have been delivered from ship to warehouses in the cities; therefore, the railroads have a third rate, an "export rate," which, on flour from St. Paul to New Orleans, is $3 90

The above cases could be multiplied indefinitely, as they are representative of thousands of others, all of which show the injustice suffered by the land communities in the matter of freight rates. And while the paralleling railroads of our inland waterways are strained to their utmost to carry the freight offered at each crop-moving season, the waterways themselves are vast expanses of idleness.

A mistake is made by the public in assuming that it is always the river channel that causes this idleness. Nothing could be farther from the truth. Today the Mississippi affords an 8-foot channel from St Louis to its mouth, which is the best to be found on any stream in the world, and see its emptiness! An 8-foot channel is all that the most efficient service requires The Government works unremittingly to develop waterways, only to see the water-borne traffic on our inland rivers grow less as the years go by, not chiefly due to inadequate depth of channel, but to this rate-making anarchism; and until the idea that the principal functions of inland water transportation is to regulate the rates for rail transportation has been untaught or made unnecessary through just rates, we will not see great river traffic

Still the average "river man" will insist that poor conditions of the channel keep our inland waters idle. This is not always true The Rhine could never compare with the Mississippi River in its advantages for transportation; its channel is narrower.

shallower and more changeable, the current is swifter, and ice is known in winter months over its entire navigable length to its very mouth. Yet, last year over 96,000 vessels passed the Dutch and German frontier on the Rhine, which means a vessel every five minutes for the entire year. In order to illustrate this point clearly, I will read page 109 of the English translation of the Trade Report of the Rotterdam Chamber of Commerce for the year 1913.

RHINE NAVIGATION

"We could almost suffice by referring to our review over 1912, seeing the slight difference between 1913 and its predecessor.

"Arrivals were plentiful till the autumn, and the water level was satisfactory during the whole of the year; only during nine days, from the 30th of October to the 7th of November, a short period of low water on the Rhine was witnessed when the water mark recorded a level of 1 20m. (four feet) and below that to 1 14m. (3 feet 9 inches).

"The not normalized lower part of the river was, as a channel, in a rather favorable condition, the occurring sand deposits were for the greater part removed by dredging operations, whilst, by altering the fairway in the second half of the year a sufficient channel was maintained

"The average Rhine freights were during 1913 for cargoes of 800/1000 tons, including towage·

"For ores and other crude commodities to Ruhrort, Duisburg, Hochfeld, Alsum, Walsum, or Rheinhausen: $0.26 per ton or 1.2 mill per ton-mile.

"For ores (copper ore, phosphate, etc.) to the upper Rhine and Mainz stations· $0.56 per ton or 1 1 mill per ton-mile.

"On the whole the freights were rather satisfactory as well as the water level, which only from the middle of October to the beginning of November was low.

The total traffic across the German-Netherland frontier was in tons:*

	1912.	1913.	*More in* 1913
With Netherlands . .	25,619,771 0	27,941,378 0	2,321,587 0
With Belgium	8,523,472 0	9,073,140 5	549,668.5
Rhine Sea Traffic . .	485,117.5	514,634 5	29,517.0
	34,628,360 5	37,529,153 0	2,900,729.5

The tables given hereunder give a comparison of the Rhine traffic during the last ten years in tons.*

	Rotterdam.	*Amsterdam*	*Belgium.*
1904 . . .	10,684,261	428,589	4,104,306
1905	12,771,307	478,320	4,435,580
1906	13,357,575	538,945	4,821,229
1907 . .	14,762,526	597,518	4,937,736
1908 . . .	12,938,898	716,035	5,013,609
1909 . . .	15,134,175	798,535	6,205,324
1910	17,663,521	990,927	7,727,219
1911 . . .	19,042,847	1,042,603	7,956,855
1912 . . .	20,818,991	1,360,280	8,523,472
1913 . .	22,764,241	1,531,772	9,073,140

"The following number of vessels passed Lobith from and to Germany

In 1904	67,519 vessels, of which	46,584 under Dutch flag
In 1905	72,029 " " "	48,941 " " "
In 1906	75,306 " " "	49,821 " " "
In 1907 . . 79,640 " " "	52,508 " " "
In 1908	71,206 " " "	47,021 " " "
In 1909 . . 77,909 " " "	50,692 " " "
In 1910 . . 85,372 " " "	55,740 " " "
In 1911	90,129 " " "	59,122 " " "
In 1912	91,904 " " "	58,978 " " "
In 1913 . 96,768 " " "	62,249 " " "

* Metric tons = 2,204 6 pounds.

Mississippi River Trip With Self-Propelled Barge

Most of our inland waters would show life instead of idleness (were not the sanctioned ratewalls effective), even without the much-needed improvements to let inland navigation bear its full economic fruit, as it would under proper working conditions of fair channels and terminals, but, even so, most of our important waterways are sufficiently navigable to yield profits, for instance the Mississippi River. To prove my contention that this river is navigable, if properly navigated, I sent, during the low water season of this year, a 1,000-ton, self-propelled, twin-screw, shallow-draft, steel barge from New Orleans, La., to St. Paul, Minn, and back, so that it might become a public fact that water transportation on our rivers in general, and on the Mississippi River in particular, is an economic possibility and should be a profitable undertaking

A strange craft it was, that steel barge, but strange alone because it was economical and modern, which are rare qualities for any craft on the Mississippi River On this river we are still living in the antebellum days and happy memory of Mark Twain, and the ideal river boats are still, in the eyes of many, the palatial stern wheelers like the "Robert E. Lee" or the "Natchez," where the gentlemen of old gambled and fed, and drank and bled, where the drowsy negro roustabouts, as drones, whiled away in slumber hours of idleness, drawing preposterous wages of $80 to $100 per month, barring modern loading and unloading apparatus We, on the Mississippi, are still content with mud levees, slippery and cumbersome, and feel fully compensated· for economic inefficiency by the great smokestacks. belching forth clouds of smoke, by the large whistle, able to be heard for miles, and by the wheels, that beat the water up in waves higher than a man, of our present steamboats, the daily expense of which surpasses the weekly expense of more modern craft of a larger capacity

Compare with this the self-propelled barge, which, with a carrying capacity of 1,000 tons and a total crew of seven men for the day and night runs, is propelled through two gas engines, consuming fuel at the rate of 30 cents per hour, and proceeding quietly with a total absence of wave, so that a row boat hardly rocks in its wake. One hardly feels surprised when it was demonstrated by this trip that the cost of transportation, by means of this barge, was just one-sixth of the cost of transportation by means of the old-fashioned steamboat. The barge which I used was never meant for the Mississippi trade, but was used in the coal trade between Alabama and New Orleans, but. even under these adverse conditions, is so much more efficient than the old style river boat that I did not feel any hesitancy in sending it over this almost 4,000-mile journey.

Obsolete Mississippi River Craft

In order that it might be clearly brought home to you why I call the present Mississippi River boat obsolete, I will give you some comparative data between this barge and the prevailing Mississippi River boat. For comparison, I have used the average Mississippi River craft, the like of which in one instance constitutes the entire fleet of one of the least inefficient companies on the Mississippi River.

The cost of this 1,000-ton barge complete, with all equipment, is $32,000   The average cost of a like capacity Mississippi River boat is $60,000 to $70,000   The total crew of this barge is seven men, on the Mississippi River craft fifty-four   Insurance on the barge is 4% marine and fire; on the steamboat 12 to 15%; fuel consumption on the barge is 30 cents per hour and on the Mississippi River craft $4 per hour, both at a speed of eight miles per hour. Total cost of operation of the barge, including 6% interest and all other charges (wages, fuel, supplies, subsistence, repairs, insurance, depreciation, etc) is $2,100 per month; on the Mississippi River steamboat, $8.100 per month.

That these barges can be constructed strongly is shown by the fact that Lloyds classified one of this type recently as "A 1" for ocean travel. Compare against this the remarkable weakness of the present steamboat, which might easily be described as a raft, with several thousand dollars' worth of junk about it; the prevailing Mississippi steamboats are built of wood, tin, shingles, canvas, and twine, and look like a Bridge of Babylon.

"No," the river men object, "our boats are not obsolete; we have kept pace with time, and our boats are today a great improvement on those of the fifties." Why, the other day, a captain, accepted as the Nestor of the stern wheeler, said to me: "You are not familiar with the improvements we have brought about on our river craft. Our steamers are now almost fireproof; we have patent tapered floors, balanced rudders, steel and asphalt decks, swinging stage; we have the improved tandem compound, or cross compound piston valve engine, steam capstan and steering machine, a locomotive type of boiler, wire railings and tiller ropes, electric lights, combined breeching, shield and furnace damper, insulated pipe coverings, and many more important improvements that substantiate the statement that our present side and stern wheel steamers are the best type of boats for river craft in the world."

This enthusiastic description of the important improvements of the present Mississippi River boat from one of its ardent champions illustrates better than anything I can say their total obsolescence and inefficiency. But it is not only the type of boats that make practical navigation on the Mississippi River of lucrative interest to the transportation engineer, but the many other prevailing difficulties which were brought out in this memorable barge trip

DIVERS DIFFICULTIES

Immediately upon departure from New Orleans we were shown very forcibly some of the difficulties of Mississippi River navigation. Under the United States laws I know of no other business that forces any industry to employ Government licensed persons except navigation, which demands the employment of licensed captains, pilots and engineers, which licensed persons are permitted to form unions and thereby create the most absolute monopoly one can dream of   The pilots were hard to get and I had to bring two from St Louis to New Orleans at a cost of $32 per head travelling expenses and $5 per day wages; on the moment of departure they demanded a change in employment conditions, which were $150 per month, to $10 per day for the first 10 days and $5 per day for each day thereafter

This at the final settlement brought out another serious menace to the boat owner, embodied in the very unjust laws pertaining to navigation. For instance, anyone without credentials or proof may have the United States marshal in any city attach any boat anywhere in its harbor for any claim that one might trump up, and the boat, regardless of financial consequences or any other consequences, is tied to shore under a daily charge of at least $5 per day until either the lawsuit is settled or the owner of the boat brings up a surety bond twice the value of the claim.

The Government lights, "aids to navigation," are closely affiliated with another serious trouble. Great difficulties are caused by the late adjustment of the Government channel lights, which are as a rule so much behind time of actual changing of the channels, that the Government marks do not show where the channel is, but where it was.

And so we slowly climbed the river, as it were an endless winding stairway, dizzy from lonesomeness. For days at a time, in the heart of as rich a farming country as there is in the world, we did not meet enough traffic to fill a dozen freight cars or even enough people travelling to fill a sleeping car, and yet this river was once supposed to be the key to the continent, the river which nearly interrupted the Peace Conference at Ghent 100 years ago, when Great Britain demanded that her commerce should have full rights upon that stream. France, England, and even Spain, saw the possibilities of the Mississippi River. yet its actual owners are today not only allowing it to become a wasted opportunity, but an annual source of devastation. Let us place this American "River of Doubt" back upon the map and aid in dispelling the indolent skepticism which has for years paralyzed its development. (Applause.)

Banking Facilities

Many other obstructions to economical navigation are caused by the total absence of banking accommodations; bills of lading are frequently considered banking securities, unless they happen to be for freight on inland water craft, and then the bank throws up its hands in holy terror, and you leave their marble halls without a penny more in your pocket. You lead a blind mule to the bank or buy an automobile, and with that as security you can get at least a certain percentage of its value as loan, but should you be patriotic enough to own the cheapest tool of transportation, a river boat, you might well have to sift the entire United States in order to find a single man or bank that is willing to finance you, or even give you reasonable banking accommodations.

When the barge left I had the hull insured against marine and fire risk, public employers, life and property liability, carried cargo insurance, and had even the freight money insured, yet in six attempts I failed to find a bank that would advance me money on the freight receivable, although assigned to me with cargo as security. Yet the combined ship mortgage banks in Holland, including all their losses, have made in the last five years an average profit per year of 18%. You can get there almost invariably with a boat as collateral up to two-thirds of its estimated value as a loan, at a rate that would total in all expenses 6½%.

INSURANCE

While mentioning insurance another important obstacle comes to my mind, this is the insurance rate. The barge carried from New Orleans to St. Paul, a distance of 1,921 miles, 90 tons of coffee, on which a freight rate of $4 25 per ton was paid I paid an insurance rate of 90 cents per $100 value, or $2.70 per ton, and the terminal charges were 43 cents, which leaves a total of $1.12 per ton, yet even at that rate the barge would have yielded handsome profits had it been fully loaded both ways, or only carrying an average of one-third of its capacity. This rate of insurance is actually ten times larger than the insurance on the same commodity from Brazil to St Paul providing it is moved by rail from New Orleans to St Paul, and why is this?

There are three reasons for this flagrant injustice (A) The small amount of inland water-borne traffic makes it no fair average risk; the law of averages is hardly applicable to this limited movement.

(B) The insurance companies, like most of the people in the United States, do not take water transportation seriously; they are not willing to accept the movement as a growing one, as one with a bright future, and, therefore, do not care to foster it because they only see possible losses, and not even promises of a future.

(C) Most of the insurance companies have invested their securities in railroad bonds, which circumstance rather seems to strengthen their belief that water transportation should not be taken seriously, at least they have no burning desire to foster it.

Some one might feel inclined to add a fourth reason by speaking of the "River Pool," but I prefer to ignore this factor, as I have been successful in doing my business as a carrier and, therefore, perhaps know precious little about the working of this combine

RIVER TERMINALS

Of all the serious handicaps that inland navigation has to contend with, the terminal or shore problem is the most important—so important, that it might often be said that the problem of inland navigation is more a shore than a water problem; almost invariably are the shore expenses higher than the actual cost of transportation from harbor to harbor.

With the present river terminals the height of inefficiency seems to have been reached   The shipper must carry his freight by wagon over poor roads, move it somehow down a poorly paved, and usually very steep, bank, laboriously unload it by hand, roll it to the edge of a muddy levee, watch it until the steamboat may arrive, when it is carried piece by piece and stowed away under the towering superstructure of an American steamboat amidst a forest of deck supports, and reverse the process at the other end   The only exception to these conditions is the city of New Orleans, where covered sheds are provided and where now mechanical loading and unloading devices are tried   Economical navigation of the stream and efficiency of the carrier are greatly handicapped under such conditions.   The elimination of the steamboat gangplank as the highway of water traffic, and of the roustabout, are necessary for the restoration of commercial activity on the river   Modern river terminals, constructed at the combined initiative of State and municipality, with a municipally-owned belt railway, must take their place. (Applause.)

The present excessive terminal cost offsets often the advantage of the lower river rate as against the higher rail rate Without an exception, there is no port in the Mississippi Valley at which freight can be transferred directly from car to boat, or *vice versa,* except with a heavy arbitrary, or by an added labor cost of from 20 to 50 cents per ton   These high terminal expenses, a serious menace to water transportation with the old-fashioned stern- or side-wheeler, are out of all reason where modern craft is used.   The 1,000-ton, self-propelled barge that went to St. Paul from New Orleans last August brought this forcibly to light.   The most serious handicaps this barge encountered were terminals; in almost every instance it cost more to load and unload the cargo than it cost to carry it to place of destination.

LOADING AND UNLOADING CHARGES

The New Orleans freight was received, watched and loaded, including receiving clerk's time, for a total of 26½ cents per ton The time consumed for loading was five hours, or 46½ tons per hour, during which time the barge expenses increased at the rate of $3.86 per hour, or a total of $19.30, since charges that increase with every additional hour the barge takes for the round trip amount to $3 86 per hour   At Jeffries, La , 554 6 tons of lumber was received, which lumber was loaded and unloaded by the shipper   The loading took from Thursday, 3 P.M., until Monday, 10 A M., working night and day and Sunday, a total of 91 hours, or 6 1 tons per hour   The cost of loading was to the shipper 27 cents per ton   The cost of loading the lumber on the barge was in time loss 91 hours, or, in cost, $351.26 The entire cost of loading and unloading to the shipper was $245.72, and this, together with the time loss to the barge, expressed in dollars and cents, makes a grand total of $807 35, as against a transportation of the entire lumber cargo of 554 6 ton_ for $998 37, or $1 80 per ton to carry the lumber 1,000 miles and $1.46 to carry it to and from the barge. With any decent semblance of an opportunity to load the barge with this lumber, it should have been loaded in 12 hours, causing a saving alone in loading time of 79 hours, or $305, and it is safe to say that what cost $807 35 to load and unload should not have cost over $210 under fair conditions   The total cost of loading and unloading the barge on this trip was $1,733 12, or 63 per cent of the gross freight receipts.

QUARANTINE

As a final word about the problem of inland navigation the quarantine regulations we have to contend with are worthy of a few remarks. Should there be bubonic plague in New Orleans, and should a vessel leave for foreign harbors with a health and inspection certificate from the Federal Health Officer, then such vessel will see this honored wherever it goes, but should the authorities in the first harbor it touches desire to have it go through certain formalities then at least all subsequent harbors will not further bother the vessel regarding its stay in New Orleans; but should a craft turn its prow upstream, and dare to remain within the United States officials' own jurisdiction, then any State or city health officer, regardless of any reasons to the contrary, indifferent to the number of former inspections or fumigations, may, upon the boat's arrival in their own sphere of influence, stop, inspect and fumigate to their heart's content   So it came about that this steel barge, which only had been in New Orleans six hours during daytime while the loading was in progress, and which was officially declared "absolutely rat proof," was frequently detained by the various health officials along the route till the very end of its journey, St Paul, where, 1,921 miles from New Orleans, 35 days after its departure, it received its last health inspection, although it had lain five days in Jeffries, three days in St Louis, and shorter periods at various other places, had been officially fumigated, and had had hundreds of visitors; and today I firmly believe it escaped more serious delay because many officials were puzzled how to fumigate this steel, air-tight can, which has an open engine room and pilot house, carried its freight out in the open on deck and had its hold sealed with water-tight bulkheads, and a deck without hatches. I have a faint suspicion that some of these inspections were more due to curiosity about the construction of the barge than to sanitary reasons.

Detailed Figures About Barge Trip

The barge left on July 6th at 4 P.M., and returned on August 29th at 2 P.M , a total of 54 days and 8 hours, including loading and unloading   During that time she covered 3,842 miles, spending a total of 240 hours and 45 minutes in loading and unloading a total of 1,182 tons.   She lost 8 hours and 4 minutes on account of engine-room trouble, was grounded for 174 hours and 10 minutes, or waiting for the pilots to learn where the channel was, notwithstanding the fact that at no time we found less than six feet of water.

The barge carried coffee, rice, sugar, cement, molasses, lumber, flour, paper and chemicals   Out of the total of 1,921,000 upstream ton-miles capacity it delivered 1,066,986 ton-miles, and of the 1,921,000 downstream ton-miles capacity it carried 183,-181 ton-miles or a total for the round trip of 32% of the barge's capacity   The total gross receipts were $2,762.57, or 2 21 mills per ton-mile   The same freight moved by rail would have cost $4.932 98. or the water rate was a saving of $2.170 41 or 45% of the rail rate, which was an average of 5.98 mills per ton-mile (as against 2 21 mills per ton-mile by water) or 4 mills per ton-mile over the same mileage (the rail distance being shorter than the water distance).

The total expenses of the barge were high, and in some items out of all proportion, on account of the lack of organization and other consequences of the single "isolated" trip   For instance. the extra pilots, needed because the crew was totally unfamiliar with the route, received for this single trip in wages $1.014 13, or $18 67 per day, an item entirely in addition to the usual payroll   Heavy expenses incurred through slow loading, etc., to a large extent caused by the fact that this was just one isolated trip. all made the expenses for this trip extraordinarily high.

Where, under usual conditions, with a regular service and more boats than one to carry all the overhead and administration expenses, the total expenses for this trip of 3,842 miles would have been less than $3,500, they actually were $5,740 22

The overhead charges, including 6% interest on investment, 6% depreciation, ½% for repairs not covered by insurance, harbor dues, taxes, traveling expenses of traffic manager (who was on account of this trip six weeks on the road) his wages, advertisements, photos, traveling expenses of general manager, office and administration expenses, telegrams, telephone, soliciting expenses, salary of clerks, etc, gives a total of $2,011 66   The other expenses were as follows· Fuel, $261.37; deck supplies, $270 72; subsistence, $400; engine room supplies, $140, wages of crew, $1,230; extra pilots, $1,014 13; insurance, $412 34.

The total expenses were equal to 1 65 mill per ton-mile carrying capacity   Had the barge been fully loaded both ways, her gross receipts, at the rate of 2 21 mills per ton-mile (the average of her freight charges), would have been $8,491, yielding a profit of $2,750 78, under even these adverse conditions, on this single trip, and this, notwithstanding the fact that in mills per ton-mile the freight rate of the barge was 37% of the rail rate, so that on the lumber alone we saved the shipper $1,300.52, making a rate of $998 65 against a rail rate of $2,300.17; $2,750 78 profit on a single trip or 8½% on the investment

River Navigation Profitable

On the strength of figures I have recently compiled, a group of financiers have agreed to furnish the needed capital of $5,000,-000 for the Mississippi River Navigation Company   This company expects to place on the lower Mississippi River, by May, 1916, five barges with a carrying capacity of 3,000 tons each on a draft of seven feet and an upstream speed of fifteen miles per hour, so that a schedule may be maintained of three sailings a week from both New Orleans and St Louis, with one barge in reserve.   These barges will be of steel, 310 feet long, 56 feet beam and nine feet in depth, with a weatherproof cargo box They will be driven by four propellers, power being furnished by four producer-gas engines having a total of 2,400 horse-power. Each barge will have fifteen watertight bulkheads and will be equipped with wireless, three 9,000 C. P. searchlights, motor launch, distant anchor-placer (new patent), and many other features which will contribute to economy and efficiency.

These barges will make 140 trips to St. Louis between April and December, 8 trips to Cairo during late spring and late fall, 12 trips to Memphis in early spring and early winter, and 27 trips to Vicksburg in midwinter. When the barges are unable to run directly to St Louis, freight will be forwarded from these other points by rail. If the barges could be fully loaded each trip, we could move freight between New Orleans and St. Louis for $1.00 per ton (not including terminal and switching charges), declare a dividend of 26 per cent a year and have a 100 per cent sinking fund in twelve years

At first, however, it is intended to make a rate, for transportation proper, of $1 50 per ton, or a total, including switching and terminal charges, of $2 20 per ton This charge will be reduced to $1.92 as soon as the Interstate Commerce Commission has readjusted, or, rather, corrected, the present switching and rate arbitraries and, with the development of traffic, will ultimately be reduced to $1 45. This is equal to 1 2 mills per ton-mile for the river distance, or 2 mills per ton-mile for the railroad distance.

TRIBUTARY LINES

The tributaries will be served by similar barges of smaller proportions For instance, the Upper Mississippi River will have ten barges of 1,000 tons carrying capacity each, 270 feet in length, 45 feet beam and four feet draft, driven by two propellers and one stern center wheel. It is expected that these barges will make the trip from St. Louis to St Paul in three days and a round trip each week Thus, freight received at New Orleans on Monday will be delivered the following Monday at St Paul, and the bill of lading will guarantee delivery by the following Thursday.

Cᴏᴍᴘᴀʀᴀᴛɪᴠᴇ Rᴀᴛᴇs

How our proposed rates between New Orleans and St. Louis will compare with the present rates by rail is shown by the following table:

Rᴀᴛᴇs Bᴇᴛᴡᴇᴇɴ Nᴇᴡ Oʀʟᴇᴀɴs ᴀɴᴅ Sᴛ. Lᴏᴜɪs

| | *Rail Rate* | *Per Ton* | |
Commodity.	*C L.*	*L. C. L*	*Water Rate.*
Baking powder . . .	$7.50		$3 20
Beef	5 00		4 10
Beer	4 20	$5 20	2 30
Bridge material .	3 50	5 40	3 25
Butter	18 00		4 00
Canned goods . . .	5 20	6 90	2 80
Cement	2.50	6.10	2 25
Chairs	19.50		6 00
Cocoa	13.50		5.40
Coffee	4 60	6 00	3 10
Condensed milk . . .	4.20	8 70	3 15
Copper ingots . . .	7 00	13.00	2 50
Copper castings . . .	15 00		4 00
Dry goods	13 00	18 00	4.50
Flour	2 80	5 20	2 50
Furniture	8 50	11 50	5 80
Glassware (bottles) .	10 30	13.50	3.70
Guano . . .	61 00	73 20	8 00
Hardware	6 00		3 60
Liquors . .	8 00		3.10
Lumber	4 00		2.28
Molasses . . .	4 10		3 00
Nails	4 40		2.80
Nitrate of soda .	3 40	73 20	3.10
Paint .	4 60		2.60
Paper	5 60	10.00	2.50
Plumbing material . .	6.00		3 40
Pickles	76 00		2 40

Commodity.	Rail Rate C. L.	Per Ton L. C L.	Water Rate
Refrigerators	$10 00		$2 90
Rice	4 80		2.40
Rubber	18.00		3 00
Salt	4.30		2 95
Shoes	18 00		6.00
Soap	4.60		2.40
Stoves . .	7 00		3.00
Sugar	3 40	4.80	2.70
Tin	10 00	15 00	3.80
Vehicles	5 00		4.00

Shipment of a ton of each of these commodities would have cost $541.10 by rail and $138.28 by Mississippi Navigation Co., a saving of $402 82 or 75% of the rail rate I have only used the rates between New Orleans and St Louis, but all similar rates are similarly compounded.

Available Trade

To load a 3,000-ton barge each way every other day would mean 561,000 tons of freight per year in each direction   Large as this figure might seem, it is only a fraction of the possible freight that could be had   The Mississippi River Navigation Company has already pledged to it 700,000 tons of freight, covering almost every variety of commodity that can be named

The Panama Canal is open and the opening is the cause of great rejoicing on the Pacific Coast, in token of which an exposition costing millions of dollars is going to be held   The Pacific Coast people expect to trade largely, not only with New York, but with New Orleans and the Middle West   Hitherto they have been barred by rail rates like $11 00 for lumber and asphalt. $15.00 for wines and canned goods, $17 00 for beans, and $22.00 for fruit. Now, considering the fact that these commodities could move by water from the Pacific Coast to New

Orleans for from $3.00 to $6 00, and from New Orleans to St Paul within $5.00 for the highest class commodities, or to St. Louis for $3 00, it is safe to say the average rate by water from the Pacific Coast to points lying on the Mississippi River or its tributaries would not be more than $7.00 a ton. Counting the average railroad rate at 8 mills per ton-mile, we could reach for an additional $3.20 territory 400 miles on either side of the river or its tributaries. This practically means two-thirds of the United States, or the entire Mississippi Valley drainage basin   To the water rate should be added $1.25 per ton for canal tolls, the insurance rate and the cost of loading and unloading at terminals, giving a total average rate of $10 00 per ton throughout the valley and a maximum of $15.00 from the Pacific Coast to any point in the valley.

If the Mississippi River and its tributaries are used there would also develop a large trade from the Atlantic Coast to New Orleans, and thence by water to points in the valley, but, unless the rivers are used, this trade cannot be carried on and the Panama Canal will be of little or no use to the people of the Mississippi Valley.

CAPACITY OF INLAND WATERS

The capacity of the railroads, at present our only arteries of transportation, constitutes at once a very serious menace or obstacle to successful progress   I will not this time cite the so oft-repeated statement of James J Hill, that there was not sufficient money in this country to develop the railroads as they should be, nor sufficient material or workshops to build railroad material, should there be sufficient money. This was said at the height of the prosperity mark in 1907, and will come true sooner than has ever been expected; but the following facts may give you some new light on this subject   The average tonnage of freight trains of one of the best railroads that moves east or west is 489 tons. A barge of 3,000 tons only requires a length at the river front of 310 feet, the same tonnage moved by rail would require a train not shorter than 8,000 feet. Truly, compared to the railroads, the rivers are unlimited in their capacity. I would not fear to say that all the traffic of the entire United States could be moved on the Mississippi River without crowding it (Applause.)

Now, to shortly recapitulate, the present obstacles to water transportation are placed in accordance with their importance as follows· the railroad rates, terminals, Government lights, insurance, labor, pilots and labor laws, financial accommodations, interchange of freight between railroads, lack of shipyards and supply houses, lack of organization and leadership, obsolete craft and failure of standardizing same, ice, total absence of connecting links between various water channels, great variations in channels and lock dimensions, failure of the public to properly understand the importance of water transportation, poor means of communication between water front and the interior through the absence of rail connections, streets, trolley cars, telegraph and telephone stations.

Yet with all these obstacles there is none that cannot be overcome by a well-organized company sufficiently financed Even under the present obstacles this Mississippi Navigation Company will give cheaper, more regular, more reliable and speedier freight movement, between such communities as are connected by water, than any railroad can offer, with a system which is far more elastic.

At present water transportation conditions in the United States absolutely demand and justify the fullest attention of the Government, and it should not shrink at any justifiable expenditure This country has spent far too little on its waterways One only needs to look to our neighbor, Canada, or the A B C Republics, to feel that we have spent very little on our waterways. Why, if this country added up all its expenditures on its waterways, it would only show a figure one-fourth of that which a country 1-250 part in area could show, my native country, little Holland (Applause.)

Transportation is the most important thing in our lives; in fact, as I often have said, it is the best word to define life from death; life might be said to be the ability to transport; every dollar we spend every day of our lives represents 100 cents for transportation Gold has no value until it has been moved out of the vein; moved to the surface of the earth, where the impurities are moved out of it   The polishing of the metal means the removal of the very small part that gave this a rough surface. Writing a letter is transporting ink to paper

It was with some timidity that I spoke like this, with the bluntness that is a Dutchman's privilege   Knowing that my accent would betray me as a foreigner, had not your Chairman announced me as such, I feared that my address would sound too much like adverse criticism.   Far be it from me to wish even to criticise for a moment this great commonwealth of clean-minded men and women   Let me, therefore, not finish without giving my views as to what I believe is necessary on behalf of inland navigation   Since the Government controls all the harbors and navigable streams, individual communities cannot undertake to improve our waterways, and will look to the Government as trustee for and responsible to the entire universe for the highest development of rivers and harbors of this country

Many South American cities, practically unknown to even the well-informed, have carried out harbor improvements on a far larger scale than any of the largest cities of this country, and yet a fight for improvement of rivers and harbors is made by ignoramuses the butt of ridicule and is fought by interests that would benefit rather than be harmed

The suggestions that times of adverse business conditions are not the times for rivers and harbors expenditures are absolutely without merit; of all times this is the time that our Government should carry forward on a large scale much work of this character, even if it had to issue 500 million dollars in bonds covering years of construction, rather than halt the work at present. (Applause.)

It has been my privilege to learn that there has been less wastage and unwise expenditure made in the rivers and harbors work than in any other governmental or industrial expenditure of like magnitude, and I heartily state that in my opinion there are few nations that can and may so proudly boast of their splendid Corps of Army Engineers, and your illustrious body of Senators and Representatives who are responsible for this work of natural waterways   To look upon their work alone makes us feel how highly privileged we are to meet them. Mr. Chairman, ladies and gentlemen, I will wind up my address by mentioning some of the great necessities taught me through practical navigation.

MY WATERWAYS CREED

1. I believe that waterways, harbors, bridges and quarantine should be combined in a new department with a Cabinet officer as head, this department to employ engineers specially educated for this; these engineers, while commissioned officers in the U. S. Army, not to be under direct charge of the army officials during the time they are engaged in this waterways department.

2. I believe further that the decision, which of the new waterways are a commercial necessity, should not be taken by such engineers, but considered by a group of transportation experts, specially employed by the Government for such purpose.

3. I believe that a definite, concise, uniform plan, a system of waterways improvement and development, etc., should be prepared by this department for the entire United States, Congress to change or improve this and appropriate a yearly lump sum to be spent in the approaching of this ideal of approved waterways

4. I believe flood control to be entirely a Government question; the Government to own the river bed, not States or individuals.

5. I believe that there is not such a thing as a hard and fast levee system for the Mississippi River, nor of reservoirs and dams, but that the entire control of the Mississippi River should be referred to the Government Waterways Department, which should decide upon a plan, Congress to approve, change or reject.

6. I further believe that all States and communities are in duty bound to build inland water terminals, just as they now feel that they are obligated to build sea terminals (harbors)

7. I believe in the educational campaign in municipalities for the building of belt railroads, warehouses and other facilities of communication to the harbor

8. I believe in public ownership of the river front, but decline to accept this as antagonistic to private ownership, or at

least private leases ranging from periods not shorter than 20 years, unless desired by the tenant

9 I believe in the absolute necessity of stopping the abuse of the rail rate to meet water competition, and I am convinced that successful water transportation means rail rates tied down to fixed charges per ton mile, plus terminal charges, and enforced exchange of freight through water and rail terminals.

10. I am opposed to the licensing of pilots or to the compulsory employment of licensed officers.

11. I believe in a uniform and Federal quarantine law

12. I believe that our water and coasts should be open for navigation for any nationality or any trade. It seems to me that the United States needs all these waters used; this will bring work to our shipyards and supply houses and employ, under the present laws, American labor; the stimulation of the business depending on water transportation brings life where there was death and results in better living conditions on the water and along the coasts of the United States for any water transportation company, no matter what nationality

PRESIDENT RANSDELL—There is still another interesting number on our program—Hon Peter G. Ten Eyck, Member of Congress from New York, will discuss "The National Government, Its Obligations and Governing Powers."

THE NATIONAL GOVERNMENT; ITS OBLIGATIONS AND GOVERNING POWERS

Address—Peter G. Ten Eyck, M. C.
Albany, N. Y.

MR PRESIDENT, FELLOW MEMBERS NATIONAL RIVERS AND HARBORS CONGRESS:

Three or four weeks ago. on my way to Washington, my heart was gladdened to see tied at the docks at Poughkeepsie, N. Y., a trans-Atlantic steamer with a cargo of lumber that had been shipped through the Panama Canal from the Pacific slope. The dock to which the vessel was tied is a new dock built by a syndicate who are interested in lumber on the Pacific slope. This location was chosen on account of the channel in the Hudson River at this place being deep enough to permit a trans-Atlantic steamer to dock. From here will be distributed lumber from the Pacific slope throughout the Middle and Eastern States

This question is too broad to treat as a local or State issue Therefore I am going to discuss it as a national and an international project for the progress and the extension of trade not only with ourselves, but with all the other nations, both on the Eastern and Western Hemispheres I believe in conservation of our natural resources, but conservation without utilization will cause stagnation of business and commerce. This not only holds good of our forests, our coal and mineral lands, but our waterways for power and transportation purposes The United States is nothing more than a big corporation run by the stockholders, who are the citizens; the legislative, judicial, and executive branches are the same as a board of directors in a large corporation

All corporations have overhead charges, all corporations have what is known as an account called "Betterments or improvements ' This is the account that I intend to deal with today The legislators, or the legislative branch, must put the soft pedal on the continuous changing of the constitution and by-laws of this great corporation and look to the promulgation of proper laws to govern our betterment account, and see that out of the moneys expended each year a sufficient share is allotted to betterments, which, if properly expended, will tend to increase the business of the country without increasing the expense account

One of the greatest controlling forces of business and commerce is the transportation facilities of any nation—the railroads the waterways, and the highways—all of which bear the same relation to a country as the veins and arteries to the human body. Commerce is its blood, and particular care must be taken that it is not contaminated or its flow interfered with by cutting or severing of its veins or arteries If we do, the business of the country will die, just as the body will die if the veins and arteries are permitted to wither I intend to treat of the waterways of this great country, not in antagonism to railroads but in cooperation and conjunction with them.

The great Empire State, which has won its name and rank because of its commerce, wealth, and population, has constructed entirely at its own expense the longest and greatest artificial canal system in the world, which has done its share toward making this country the first nation among nations in wealth and commerce One State can not improve itself materially without having a beneficial effect upon the entire Union of States. The United States can not be benefited or improved without having a beneficial effect upon the nations of the world. Our interests are so entwined with each other that the waves of prosperity in one country vibrate and extend so far that they are felt at the uttermost parts of the earth The Government of the United States is obligated to its people, to the various States and Territories, and to itself It is bound to maintain peace throughout its borders, and it is bound to look after the prosperity of its people in times of peace To accomplish this, it is called upon to construct, regulate, govern, and improve enterprises which are too large for one State to build, control, regulate and improve—projects which pertain to the entire United States rather than to any one State.

The authors of the Constitution of the United States, through the great article of particulars, delegated to the National Government certain obligations and governing powers, and within its jurisdiction are its navigable streams.

The great changes which are taking place in our rivers, due to the alterations in the topography, the clearing of the lands of timber, and the cultivation of the lands in the various watersheds, by the increasing population in the different sections, demands increased facilities for water and railway transportation and flood protection Most of these navigable rivers are used for interstate trade; most of these rivers drain a number of different States. Therefore flood protection and improvement for transportation are National rather than State projects The same is also true of our great streams which are adaptable for power purposes It is, therefore, imperative that the National Government construct such improvements and pay for them out of the National treasury, wherever the expenditures are too large for any one State or when the State is prohibited from making these improvements itself on account of constitutional restrictions

The State of New York, which I have the honor of being one of its Representatives in Congress, is willing and also able to take care of this worthy project, in which the people of the United States are so much interested and which will be so valuable to the general public good. It is this project which I intend to discuss here today, and I wish to assert that when this project is constructed, which it will be, it will not only be beneficial to the people of New York State, but of the greatest service and benefit to the entire United States, and will also render the greatest service to all civilization. We are, however, prohibited from improving this navigable river on account of constitutional limitations, as the Federal Government has entire control over all navigable streams

The total receipts of the United States from all sources during the fiscal year 1914 amounted to the enormous sum of $380,-800,893.96 Of this amount the State of New York furnished $62,116,763.34, or 16 34 per cent of the entire amount. I merely bring this to your attention as a reminder that it should have all consideration when it requests that some of this money be returned to it in the form of a betterment for the use of the people throughout the entire Union of States

The deepening of the channel in the Hudson River, which will make of the capital district of the State of New York a seaport, which capital district represents a population of half a million people, will also prevent the devastating floods which destroy property to the value of millions of dollars annually

New York State has expended approximately $150,000,000 in the construction of this unexcelled canal system, including terminal facilities at points of vantage This great artificial waterway was not built by the State of New York for the exclusive use and benefit of the people of the State, but it was constructed for the use and benefit of all the people of America. not only for domestic and interstate commerce. but for coastwise, trans-Atlantic, trans-Pacific. and South American commerce. Every State and every Congressional District bordering on the Great Lakes is more interested in this waterway than the Empire State   In addition to these, all the people in the States and Congressional Districts bordering on the Atlantic and Pacific Oceans and their tributary rivers are vitally interested in a deeper Hudson River and in the Barge Canal, which is the connecting link between our coastwise trade and the Middle and Northwestern States. If their Representatives have not already taken an interest in this project and in the various projects in the Rivers and Harbors Act, they will realize their obligations in the future

It is estimated by competent authority that the freight carried on the Hudson River after the completion of the Barge and Champlain Canal system will exceed the freight which passes through the Panama Canal. Freight from Duluth, Chicago, Cleveland, and Buffalo on the Great Lakes can be transported by water to San Francisco or Seattle from $1 to $2 a ton cheaper than by rail across the Rocky Mountains to San Francisco or Seattle, and where it has to be retransported to Alaska the saving is double this amount   On account of the natural topography of the Hudson River valley, and the simplicity of construction of this project, it should be improved at once   The Hudson River, as far north as the Government dam at Troy, is an arm of the sea extending into the interior for one hundred and fifty-odd miles, and the tide rises and falls 3½ feet at the Federal dam at Troy; the mean level of the surface of the water in the Hudson River at the dam is only 1½ feet higher than the mean level of the surface of the water in the harbor at New York City   This natural transportation and commercial route of water, rail and wagon, from the Great Lakes through the Genesee, Mohawk, and Hudson Valleys, has made its terminal, New York City, the greatest market of exchange in the world, as it connects one of the richest producing localities of this continent with ocean transportation

As the demand grows upon this market for greater facilities, greater space, and for more economy in exchange, this demand will have to be met by improving the natural highway, which in its crude form in years past started this growth   When the United States Government restricts the State of New York, by its constitutional right, from making its own improvements, it must reply to the demand of the people of the State of New York by making the improvements which they request. You must keep in mind that, when the people of New York State unanimously request the Government to assist and aid in this project, it is a request of approximately one-tenth of the population of the United States, who pay approximately one-fifth of the revenue, which is their proportion toward any amount expended for any improvement within their own State, as well as one-fifth of the amount expended by the Government for any improvement, whether it be railway, waterway, roadway, or any other project in any of the other States.

This project is of the utmost importance and will be directly beneficial to 80 per cent of the population of the whole United States and will serve those people who pay 90 per cent of the total revenue of the Government. This waterway route through the Empire State is the one real competitor of the Canadian canals and St. Lawrence waterway system for export trade Canada, on the construction of the Welland, Trent and Lachine Canals, and the improvement of the harbors of Toronto, St. Johns and Montreal, has already spent millions of dollars As a result, they have secured a great trade, and to hold and increase this trade they contemplate spending many millions more to increase their waterway facilities, and thereby cut out the competition of the United States.

The foreign commerce of the Great Lakes has reached the enormous sum of approximately 20,000,000 tons annually To quote from an article in the *Saturday Evening Post* "Peru has four and a half million people and has a coastal length equal to the distance from Maine to Georgia; Chile has 3,000,000 people, and its coastal length would measure from California to Alaska; Columbia has 4,000,000 people, and is the size of the Louisiana Purchase; Mexico has 16,000,000 people, and if transposed on the map would cover the German Empire, France, and Great Britain; Cuba, with her 2 000,000 people, would just nicely cover the area of Pennsylvania; Argentina, with a population the same as Canada, is the size of half of the United States, Bolivia equals the area of all of the Rocky Mountain States together.' Brazil, having a population three times that of

Canada, has the area and resources of the United States with Germany thrown in. Here in South America are Republics with three times the area of the United States and with 70,000,-000 people, just beginning to realize their size as the United States began to feel her strength and growth 20 years ago, and we are getting a bare third of that continent's enormous commerce Germany and England, Japan, yes, even Canada, so far as investments in Brazil and Mexico are concerned, are in the field reaping the profits of South American trade to which the United States was indifferent prior to the construction of the Panama Canal "

There will be built at either or both of the terminals of the Panama Canal a city which will rival our greatest seaports on the Western Hemisphere. This city, or cities, will be the market of exchange for all the packet cargoes of South America, both on its Atlantic and Pacific slopes, the packet cargoes of the western slope of the United States, the Hawaiian and Philippine Islands, Australia, New Zealand, Japan, China and Africa Who will be the purchasers, other than Europe? It will be the population of the United States, principally that portion bordering on the Great Lakes and which live adjacent to and connected by this waterway system with the markets in New York City

With only a depth of 5 feet, the Erie Canal, before it became obsolete, carried as high as 6,442,225 tons of freight in one year, and as late as 1906, with a greater depth, it carried 3,540,907 tons of freight after the State of New York had decided to change the entire water traffic by the construction of the Barge Canal This of necessity changed the class of boats plying on these waters, so that practically all the tow lines which operated on the canal stopped extending, which permitted Canada's competition to become more formidable and take that tonnage which we hope to again secure

The following data will give you some idea of the Barge Canal:

NEW YORK BARGE CANALS

Erie branch	miles	323 3
Number of locks		35
Oneida Lake, forming part of the route	miles	19
Spurs to Syracuse and Rochester	do	10 26
Champlain branch	.do.	61 5
Number of locks		11
Oswego branch	miles	22 8
Number of locks		7
Cayuga and Seneca branch	.miles	27 3
Number of locks		4
Cayuga and Seneca Lakes connected with Barge Canal	miles	65
Width of channel, land line, surface section, bottom, minimum	.feet	75
Width of channel, land line, water surface. .	. do....	123 to 171
Width of channel, land line, lock section, bottom, minimum	. .do.. .	94
Width of channel, river line, bottom, general	....do .	200
Depth of channel, land line and minimum river line	do	12
Locks, length between gates .	do	328
Locks:		
Various lifts	..do	6 to 42
Triple lock at Troy, distance between outer gates	do .	450
Available length, regular locks	.do.	310
Width of chamber	.do..	45
Depth of sills	do.	12
Dams		
New		28
Old, with new crests		6
Old, without change		5
Boats		
Capacity utilizing full lock width	tons..	3,000
Built for two to pass in narrowest channels, and for two traveling tandem, to be locked at one lockage	.tons	1,500
Appropriation·		
Erie, Champlain, and Oswego Canals		$101,000,000
Cayuga and Seneca Canals		7,000,000
For terminals		19,000,000
Total		$127,000,000
Total length	.miles.	529 16
Total number of locks		57
Total number of dams		39
Total carrying capacity	tons	25,000,000

Running time, between Buffalo and Albany, four to five days

The descent from Lake Erie level to the Hudson River level is 565 feet. The original canal was constructed with a depth of 3 to 3½ feet and was built to accommodate 30-ton barges which carried less freight than the ordinary railroad freight car does today, while the present canal is constructed so as to accommodate barges of 3,000 tons capacity, one hundred times greater than the original canal boat. Approximately 90 per cent of the population of New York State lives within 25 miles of the navigable streams and waterways so that they all are within its commercial advantages. This population occupies one-half of the total area of the State

The representatives of the people in the National Government should make it their paramount interest to cheapen both the cost of our natural and manufactured products to the consumer. The merchandise of the Pacific Ocean from the Orient, North, South, and Central America, and the West coast of the United States and Alaska should be brought into close touch with our Atlantic Coast and the great interior of the United States With a port at Albany there will be a saving of 150 miles by railroad for all points reached by the New York Central, the Rutland, the Boston & Maine, the Delaware & Hudson, the West Shore, and the Boston & Albany Railroads.

EFFECT OF PANAMA CANAL

An article in the *New York Herald*, Monday, December 7, 1914, says:

"The canal has shortened travel routes between New York and Yokohama by 3,700 miles; between New York and Shanghai, about 2,000 miles; between New York and Australia, about 3,000 miles; and between New York and western South America by from 3,500 to 7,000 miles It also reduces the distance from Europe to western South America by more than 5,000 miles International commerce doubled in the 30 years following the opening of the Suez Canal, and

business and personal interrelationship between the
Occident and Orient was increased in like proportion

"Highways of travel on the ocean are influenced by
surrounding conditions just as are those on land, so
that the shortest distance between two given points is
not always the best   Plentiful freight supplies, inter-
changeability of the products of the countries forming
the termini of the routes, 'way stations' on such routes,
plentiful coaling stations and cheap coal of a quality
suitable for steamship engines, and even favorable
winds and ocean currents are among the factors contributing to the success of routes of travel upon the
ocean

"The sections of the world which may be considered as probably within the 'sphere of influence' of the
Panama Canal are the eastern and western coasts of
America, the eastern coast of Asia, and the islands of
the Pacific   All of western America is nearer to
Europe than formerly, and all of western America and
most of eastern Asia and Oceania are nearer to the
eastern coast of America

"Study of the production and consumption of the
various countries lying within the canal's sphere of
influence shows that their various products are thoroughly interchangeable   A study of distances also
shows that both New York and New Orleans are now
so much nearer to all of western America than is Liverpool that we may expect an increasing share of the
trade of that section to fall to the lot of eastern North
America; that the eastern ports of the United States
are considerably nearer to Yokohama, Melbourne,
Sydney, and Wellington than is Liverpool by her
shortest route; but that Liverpool is still nearer Hong-
kong and Manila than either New York or New Orleans via Panama "

In conjunction with this I wish to give you a table of distances from New York and Albany, the distance from New

York being via the Pennsylvania Railroad and the distance from Albany being via the New York Central.

Cities	New York. Miles	Albany Miles.	Difference. Miles.
Chicago	908	837	71
Buffalo	411	296	115
St. Paul	1,318	1,247	71
Duluth	1,391	1,320	71
Detroit	759	547	212
Cleveland	579	479	100
Cincinnati	751	743	8

Wheat being one of the principal articles of export trade which is carried by this waterway, I take pleasure in giving you below the export, both from the United States and Canada, in 1901, in 1913, and 1914, as follows

United States and Canadian Exports of Wheat

1901   Busheis.

United States and Canada, exports of wheat (largest).	150,173,000
Of this amount New York exported.	30,202,000
Of this amount Montreal exported.	13,582,000
Of this amount St John exported.	1,085,000

1913

United States and Canada, exports of wheat		195,774,000
Of this amount New York exported	49,019,000	
Of this amount Montreal exported	33,252,000	
Of this amount East St John exported	8,236,000	
Inbound through United States	70,850,000	
		112,338,000

Balance of United States wheat shipped from American ports   83,436,000

	1914	*Bushels*
Montreal, since opening of navigation, May 1st to October 3d (on account of ice she could not ship from January 1st to May 1st; she is what is termed a seven-months port).		46,264,000
New York, January 1st to October 3d.		26,533,000
Galveston, " " " " "		19,804,000
New Orleans, " " " " "		18,793,000
Baltimore, " " " " "		16,456,000
Philadelphia, " " " " "		12,471,000
Boston, . . . " " " " "		11,430,000
Total exports of United States and Canadian wheat to October 3d		166,264 000
Exports same time, 1913		145,696,000
Increase of exports of wheat to October 3, 1914		20,568,000

From the Great Lakes in August the shipping prices for wheat
were substantially as follows:

EXPORT WHEAT CONDITIONS TO OCTOBER 3, 1914

	Per bushel
Lake freight, etc., Duluth to aboard ocean-going steamer at Montreal, Canada	$3\frac{7}{8}$c
Extra ocean freight, tramp steamers, Montreal, over New York to United Kingdom or Continent	1c.
Extra marine insurance (St Lawrence route)	$\frac{1}{4}$c.
Total cost, Duluth to f o b ocean carrier at Montreal, Canada.	$5\frac{1}{8}$c
Chicago to Buffalo lake freight on wheat	87c
Inland freight, Buffalo to New York.	5 50c
Charge for putting grain f o b. vessel in New York Harbor	90c
Total	7.27c.
Cost of shipping via New York	7 27c
Cost of shipping via Montreal	5 12c
Showing cheaper cost of shipping via Montreal route	2 15c.

From which you can see why all of us that are gathered here
today, representing the country geographically as well as commercially, are all interested in this project of deepening the channel in the Hudson River to 27 feet, about which I have had the

pleasure to speak today, as it, with the Barge Canal, is the connecting link between the Great Lakes and the Atlantic Ocean. It is of paramount interest not only to the producer, but to the consumer, not only the exporter but the importer, as this project is the one scheme of all others that connects the most westerly city of Lake Superior—Duluth—as well as Chicago, Cleveland, and Buffalo, with a 40,000-mile water route around the world via the Barge Canal, the Hudson River, the Atlantic Ocean, the Gulf of Mexico, the Caribbean Sea, the Panama Canal, Pacific Ocean, the Indian Ocean, the Red Sea, the Suez Canal, the Mediterranean Sea, the Straits of Gibraltar, the Atlantic Ocean, back through the Hudson River, the Barge Canal, and the Great Lakes, which waterway washes the shores of approximately every civilized nation of the world and forms the greatest interstate and international waterway route known to man. (Applause.)

President Ransdell—The next speaker will show us beautiful pictures which I think will demonstrate that there are some terminals on the Mississippi which are not obsolete. Some of these pictures will also show you, not what the terminals are now, but what they are to be in a very few years.

Before introducing this speaker, I wish to remind the audience that we are to have a very unusually interesting program this evening. There will be an illustrated lecture by the Chief Engineer of the New York State Barge Canal system. The State of New York, as you all know, has been spending millions of its money for the benefit of the Nation

We are also to have a lecture on "Constructive Cooperation vs Cut-Throat Competition," by Louis D Brandeis, of Boston, Mass., who is known to all of us

Last, but not least, we are to be told about "Trade and Transportation in the Amazon Valley." By whom? A man whom all of us know and love, Captain J. F Ellison, who for many years was our Secretary   (Applause)

We want all of you to be present this evening, and bring your friends.

Now we will have the illustrated lecture on "Water Terminals," by Mr Irving C Norwood, Davenport, Iowa, Secretary
of the Greater Davenport Committee   Let me present Mr.
Norwood. (Applause.)

WATER TERMINALS
Illustrated Lecture—Irving C. Norwood, Davenport, Ia.
Secretary Greater Davenport Committee

The cities of the Upper Mississippi River have awakened to
the importance of utilizing the great waterway as a freight carrier. They have begun to appreciate the necessity of cooperating
with the Federal Government in the rehabilitation of the river;
to understand that modern terminals and the proper type of boats
are just as important as an adequate channel; and to realize that.
while the improvement of the channel is a Government function.
the building of terminals must be undertaken by the cities themselves and the construction of boats by private capital

Well-informed people in the upper river cities no longer
waste time discussing the reasons why freight is not carried on
the stream under present conditions   They are more concerned
with remedying those conditions. They are familiar with the
evolution from keels and flats to the present type of river
steamers and understand how it happened that the railroads,
paralleling the river, having excellent terminal facilities and
being uncontrolled in the use of competition-killing rates and
methods, were able to absorb the business and reduce the amount
of river freight to a negligible quantity. But, of much greater
moment, the public of the upper river cities has come to see that
at the present time the real obstacle in the way of an immediate
revival of river transportation is the absolute lack of modern
freight handling facilities at industrial centers along the river
(Applause.)

During the recent fight in Congress against river and harbor
appropriations. almost every project undertaken by the Government in recent years came in for a share of criticism   The
project for the improvement of the Upper Mississippi probably
was subjected to less abuse than many other waterway improvements. but doubt was nevertheless expressed in some quarters as

, to the Government's justification for carrying through the plans for a six-foot channel from St Louis to St. Paul at a cost of $20,000,000, of which approximately $5,000,000 has been spent since work was begun in 1907

The justification of this project may be discussed under three heads. First, is there sufficient potential water freight along the Upper Mississippi to warrant this expenditure; second, will the cities of the Upper Mississippi, by building terminals and installing machinery, make it possible to handle this freight rapidly and economically; and third, will the enterprise of private capital keep pace with the efforts of the Federal Government and the cities, so as to assure the building of a sufficient number of boats of the proper type?

Let us consider these questions in order. That as to the freight possibilities of the upper river is readily answered by available figures From Alton, Ill., just above St Louis, to Minneapolis, there are sixteen cities with an aggregate population of more than 1,000,000, housing 3,370 factories which produce more than $400,000,000 worth of manufactured products annually The freight in and out of these cities amounts to about 35,000,000 tons annually, of which 33,500,000 tons now move by rail and 1,500,000 tons by water. A study of the classes of freight that go to make up this total indicates that there are approximately 4,000,000 additional tons of freight that at the present time could be and should be carried by water, and that would now be so carried if there were terminals at which it could be rapidly and economically handled and boats in which it could be cheaply moved

With reference to the second question, the attitude of the upper river cities toward terminal improvements, it is only stating a fact to say that most of them have begun to realize the economic necessity of putting the idle river to work The river has long been a rate basing point, even in its idlest periods, but its effect upon rail and water combinations on traffic passing through the Panama Canal will amount to very little Indeed, I quite agree with the statement of the Secretary of this organization in a recent circular letter, to the effect that the operation of the Panama Canal will impose an actual handicap upon Mississippi Valley shippers unless the water link to the sea is rendered efficient and is actually operated.

The Upper Mississippi River Improvement Association, whose activities were responsible, in part at least, for the great betterments already made in the navigability of the upper river, has now turned its attention to the terminal question and has been engaged in educational work along this line for the last two years   Last summer the field secretary of the organization traveled up and down the Mississippi between St Louis and Minneapolis, urging upon commercial organizations, city councils and business gatherings, the necessity of early and adequate terminal improvements.   The Greater Davenport Committee has spent much time and money in similar missionary work.   The effects of this continuous agitation are becoming apparent There are few cities on the upper river in which a healthy, intelligent sentiment in favor of the reclamation of river fronts and the construction of terminals is not being developed   There is now a much larger understanding of the fundamental proposition that, no matter how deep and wide the river's channel may be made, no matter how numerous and how perfect the aids to navigation that may be installed, no matter what type of freighters may be built, the river will never carry a large volume of freight until the cities themselves build and equip their own terminals   (Applause.)

To some of you gentlemen this may seem like placing undue emphasis upon a clear and simple proposition.   But emphasis is necessary, for it has only been of comparatively recent date that the general public in the section under discussion has been willing to admit that the lack of terminal facilities has had anything much to do with the lack of freight movement   The railroads, the Federal Government, the Mississippi River steamers, all have been blamed   The Federal Government is doing its share on the Upper Mississippi River; whatever the railroads may have done in the past they are not now in a position to exercise effective obstructive tactics; the present Mississippi River steamers are not ideal freight carriers, but have been abused beyond their deserts   The truth is the cities of the upper river are just reaching the point where they are willing to admit that the decrease in river freight tonnage has been largely their own fault They have bartered away their river frontage and their riparian rights; they have turned their levees into dumping grounds for city refuse and anchorages for river junk; they have refused to provide storage facilities for even the small amount of port to port freight carried by the river steamers and laboriously and expensively loaded and unloaded by deck hands. But nowadays they are holding tightly to what is left of their frontage; they are cleaning up their levees, and those cities which, by reason of lack of frontage or lack of money, find themselves unable to construct industrial terminals, are at least contemplating the building of docks and warehouses

Let. us see what the situation is in the principal upper river cities. In the progressive city of Minneapolis, with a population of 301,408. soon to be at the head of navigation on the Mississippi, conditions are excellent The Federal Government has appropriated funds to complete the high dam which will make navigation possible to the foot of the Washington Avenue bridge. and the Legislature has authorized the City Council to issue $300,000 in bonds for the acquisition and improvement of municipal terminals Of these bonds, $75,000 have already been issued and sold and the money is being spent by the city in erecting a sea wall preparatory to the rise in level that will accompany the completion of the dam next summer. The installation of handling devices and the construction of a municipal warehouse will follow, answering in plain terms the question as to what this particular city will do to take advantage of the improved river. And it must not be forgotten that Minneapolis has 12,500,000 tons of freight in and out annually, much of which should logically be moved by water

Winona, Minn., a city of 18,000, has thought well enough of her river front to build a sea wall and create a park, but has no freight terminal and no handling facilities. There is frontage available for terminal purposes, but no work is contemplated in the immediate future. The same may be said of La Crosse, Wis., a city of 30,000, which has parked a portion of the river front but has gone no further.

Dubuque, Iowa, although having no public freight landing or terminal facilities at the present time, will not be long without them Plans have been prepared and sentiment is developing with a rapidity that will ensure the beginning of work on a definite improvement project in the near future.

Clinton, Iowa, a city of 25,000, has parked the waterfront in a beautiful and commendable manner, but has made no provision for handling freight This latter question has recently been taken up, however, with every indication of active work being begun next summer.

Moline and Rock Island, Ill , adjoining cities of 24,000 each, have extremely limited equipment for handling sand and coal at the present time, but are becoming extremely interested in the installation of more adequate facilities as a result of recent indications that the waterway from the Lakes to the Mississippi, consisting of the Chicago Drainage Canal, the Illinois and Michigan Canal, and the Hennepin Canal, is to be improved and enlarged in the near future.

At Muscatine, Iowa, the City Council and the City Engineer are working on plans for a small freight terminal, which will probably be financed by a bond issue. Work will be begun on this improvement within the year.

At Burlington, Iowa, a city of 24,000, there are no terminal or freight handling facilities and no definite plans under way. But as this city is the home of the President of the Upper Mississippi River Improvement Association, Mr Thos. Wilkinson, I am convinced a start will be made in the right direction before very long.

At Fort Madison and Keokuk, Iowa, there are no freight terminals, but Keokuk recently had the harbor line established, surveys made and a plan prepared for a freight terminal of the type approved by the Upper Mississippi River Improvement Association

At Quincy. Ill., a city of 36,000. a joint water front terminal committee was recently created at the suggestion of the Chamber of Commerce and authorized to prepare plans for sea wall construction, a freight terminal and a municipal belt line

At Hannibal, Mo., a city of 18,000, there are no existing freight terminal facilities, but public sentiment in favor of such an improvement on a limited scale is growing rapidly and will probably crystallize into a definite plan within the year.

At Alton, Ill, a city of 17,000, there is no freight terminal at present, but the city authorities are working out a docking system and local shippers are much interested.

The city of Davenport, with a population of 43,000, lying opposite Moline and Rock Island, Ill, and about midway between Minneapolis and St Louis, I have left until the last in order to discuss the terminal operations there somewhat in detail   In 1910, that city, which is under special charter, secured the enactment by the State Legislature of a law authorizing the creation of a Levee Commission and the issuance of terminal bonds. Before plans were drawn or work was begun the senior member of the Commission, Mr. W. D. Petersen, made a trip through Europe inspecting the terminal basins, warehouses, docks and handling facilities on the inland waterways of Germany and France   Work on the Davenport terminal has been in progress since 1911. Up to the present date nearly one mile of sea wall has been built and more than twenty acres of land reclaimed This work has cost $150,000   It is estimated the entire improvement will cost about $750,000, which will include the building of three miles of sea wall and the reclamation of 141 acres of land. This reclaimed land will be worth, conservatively estimated, not less than $3,000,000   (Applause.)

The first section of the industrial terminal has been completed This contains thirteen units of 10,000 square feet each, which will be leased for twenty-year periods at rentals ranging from $480 to $750 per year. These units are suitable, either singly or in groups of two or more, for warehouse or factory purposes.

The second section of the industrial terminal, consisting of twelve units of approximately 10,000 square feet each, is now under construction. The sea wall has already been built to the twelve foot stage and the fill begun. This section will be completed by the fall of 1915   On this section will be located the municipal warehouse.

Work on the third industrial section of twenty-four units will not be begun until after the first and second sections have been entirely completed, front and rear tracks laid, the municipal warehouse built, and the locomotive cranes, moving platforms, etc., installed. The entire terminal will be under the direct control of the Levee Commission, which will operate the warehouse, the handling apparatus and the levee railroad, a switching proposition connecting with the four trunk lines serving the city of Davenport.

In building the terminal in this way it has been the idea of the Levee Commission to make each section self-supporting. The rentals per unit of 10,000 square feet have been based on the cost of construction of the units and the charges that will be made for switching and freight handling will be based upon the actual cost of these operations, plus a reasonable charge for interest and depreciation. Under the Commission's plan it will be possible to retire the construction bonds covering a given section within twenty years of their issuance, and this without asking the Davenport taxpayer to contribute one cent toward the improvement. (Applause) At the same time the completion of each section adds extremely valuable acreage to the list of city property.

The Levee Commission has fixed January, 1915, as the time when formal applications may be made for lease of the thirteen units in the completed first section   Already more than twenty preference claims have been filed with the Commission for these units.

Now as to the third and last question—whether or not private capital will become interested in the building of boats and thus complete this necessary link in the rehabilitation of the river. With the improvement of the channel by the Federal Government and the construction of terminals by the cities, ample private capital will be provided for this purpose. An excellent concrete illustration of this fact is contained in a letter I received just a few days ago from John H Bernhard, of New Orleans, a successful builder of steel, self-propelled, light draft barges Mr Bernhard has developed a cargo carrier that is ideal for use on the Mississippi, and in his letter informed me that he had raised five million dollars with which to finance a Mississippi River transportation company to operate between Minneapolis and New Orleans and to touch at intermediate points where terminal facilities were provided. The building of barges will be begun in May of 1915, and the company will begin operations in May of 1916.

Mr. Bernhard is not a dreamer. He is a hard-headed, successful business man, thoroughly familiar with inland waterway transportation problems in this country and abroad. He proposes to run on the Lower Mississippi River, between New Orleans and St. Louis, barges of 3,000 tons carrying capacity, with four propellers, seven-foot draft, weather-proof cargo boxes and an upstream speed of fifteen miles per hour. On the Upper Mississippi he expects to run barges of 1,000-ton carrying capacity, with two propellers, and one center stern wheel and an upstream speed of 10 miles per hour.

"This company is already an assured fact," said Mr. Bernhard in his letter to me. "I am at present engaged in the preparation of plans, specifications and organization, while a firm of attorneys is engaged in the preparation of a charter, by-laws, through bills of lading and contracts conforming to the various laws of the large number of States in which we will have to do business."

Even lacking this announcement from Mr. Bernhard, I am confident that in Minneapolis, in Davenport and in most of the cities on the upper river very material sums could be raised with which to finance an upper river freight line. In fact, Davenport shippers have repeatedly suggested that a company be formed in Davenport to build barges and operate as a transportation company and that the shippers of other upper river cities be invited to cooperate by investing money in the stock of this company and by shipping their freight by water. I have been inclined to wait, however, before undertaking the organization of such a company until the first two sections of our terminal were entirely completed and until there were indications that other upper river cities would soon have terminals and handling facilities.

This announcement of Mr. Bernhard was very welcome at this time, however, and simply serves as an indication that there is plenty of available capital for this purpose. With the Government doing its share in improving the channel and the cities taking hold of the terminal question, private capital will not be backward to invest in the securities of Mississippi River transportation companies.

The day is not far distant, in my judgment, when those cities on the Upper Mississippi River, which have not been farsighted enough to build and equip their terminals, will labor under a very heavy handicap indeed and will be left far behind in the race for industrial and commercial supremacy. (Applause.)

Following this portion of the lecture there was thrown upon the screen a series of pictures showing the great improvement already made in the water front of Davenport, and terminals, improved and unimproved, in various cities, after which the Convention recessed until eight o'clock.

THIRD SESSION

Wednesday Evening, December 9

The Convention met pursuant to recess, President Ransdell in the Chair.

President Ransdell—It is unnecessary to make any introduction of the gentlemen who is now to speak to us. Most of you here have been attending our Convention for a number of years, and you know this gentleman as well as I do. For a long while he was the Secretary and the moving spirit of the National Rivers and Harbors Congress. Several years ago he resigned his position with us to take charge of the greatest inland fleet in the world, a fleet of forty odd steamers on the river Amazon, by all odds the greatest river on the earth—I say that although I live on the banks of the Mississippi.

Recently this gentleman was sent by his company from the Amazon to Paris. Although temporarily in America, he is still in charge of the affairs of that great company. It is needless to say that I refer to Captain J. F. Ellison, of the United States. (Applause.)

TRADE AND TRANSPORTATION IN THE
AMAZON VALLEY

Address—J. F. Ellison, Cincinnati, Ohio
Ex-Secretary National Rivers and Harbors Congress

Mr. Chairman, Ladies and Gentlemen:

Your President, in the seven years we were associated in the work of this organization, grew so accustomed to issuing me orders, that, upon learning of my arrival home, he immediately sent out a written order that I should come to this Convention prepared to make an address.

In fulfillment of instructions received, which, however, did not specify my subject, having in mind the great interest in, or perhaps I should say the widespread publicity being given to, the possibility of capturing for this country the trade of South

America, formerly held by Europe, I have decided to tell you some of the trade and other conditions as I found them in the Amazon Valley.

If what I say does not bear out some of the rainbow-tinted stories so beautifully told by writers, the majority of whom, judging from what they say, have never been far enough south to lose sight of the North Star and pick up the Southern Cross, or those of gentlemen who have been down there on trade excursions and pleasure jaunts, please remember that, having lived and transacted business with its people, mine is a different viewpoint Also—and I want to emphasize this—if anything that is said seems a criticism of the people or the country, I do not mean to be critical, but do mean to tell you the truth as I saw it

For Brazil and its people I have not only good feeling, but warm regard. The climate of the Amazon Valley, located as it is in the very heart of the South American tropics, can truthfully be called good Para, where I was located, is only eighty miles from and south of the equator, yet the thermometer rarely ever goes above ninety degrees Fahrenheit. In the various trips into the interior, made necessary by my business, I covered about 14,000 miles; one of these took me 3,300 miles up rivers and into localities where health conditions were not good yet I never had a degree of fever.

My reception into business, social and official circles was most cordial. The educated Brazilian is invariably a courteous, polished gentleman, a charming host, and if he becomes your friend, is one upon whom you can count.

My experience leads to the belief that people from the States are more cordially received and better liked than those from any other country. This, I think, is due first to the fact that our Consul, Mr George H Pickrell, ranks in business and official circles higher than the representative of any other government. Second, there have been so few of us down there, that they have not grown to know us as we really are   (Laughter.)

The Amazon Valley, as possibly you know, has but two Brazilian ports of entry Para, the principal one, is not located at the mouth of the Amazon, but on the navigable entry into the great river, the true mouth of which to mariners is an unknown and uncharted sea. Manaos, the second, and scarcely less in importance than Para, is 1,000 miles inland at the mouth of the Rio Negro to which port from New York, Liverpool and Hamburg, ocean steamers ply regularly regardless of draft, and drop anchor in that harbor, 1,000 miles from the sea, in from 16 to 20 fathoms of water. Both these ports have well-equipped docks, those of Para being equal to New Orleans, and Manaos having beyond question the best dock facilities of any strictly river port that I have knowledge of. The Rio Negro has a rise and fall of 60 odd feet, but neither high water nor low water interferes with the loading or unloading facilities. There is a third port in the valley, but it is in Peru—Iquitos, 2,100 miles from salt water, to which steamers can and do go regularly the year around from New York and Liverpool, on a draft of 21 feet.

You will please understand that I make no pretense to any special knowledge, but only a slight general knowledge of Brazil as a whole. It is too big. If you will except Alaska, Estados Unidos de Brazil is territorially as large as the United States of America. At Para I was 3,100 miles from New York, and 3,000 miles from Rio de Janeiro, the capital of Brazil, which serves to illustrate and emphasize the fact that a man in North Brazil cannot know much more about conditions prevailing in South Brazil than a man in Maine knows of conditions in Oregon.

To be of benefit, any discussion of the Amazon Valley, as it relates to the possibility of exchange of business between this country and that must cover, in part at least, transportation, production and consumption.

As an advocate of, and believer in, water transportation, it is pleasant to tell you that the Valley of the Amazon is the *one* place in all the world of which I have direct knowledge, where rivers have nothing to fear from rails. In that country waterways reign supreme, and no man can see far enough into the future to offer a prophecy as to when railways will become competitors of waterways.

Nature has been most bountiful in supplying that part of the world with wide, deep rivers; that some of them in their extreme *alto*, or upper, reaches would be better for navigation if improved, admits of no doubt; but the Brazilian Government is even more content than ours to let Nature's work alone, and none of the rivers have been improved in the slightest way since time began, or water commenced to flow.

The improvement of harbors in Brazil, as in this country, is quite another story Along the coast of Brazil there are many good harbors, thoroughly improved and as well equipped to handle deep sea traffic as any in this country or in Europe, which reminds me that from this platform the National Rivers and Harbors Congress has been told, by an able, active and most distinguished gentleman, of the immense sums Brazil and other South American countries were spending on the improvement of their harbors.

The gentleman I refer to has been accepted as an authority on Latin-America That he is well informed, possibly the best informed man in the States on a good many subjects concerning those countries, admits of no more doubt than that he is misinformed on the subject of harbor improvements in Brazil As a matter of absolute, concrete fact, Brazil has never spent anything from its treasury in the improvement of a single harbor from Rio Grande do Sul, in the South, to Manaos in the North. All have been improved by foreign concessionaires, who have used foreign money, brains and skill to effect the improvements, and who, to cover investment, interest and capital stock, are allowed by the Federal Government to tax every pound of freight that comes into or goes out of the country by the ocean routes. This applies even to the capital city of Rio de Janeiro, whose harbors and docks are in the hands of a French Company I might say in passing, that the Latin-American is rarely, if ever, a constructor, but invariably he is a Prince of a Promoter. With but three exceptions, I neither know nor have heard of any public utility, railroad, electric road, lighting or power plant in all of Brazil that has not been built by foreign money, and if successful, owned, run and managed by foreigners

This statement has a big bearing on the possibility of trade between that country and this, for the capital thus invested, and the amounts are very large, did not come from the States but from Europe, principally from England, France and Belgium It is my opinion that *trade follows more closely the investments of a country than it does the flag of a country.*   It is, however, very pleasant for me to tell you that one citizen of the United States, using his own and French and Belgian capital, has done more to give both North and South Brazil good harbors, and rail and water transportation, than any or all the Brazilians, either living or dead, have done for their own country.   I refer to Mr. Percival Farquhar, of York, Pa.   (Applause.)

Having said that the Amazon Valley, which means practically all of North Brazil, does and must depend for transportation on its waterways, just one more statement and I have done with that part of my subject.   I trust you will pardon a personal reference.

In many of the articles that have appeared in magazines and newspapers attacking appropriations for our rivers, stress has been laid on the decadence of traffic on western and southern rivers, the chief reason given being that our steam craft are of an old, obsolete type; that we have not kept pace with modern practice and the improvement that has been going on in other parts of the world.

If thirty-five years of actual practical experience, covering every detail of river business from mud clerk to captain, and from captain to general manager of steamboat lines, on two continents and under two flags, qualify me to express an opinion contrary to that of writers of theory, then I say to you that the American river steamboat, particularly the stern-wheel type, on alluvial rivers, obstructed, as all such are, with sandbars, snags, changing channels and currents, stands today at the head of all river craft that the world has yet produced.   (Applause.)

It has been my privilege during the past three years to handle a steamboat company having a fleet of sixty-two river steamers, of the combined freight and passenger type, among which were steamers from the yards of the best builders in England, Holland and Germany.   The last addition to the fleet was 14 stern-wheel steamers from Pittsburgh, U. S. A.   These boats have worked a revolution in the river business of the Amazon.   They have penetrated further into the *alto* regions than any other steam craft, carry their full load on less water than equal size boats built in Europe do without any load, and in two years continuous service their cost of operation and upkeep have been

lower than any other steamers of the entire fleet. These are
Facts vs. Theory.

If additional proof be needed of my statement that the American stern-wheel river steamer is neither antiquated or obsolete,
as was stated from this platform this afternoon by a gentleman
who tells you that he has studied Mississippi River navigation
for some time, and who, I am told, has fifty-four days (the time
it took a craft he had designed to make one trip from New
Orleans to St. Paul and return) actual practical experience, let
me point out the fact that one firm in this country has built and
sent this stern-wheel type of boats to most of the principal countries of the world that have real alluvial rivers, their boats being
in successful operation on the Volga in Russia, the Nile in Egypt,
the Congo in Africa, the Magdalena in Columbia, having a fleet
of more than thirty-five on that river, on the Guapore and Beni
in Bolivia, on rivers in Mexico and Venezuela, and, lastly, on
the Amazon in Brazil; and that within the present month another
firm of builders, the head of which is now in this hall, has con-
tracted to build and deliver in Australia one of their stern-wheel-
ers so much derided by theoretical writers and gentlemen who
have so much as fifty-four days actual experience. (Applause.)

No, gentlemen, it is not lack of proper craft, but lack of
dependable channels, that has caused the falling off in traffic on
our rivers.

Now as to production in the Valley of the Amazon—speaking broadly, as it applies to world commerce, production com-
prises just *two* articles, Norracha (Rubber) and Castanha
(Nuts), neither being products of cultivation, but natural products of the tropical forests. In both of these products this
country is commercially interested. The States buy 55% of
the rubber, and 40% of the nuts, that Amazonas produces. .

With production limited to two salable articles, and under
the necessity of purchasing and importing from other parts of
the world practically all that is needed to sustain life, the weakness of the Valley, commercially speaking, is at once apparent,
for it is an accepted truth, that no country that imports more
than it exports can be permanently prosperous

In the last quarter of a century, agriculture, never extensive, has been almost entirely abandoned. All efforts of capital and labor have been given up to gathering rubber. During the first quarter of this year I traversed about 8,000 miles in the interior of the Valley, using our own Company's steamers on the main Amazon, Rios Purus, Solimoes, Negro, Acre, and Yaco, going on the Alto Purus to the Peruvian boundary at Santa Rosa; on the Yaco to Guannabara, the head of steam navigation; on the Alto Aen to Toena, a point where Brazil, Peru and Bolivia come together, with only a little river separating the three countries. It is hardly necessary to say that to get to these extreme points I used the American stern-wheel steamers.

I did not, however, in my journey into the interior of Amazonas traverse the "Rio Duvida," as another distinguished citizen of the States was at that very time engaged in putting that river on the map; but in 8,000 miles of the best rubber-producing territory in the Valley I did not see as much cultivated land as I can show you from a car window in thirty minutes in any direction from Washington; and the rivers I was on, except in their extreme upper reaches, were rivers that have had steam navigation for full fifty years.

Rubber, for the past twenty-five years or more, has been both the Gold and the Curse of Amazonas. Gold, for the reason that it has furnished all that that metal would buy, and at times has been of almost equal value; Curse, for the reason that it has caused abandonment of agriculture and production of foodstuffs to such an extent that the Valley does not now, and cannot for some years to come, be put into condition to feed itself.

A Crown of Rubber, pressed down on the brows of a people, can be as hard and uncomfortable as a "Crown of Gold."

From the time that rubber became an important factor in the commercial and manufacturing world, the Amazon Valley, the natural habitat of the Hevea tree, which produces the best and purest rubber, held a monopoly on fine rubber up to 1912. In that year her supremacy as the greatest rubber-producing center was threatened by the product from Far Eastern plantations, in Malay, Ceylon, Java, Sumatra, Borneo and the other sections of the East, where seeds taken from the Tapajoz dis-

trict in the Amazon Valley had grown into a forest of producing
trees that covers over two million acres   In 1913 the East produced more good rubber than Brazil. Starting with four tons to
the London market in 1900, the East sent in 1913 to London and
New York 42,750 tons of high grade rubber   65,000 tons was
the estimate from the plantations this year, and 90,000 in 1915

When it is understood that up to 1912, just two years ago,
the world's production and consumption of rubber was between
fifty-two and fifty-five thousand tons, you will understand and
appreciate what the Eastern competition means to the Amazon,
for the plantations can produce and market it cheaper than the
Briselleiro can go into the forests and gather the wild native
product. The reason is simple; the East feeds itself. No food-
stuff for laborers is imported into that country, and cheap food
means cheap labor the world over. In 1913, according to government figures, there were imported into the Amazon Valley
through the ports of Para and Manaos, 7,000,000 kilos of beans.
6,000,000 kilos of rice, 14,000,000 kilos of sugar, 10,800,000
kilos of *xarque* (dried beef)), 1,000,000 kilos of *baccalau* (dried
fish), canned goods to the amount of $863,000 (our money) and
tobacco amounting to $332,000 (our money).

The list could be truthfully extended until it comprised practically every necessity, and actually every luxury that the people
of the country used—all imported into a valley that will grow
in plenty every one of the articles I have mentioned, in quantity
and quality equal to the lower Mississippi Valley.

Is it any wonder that in Para the failures and protested drafts
and bills in 1913 amounted to eighteen million dollars (our
money), and in Manaos, the other rubber center of Amazonas,
to twelve million dollars?

Europe furnished 86% of the imports and the States 14%;
whether the losses were on the same ratio, I do not know, but
it is known that the conditions I have just related have brought
about a great commercial crisis   Not only has business been
affected, but State and National credits as well

Business is now, and has been for nearly two years, at the
lowest possible ebb. Revenues of the States of Para and Amazonas, and that of the National Government, have seriously fallen

off. What these revenues formerly amounted to is told by the Chairman of a Federal Commission appointed from the Senate and Chamber of Deputies to examine and report on the crisis in the Amazon. Senator Eloy de Suza in his report states that in the twenty-four years of the life of the Republic, the Federal revenue from imports and exports into and out of the Amazon, has amounted to 656,000 *Centos de Reis*, in our money $217,-696,000; that the States of Para and Amazonas have collected in the same time and from the same source another $199,200,-000. State and municipal taxes in the two states named have provided a very large additional sum—and these great amounts have been paid by a population of *less than one million people.* Think of these figures, gentlemen, the next time you discuss, or "cuss," our tariff, or grumble at your tax bills. (Applause.)

Let me give you just *one* illustration *each* of import and export duties that the people of the Amazon have had to pay. Up to the present year every kilo of rubber originating in either of the States of Para or Amazonas paid to the state government twenty per cent of its selling value. Rubber from the Federal Territory of the Acre paid a like amount to the National Government.

You know that the tropics are not as a rule considered health resorts; the Valley of the Amazon is no exception to the rule. Dr. Oswaldo Cruz, the most eminent medical authority in Brazil, reporting on health conditions in the Amazon to the Federal Government, uses these words: "Outside of the cities in the Valley (there are but two), sickness is the normal condition of all the inhabitants." In the San Antonio district of the Madeira River, no native-born inhabitants were found; *they all die.* And yet medicine pays an import duty that ranges from 200 to 300 per cent *ad valorem.* Think of it! Brazil has but few infant industries to protect; hers is a "tariff for revenue only." That she gets the revenue admits of no doubt.

The picture of conditions in the Amazon Valley that I have drawn is not a bright one, but is, at least from my viewpoint, a truthful one, but one that I fully believe can and will be changed. In no part of the world have I found better or more enterprising merchants, more industrious or faithful laborers.

Given these, and a climate and soil such as the Valley possesses, and progress is bound to come. The governments have at last awakened to the fact that they cannot continue, under the changed conditions, to levy and collect such enormous taxes as heretofore, and are now actively and earnestly seeking ways and means to help the people.

Particular efforts are being made to foster and encourage agriculture. With the Valley cultivated as it should be, and in time will be, the people of the Amazon, instead of being buyers of the necessities of life, will be sellers; and this, in addition to the great natural riches of her forests, will bring the prosperity these people so well deserve.

In conclusion, if my experience in one of our "Sister Republics in the South" has taught me anything of value, it is to be more content with our country, our institutions and our Government; for I have come to know that our Government is the only one on the Western Hemisphere that is really and truly a government of, for and by the people; and I have come back from South America thanking God, and I say it reverently, that no matter which political party is in power, whether it be the Democrats or the Republicans, it is as much my Government under one as under the other (Applause), and, mark you! I am making this statement after having carefully read the Congressional Record of the first regular session of the Sixty-Third Congress (Applause.)

PRESIDENT RANSDELL—We knew we would not be disappointed with what the Captain had to tell us.

We are now to have the very great privilege of hearing from one of the closest students of transportation in America, and one of the very best known writers on that difficult subject. He is going to talk to us on "Constructive Cooperation vs Cut-Throat Competition"

It gives me very great pleasure to present Mr. Louis D Brandeis, of the City of Boston, Mass (Applause)

CONSTRUCTIVE COOPERATION vs. CUT-THROAT COMPETITION

Address—Louis D. Brandeis, Boston, Mass.

MR. PRESIDENT, LADIES AND GENTLEMEN:

The United States has, in widely varying degrees, developed four methods or systems of transportation—the railroad, the water-carrier, the trolley and the auto. Each of these has, to some extent, competed with the others. The results have not been altogether satisfactory. The railroads complain, not without just cause, that their net earnings are smaller than they should be; and this Convention testifies to the fact that there is a widespread demand on the part of the public for greater transportation facilities at less cost.

The question that is bound to come up in connection with the development of these facilities for which you are working is this: "What shall be the relation of the different methods or systems of transportation, one to the other?" And on that question we may get some light from the experience of the past. We have made many experiments.

We began, in the first place, with free and unrestricted competition. The results were largely disastrous to the carriers and were unsatisfactory to the community. Free and unrestricted competition involved, among other things, charging "what the traffic would bear." It meant on the one hand that, where there was no competition, the traffic would have to bear everything which the carrier attempted to put upon it—everything that it could bear and still move. That was a great hardship, not only upon individual shippers, but even more upon particular communities not blessed with competitive methods or systems of transportation.

But "what the traffic would bear" involved, on the other hand, something extremely bad for the carriers; it involved charging no more than the competitive traffic would bear; and the result was a scramble for traffic among competitive lines, in which many carriers became bankrupt.

So free and unrestricted competition was recognized as a failure. Having reached that conclusion, the next step taken

was combination, resulting in monopoly of transportation   The
most striking modern instance of the disastrous results of combination, both to the community and to the carrier, is presented
by the New Haven system   The New Haven succeeded in getting, through combination, practically a monopoly of all the railroads in New England. But the company went much further.
It moved on to the water-carriers, with the result that the five
New England States with ports upon the Atlantic, free to any
traffic, had not a single line of steamships between those different States that was not owned or practically controlled by the
New Haven   But more striking still is the fact that no one
of these five New England States had a single line of steamships
to the city of New York, or to the city of Philadelphia, which
was not controlled by the New Haven; and the influence of the
New Haven extended considerably further South still.

This monopoly of transportation, however, did not merely
include the railroads and water-carriers   It extended to the
trolleys   Practically all of the trolleys of Connecticut, Rhode
Island, and Western Massachusetts, and some of the trolleys in
New York and Vermont, were also acquired by the New Haven,
with the result that it was actually impossible for any one to go
from any of the New England States to New York except by
some method of transportation controlled by the New Haven,
unless he went by auto or the old-fashioned horse and wagon

Now, there you had a combination and monopoly of practically all of the known methods of transportation in one organization; and the failure was egregious.   Why?

In the first place, the combination failed because the cost of
acquiring the monopoly was very great.   It was not merely the
cost of buying up these various systems, it was the cost of killing
the competition which was not bought up; the cost, for instance,
of killing the Enterprise Transportation Company's steamship
line, which was built to compete with the New Haven's lines.
There was also a cost very much greater than that, greater than
the cost which was incident to the buying of competing lines at
excessive valuations, or the cost of running steamships at ruin-
ous rates in order to kill a competitor   That was the cost of
inefficiency in management, the cost of bad management which

had resulted from the attempt of one organization, through one body of men, to run these various concerns. The loss in this experiment was tremendous. The limitation which is put by Providence upon the powers and capacities of the individual man was the greatest cause of the failure which ensued.

So competition failed; and combination failed also; and yet the conviction of the American people, as expressed in the Sherman Law, as expressed in the provision of the Panama Canal Bill prohibiting the ownership by railroads of competing lines of steamships, is that competition should continue between the various methods or classes of transportation. The question now presented is this: Having found that free and unrestricted competition is a failure; having found that monopoly, or combination, is a failure; having, nevertheless, determined that we are to have competition among the different forms of transportation, and among the different members of each class competing with one another, what is the rule that we are to lay down? What is to determine the proper relation of service on the one and on the other hand? How are we to distribute the traffic and the work which is to be done for the American people? I think any one of us who stops to consider this situation, to determine what shall be done by each one of four different methods of transportation, would say to himself at once, "Let each one do that which is can do best." That is the law of efficiency; and, generally, the cheapest service is what will be deemed the best.

That it is largely a question of cost, seems self-evident. It seems self-evident not only when you consider the different forms or methods of transportation, like railroad as against water-carriers or railroad as against trolley. but it is equally self-evident when you are considering what ought to be the competition between the different members or concerns in the same class. The one that can do it the best—and usually that means the one that can do it the cheapest—ought to perform the service.

Well, now. if that is self-evident, as it seems, why has it not been pursued? Why have carriers gone on doing business that was not profitable, as they have done to a very considerable degree?

I think there are really three reasons. The first reason is that with all the development of our transportation—take the railroads, which are, of course, our chief agency—with all the marvelous development of our railroad transportation the cost of the service has never yet been determined. I do not mean merely the cost of service as a whole; but, if a railroad receives $100,000,000, or $200,000,000 as the year's income, how much of that is cost and how much of that is profit has not been determined. The facts in that respect are known in a general way, but the thing that has not been determined is, what any particular service cost.

This statement will seem almost incredible to an up-to-date manufacturer, for every up-to-date manufacturer has found out, or has been in the process of finding out by the most careful methods for at least a generation, what it costs him to manufacture and sell every article which he manufactures and sells If the manufacturer simply understood how to make an article without knowing the cost of its manufacture and sale, what would happen to him, ordinarily, would be bankruptcy; but he knows better than to incur that risk, and so he undertakes to find out the cost of the manufacture and sale of each one of the articles he produces.

In this very hall not many years ago we were told by one manufacturer, who had in his catalogue one hundred thousand articles, that he undertook to find out what every article that he sold cost. Now the railroads have never undertaken to find out in detail what their service costs ' With very few exceptions they do not even know how much profit or loss there is in the passenger service taken as a whole, or how much profit or loss there is in the freight service taken as a whole. Even that first step in the division of cost, and in the ascertaining of facts absolutely essential to doing business safely, has not been taken by most railroads; and, of course, they do not know how much profit or loss they have in carrying business from one point to another. They do not know how much it costs to carry from one city to another, excluding the terminal cost in the city. They do not know what the terminal costs are in any of the cities on the articles which they are carrying.

Now the result has been one which has been disastrous to them, and which has also been quite disastrous in many instances to the development of water-carriers. The fact that there were competing water-carriers, by which freight could be carried cheaply as compared with the rail cost, resulted merely in lowering the rail rate so as to meet the water competition. But whether in meeting the water competition the railroad made money or lost money, the records kept did not show, and nothing except a guess at the cost could be made by the railroads. Therefore they have not had, up to the present time, a means of applying the rule that that carrier should do the business which can do it the cheapest, even if they had been disposed to do so.

Then there is a second reason why railroads have not ascertained transportation costs. It is in a sense historical in its nature. It is this: when you start a railroad—and, of course, that is true to a certain extent of other forms of transportation—you have not enough traffic to fully utilize the capacity of the plant. Consequently you put the rates down, and the traffic manager says, "If I can fill my cars, even if I do it for much less than the regular rate, if I can carry more passengers, if I can add another car to this train which has to run anyhow, almost anything that I get will mean a profit to the railroad, because the roadbed is there, the cars are there, the engine has to move, and therefore the additional passengers or additional tonnage that I can get must be adding at least something to the income of the railroad."

Now at one time in the history of almost every railroad there was a certain amount of truth in that; but we have long passed that period in respect to most of the railroads of the country and particularly in respect to the railroads in this Eastern district, which do about one-half of the business of the whole country. Our situation is now, and has been, for quite a number of years, say ten or fifteen years, that the railroads have reached the point of saturation of business; therefore every additional bit of business taken by the railroads imposed upon them new burdens in providing facilities. And whenever business was taken that in and of itself did not pay a profit, the railroad was subjected to an actual loss—the loss that was involved in providing the capital that was necessary to increase the facilities so that they could take care of the business   The whole situation had changed, but the traffic men who made rates and who sought business did not realize the change that had come over the situation, and they continued precisely as they had done to make such a rate as the traffic would bear, no matter how low that rate was.   Indeed, with the congestion which has come in our Eastern communities through great development and increased population, this new business added involved, in very many instances, larger investment in capital pro rata than had the original construction of the road.

You will, therefore, when you examine the figures showing the investment and the returns of the railroads in this Eastern district, find a huge increase in the invested capital.   The capital invested forms an extraordinarly important factor in the cost of running a railroad, and for every dollar of income which is received by the railroads in this great Eastern district—East of the Mississippi and North of the Ohio and the Potomac—you will find between \$5 00 and \$5.50 of capital invested.   One of the reasons, and a very potent reason, why the railroads in this region have felt the pinch, why the earnings have been inadequate, is because this capital investment has grown upon them, and the doing of more business, the great increase of business, has been done in very many instances at a loss.

Now how this works, how this scramble for tonnage operates, has been manifested in very extraordinary ways by the investigation which the Interstate Commerce Commission has made during the last year.   Take this situation: they have carried from the great grain States to the Atlantic seacoast carload upon carload of grain and of flour, on which the earnings, after paying some special terminal and similar charges, were not enough to yield the interest and cost of repairs to the cars in which the flour or grain was moved, to say nothing whatever about the cost of operating the railroad, the cost of the roadbed and the cost of the administration of the property   This all comes from failure to know the facts, from failure to deal with the bottom causes of loss and the essentials of profit.

Railroad managers will necessarily all move in the dark until they learn what a thing costs. When they do know what a thing costs then they can protect themselves against loss; then also they will welcome the fact that other people also do that business on which these others alone can make a profit. All the water-carriage ought to be welcomed, and not looked upon jealously, if carriage by water can be done cheaper, as it ordinarily can. Take the case of freight movements on our great lakes. Grain from Duluth to Buffalo is moved in bulk at one cent and a half a bushel; railroads could not get it from Duluth to Buffalo at a rate of less than thirteen and a half cents, and it would not be profitable at that rate. Take the case of ore. The ore rate in vessels on the Great Lakes, carrying as they do in bulk, is about one-eighth of the rate at which it is carried on the railroads; and probably the railroads could make no great profit, even at this much higher rate.

Now, what ought to be done is to learn these facts with reference to the individual cost of such transportation service. If men did but know these facts we could count upon it that these losses would stop—this scramble for traffic, which possibly may hurt the competitor from which it is taken, but which hurts the carrier that gets it very much more. The method which has been pursued in the past should be abandoned.

Related to these conditions is the desire for bigness, the feeling that, if the system were only large enough and if you could comprise in one unit sufficient of the carrying capacity of the country, then you would be sure of profits; but that proposition is absolutely unsound. The unit of greatest efficiency is reached before a system is very large, because the ability of every man is limited; and, having reached, through growth, the size of greatest efficiency, this also must be borne in mind— the question of profit is merely the question of how much you can earn per dollar of investment. The question to be considered is the possible return on your capital, and it does not follow that, by multiplying your five million, or ten million, or fifteen million, by twenty or thirty, and getting together a huge transportation system, you can earn more on a dollar than you did before.

Take the entire returns of the railroads of this country, and follow the history of the various systems, and you will see that after they had passed a very modest capitalization the earnings per dollar invested diminished instead of increasing. Now, let those who own, and those who manage, these various forms of transportation, keep these facts clearly before them, and if they do they will readily recognize the law which should govern the relation of competing carriers to one another—a law of business more binding than any that legislatures can enact or courts enforce.

And what you gentlemen should insist upon, you who are urging a form of transportation which can carry traffic at a cost so much below anything that the railroads have been able to reach, is simply, "Let us all stand on our merits, and let every other form of transportation stand on its merits." (Applause.) You should insist upon scientific cost ascertainment, upon a system worked out carefully, elaborately and patiently Hold that up before the managers and owners of these competing properties, and you will get what is your due. We shall then have a fair field and no favor, where the fittest will survive; and practically all can survive, if each does that for which it is best fitted

I thank you for your attention. (Applause)

PRESIDENT RANSDELL—Ladies and Gentlemen: We have heard a great deal today about the barge canal in New York It is a fact, which I presume is known to all of you, that the Empire State does things in a magnificent manner. When it wants its waterways improved, it goes down into its own pocket and improves them. It is now expending, without calling on Uncle Sam for help, something like $134,000,000 to establish a magnificent system of canals throughout its own borders. We are to be told about it this evening in an illustrated lecture by the Engineer in charge of that great work

No man is better qualified to speak intelligently and interestingly upon this subject than the Chief Engineer of the Barge Canal System, Mr. J A Bensel, of Albany, New York. (Applause.)

THE NEW YORK STATE BARGE CANALS
Address—J. A. Bensel, Albany, N. Y.
State Engineer and Surveyor

Mr. Chairman, Ladies and Gentlemen:

It may be wondered why in an Association of this kind the Barge Canal of the State of New York has any reason to put forth its claims in regard to waterway improvement; yet, without the capacity to feed the harbor or to make use of it by bringing into connection therewith the large extent of territory of this country which lies back from the sea itself, there would be less reason for the existence of the canal system of the State of New York. The New York State Canal System has gone on at a steady rate of progress and development since the early stages of the nineteenth century, commencing at the time when Jefferson was President of the United States. (Applause.)

The progress which has been made in the State of New York, phenomenal as it is among the States of the Nation, seems small when compared with our sister, the Dominion of Canada—when we consider the development of the Welland Canal. But the Erie Canal in the State of New York has made steady progress during a period extending over one hundred years of the life of the two countries. In Canada the Welland Canal is being constructed with a draft of over thirty feet so as to admit boats from the Upper Lakes into Lake Ontario and thence to various ports in Canada, and also in the United States. It is a matter of fact that the cities of New York State need to give attention to their present and future facilities in order to keep pace with our Canadian neighbors. The Barge Canal of the State of New York, however, means the intercommunication of the cities of the State which we hope will result in unexampled prosperity for our State. Its present development is wonderful as compared with conditions one hundred years ago.

This improvement is one that may be said to have originated, of course, in the selfish interest of the people of the State in order to provide a line of cheap communication which would conduce to the internal development of the State. But it must be borne in mind when considering the improvement of waterways, whether seaports or interstate communications, that whatever develops one portion of the country contributes its share' of benefit to every other portion; so there is nothing selfish about New York building this $130,000,000 Barge Canal. Our interests are the interests of the entire country We are all concerned in the elements of prosperity; they are interwoven in our statehood New York is concerned primarily in the use of its canals for commerce. They are being constructed by the people for the use of all the people. The people are paying for them and their interests are the first to be consulted New York State is pointing a way to her sister States along lines of canal development, illustrating to them the fact that the elements of nature in the way of water transportation are adequate for the uses and benefits of the people of the world.

There is this difference between the waterway and other kinds of transportation, such as are represented by railroads—the waterway is directly owned by the people and will remain their heritage forever, so that it will turn back to the people some portion of that freedom which they enjoyed when the country was young, but which has been lost by the congestion caused by the growth of population It is this feature which appeals to the young men who are connected with waterway transportation. They have a feeling that they are restoring something the loss of which is to be regretted.

The Barge Canal improvement is the greatest work of its kind ever undertaken by a single State and one of the greatest engineering projects ever undertaken by any government. The canal itself covers a length of 540 miles of construction, which, together with the adjacent natural streams, makes a total of 790 miles of internal navigation within the State suitable for boats of Barge Canal dimensions. The importance of this undertaking is not generally appreciated by the people of the country at large nor even by the people of our own State

With the opening of the Panama Canal, New York city seems destined to become one of the greatest maritime centers of the world and the new State Barge Canal, by far the greater part of which has already been completed, furnishes an up-to-date channel from this metropolis to almost the center of the continent. Many of the alert business men of the East and of the

Middle West have made preparation to use this canal as soon as it is opened, while already even the lumber merchants of the Pacific Coast are reaching out to grasp this vast market made available by the two new waterways.

New York has the proud distinction of always having taken the lead among the States of the Union in the building of waterways, and, moreover, it has done this without the help of the National Government. From the days when, in response to President Jefferson's proposal to expend surplus revenues on roads and canals, the State made its first canal survey, which, when laid before the President, he declared to be a project a century ahead of its time, saying that the idea of building 350 miles of canal through a wilderness was little short of madness; and from the time, only eight years later, when the State began its canal single handed, spurred on by one of President Madison's last official acts in vetoing a bill passed by Congress carrying financial aid—from these early days of the Republic down through all the years to the present, New York has built and maintained its own canal system and now has crowned its efforts by the expenditure of $130,000,000, in modernizing its waterways to meet the demands of present-day traffic.

In return for all this labor and money the State has, of course, reaped some of the rewards, but the whole of the country, especially the Eastern half, has been a very large beneficiary. Since New York has been such a conspicuous example for the other States and has done so much for itself, it is only just that the Federal Government should do everything in its power to render this new waterway of the greatest possible value to all who may share its benefits. (Applause.)

The Barge Canal improvement consists in the enlargement of four of the existing branches of the State Canal system— the Erie, stretching across the State from east to west and joining the Hudson River and Lake Erie; the Champlain, extending northerly to Lake Champlain from the eastern terminus of the Erie; the Oswego, leaving the Erie where the waters of the Oneida and Seneca Rivers unite and following the Oswego River to Lake Ontario; and the Cayuga and Seneca, starting south from the Erie a little to the west of the Oswego junction and running first to Cayuga and then to Seneca Lake. This improvement is distinctively a river canalization scheme, natural streams and lakes being utilized wherever available Of the whole waterway system, 70 per cent of the total length will be in lake or river channels, but in most of these river channels there is little work above the water surface which indicates any change in the river.

The Barge Canal lock which stands at the eastern terminus of the Erie Canal, where it leaves the Mohawk at Waterford, has a lift of 34½ feet and is the first of a series of five locks which are located within a distance of 1½ miles and which constitute the greatest flight of high-lift locks in the world. They will lift boats 169 feet, which is within one foot of being twice as high as the lift of the whole Panama Canal between sea level and summit. (Applause.)

These locks are placed so close together that it becomes necessary to have pools between each two of the series in order that the drawing of a lockful of water may not appreciably lower the surface in the intermediate levels Marking the canal channel through the center of these pools there have been constructed concrete dock walls, which incidentally form a walk from one lock to another

In the Mohawk River, just below the point where the canal line between the Hudson and Mohawk Rivers around the Cohoes Falls enters the Mohawk and at the foot of Mohawk River navigation, stands the Crescent dam. This structure stretches across the river with a length of nearly 2,000 feet and has a crest 39 feet above the apron

At one end of the Crescent dam there is located a power house at which electric energy for operating the Waterford flight of locks will be generated. Most of the locks will have their individual power houses for generating power for operating and lighting the lock. Within each power house two power units are installed, so that one will always be available. If, however, it happens that both are disabled, hand-operating devices are supplied for all machinery It will not be necessary to keep these plants in operation all of the time. Within 50 seconds after the water has been turned into the turbines the power is on the line ready for operation at full speed.

The Mohawk below Schenectady is canalized by two fixed dams—the Crescent dam, already referred to, and one at Vischer's Ferry. This dam is also about 2,000 feet long and of the same general design as the Crescent dam. The Mohawk between Schenectady and Little Falls has been canalized by the building of eight movable dams of bridge type. All but one of these have been completed and have been in use for creating pools in which the contractors have been able to float their dredges. In times of flood or during the winter months the gates of these dams are raised and then the uprights are drawn to a horizontal position under the bridge floor, leaving an unobstructed channel across the full width of the river.

The terminals constitute a very important part of the Barge Canal. These are being built at some fifty cities and villages along the line of the new waterway. The State did not determine to build these terminals until some eight years after the Barge Canal improvement was voted upon, but they are so important a part of the scheme that without them much of the work would have been of practically little use. In general, a terminal will consist of some place where any shipper or boatman can find dockage room not controlled by railroads or private corporations, and where there will also be warehouses and suitable freight-handling machinery available at a reasonable cost.

In the central part of the State there occurs a summit level in the canal which becomes a critical point of water supply. During the last eighty years the State has built up a system of reservoirs in the Adirondacks to the north of the canal and in the hills to the south. These sources of supply are retained and in addition two large reservoirs are added. About five miles north of Rome there has been built a large dam across the upper Mohawk River, which impounds water in what is known as the Delta reservoir. This body of water is about four miles long and two miles wide. The dam across the river is 1,100 feet long and 100 feet high above its foundation.

The work at this reservoir has been completed for about two years. During the unprecedented flood of a year ago last

March it served a very useful purpose in protecting the cities along the upper Mohawk At Rome and Utica no unusual flood conditions were experienced. The second large reservoir for supplying the summit level is being built across the headwaters of West Canada Creek at Hinckley The dam at this place will be 3,700 feet long

Throughout the western third of the canal, the alignment of the new waterway has, in general, coincided with that of the old canal and the improvement has consisted in a widening and deepening of the old channel, with new walls and structures In this western section of the canal, especially on the level which stretches for sixty miles between Rochester and Lockport, it has been necessary to place guard gates at frequent intervals. By means of these gates a short section of canal may be cut off, if any leak or damage to the banks occurs.

At several places in this western portion, the canal is carried upon high embankments At one point—near Rochester —the valley of Irondequoit Creek was filled by new embankment and the canal carried upon it in a concrete trough. This trough consists of concrete side walls and concrete floor, which are covered with tar-felt waterproofing A serious break in this concrete trough at Irondequoit showed the necessity of additional precautions and accordingly certain other sections of the canal prism were entirely lined with concrete, both the bottom and side slopes being covered.

At Medina the gorge formed by Oak Orchard Creek gave rise to some interesting construction. Early in canal operations it was thought that this gorge might be crossed by a concrete arch of long span, but it was finally decided to follow in general the alignment of the old canal, which circled the gorge, crossing the stream above its head. This alignment necessitated a considerable length of high retaining wall, so that in effect the canal runs behind a dam for about one-third of a mile, the walls reaching a maximum height of 45 feet In crossing this stream at Medina a culvert of 50 feet span was employed In order to maintain navigation in the old canal, it became necessary to perform during one winter all work which would interfere with the old channel

The locks at Lockport have always been considered noteworthy structures of canal building. In Barge Canal work two new locks replace a flight of five old ones. By means of these two locks, boats will reach the top of the ridge that extends along the western section of the State and which is known to geologists as the Niagara escarpment.

The Barge Canal has been a great engineering work largely because of the number and variety of its structures. There are nearly 700 structures of various kinds and the planning of these has entailed an immense amount of study and detail work. The building of bridges has been an exceedingly intricate and troublesome problem. In all there are about 300 bridges crossing the canal and nearly one-third of these are railroad bridges. There have been litigations and conferences with railroad officials which have been almost endless. Many of the bridges are in villages or cities, where it has been necessary to provide for large and heavy traffic.

Most of the Champlain Canal is located in the Hudson River. The canalization of this river has been accomplished largely by utilizing existing fixed dams. In much of the work of canalizing the Hudson River it has been necessary to excavate the rock bottom, and the contractors have adopted various methods for accomplishing this work. Some have built coffer-dams and have excavated in the dry; others have used drill boats and have blasted and excavated with dipper dredges. Another method has been by means of rock breakers. Upon the forward end of a scow a hammer weighing some 16 tons was so arranged that it could be dropped from a considerable height. This action broke up the rock at the bottom of the channel and allowed its removal by a dredge.

At the northern end of the Oswego Canal, where it enters Lake Ontario, there has been built a lock of peculiar design, known as a siphon lock—the only lock of this kind in America and the largest to which the siphon principle has ever been applied. Another interesting structure and one which was devised in Barge Canal design is known as the siphon spillway. This is especially useful in restricted locations where the ordinary long overflow spillway cannot be used. The utilization of the siphon principle allows the water to escape under a head and thus the flow is regulated automatically by the peculiar design of the structure.

To one who has not investigated the subject it will doubtless be somewhat surprising to learn what a large proportion of the State's population lies within a very short distance of its waterway system. In the view before us we see belts which extend along either side of the waterway system at distances of 2, 5, 10 and 20 miles, respectively. Within the 2-mile belt there is 73½ per cent of the total population of the State, while within the other belts the percentages are 77, 82 and 87, respectively. Considering the question from the point of view of area, the lines which mark the 50- and 70-mile belts show that a very large portion of the State is within easy distance of the canal, if motor trucks are used. Within the 20-mile belt lies 46 per cent of the total area of the State, while within the 70-mile belt there is 88 per cent of its total area. These figures are of great interest to a student of transportation problems (Applause.)

(Mr. Bensel's address was profusely illustrated with lantern slides and moving pictures, showing work completed and under way and the operation of locks, movable dams and the ponderous machinery used in constructing this great improvement.)

PRESIDENT RANSDELL—We have an exceedingly interesting program tomorrow, and I hope all will attend. I am especially anxious for every one to come to the session tomorrow night, as it is to be "Ladies' Night," and we are to have addresses by three very distinguished ladies whom I am sure every one of us will be pleased to hear.

We will begin tomorrow night's entertainment by a reception in honor of the ladies, which will take place from eight to nine o'clock. I hope that every delegate will attend that reception.

We now stand in recess until tomorrow at ten o'clock A. M.

Adjourned accordingly.

FOURTH SESSION—THURSDAY MORNING, DEC. 10

The Convention met pursuant to adjournment, President Ransdell in the chair.

President Ransdell—Ladies and Gentlemen: In the many assaults made upon the recent Rivers and Harbors Bill, one project was particularly singled out for misrepresentation and became the most fruitful theme of abuse of any waterway project in the Union.

The silver-tongued orator from the Lone Star State is going to tell us "The Truth About The Trinity River" today—Senator Sheppard, of Texas. (Applause.)

THE TRUTH ABOUT THE TRINITY RIVER
Address—Senator Morris Sheppard, Texas

Perhaps no other river in the world has been the subject of so much misrepresentation as the Trinity, of Texas. For nearly a decade and a half it has been an object of humor, ridicule, sarcasm, slander, denunciation. Whenever some self-styled statesman, lacking originality in thought or initiative in legislation, lost in the abysses of a hopeless mediocrity, found himself unable to attract the attention of the public, either as a debater or as a guardian of the treasury, he would invariably assume an air of outraged virtue and proceed to assault the Trinity. (Laughter.) As a savior of mythical Ciceros, imitation Pitts, make-believe Websters from a just obscurity, the Trinity River has been worked to a finish. So often has this been done that the very language of the attack has become a threadbare and thumb-worn parliamentary classic. So frequent and persistent has the practice of criticising the Trinity grown that in many quarters the impression prevails that it is a channel of sand running waterless to the sea through a dewless, fogless, rainless land. (Laughter.) If these critics of the Trinity are to be believed, the skies above it never harbor a cloud, while its bed is so devoid of moisture that the last bull frog has perished with the melancholy refrain on his dying lips: "Nobody but Theodore E. Burton knows how dry I am." (Laughter and applause.)

The favorite suggestion of the antagonists of the Trinity are that it be macadamized for good roads purposes, that it be utilized for a trolley line, or that artesian wells be distributed along its banks to furnish an adequate water supply. It has been denounced as an example of colossal graft, a fraud upon the Government, the most odious and odoriferous item in the annual rivers and harbors bill. At the last session of Congress the attack on the Trinity was especially vigorous, especially bitter. It was subjected to the most searching and hostile analysis both in the Senate and in the House. In the House a river and harbor bill was passed containing a provision for continuing the improvement of the Trinity. In the Senate, after the fullest debate, a motion was made to strike it from the bill and the motion was defeated by an overwhelming majority. Despite the ridicule that has been heaped upon it, the opposition that has been directed against it, whenever the facts in relation to the Trinity have been presented to Congress and a vote taken, that great body has always gone on record by a heavy majority for the continued improvement of the stream. Certainly a project which continues to sustain itself under such circumstances must possess substantial merit. (Applause.)

Now, what is the truth about the Trinity? As long ago as 1852 Congress authorized a survey of this river. The survey was made by Lieutenant of Engineers William H. C. Whiting, who reported in 1853 that the river was practicable for navigation during high water for about 600 miles, during low water for 100, passing through very rich cotton, wheat, corn and sugar lands; that the season of high water was generally from the first of January to the last of June, continuing at times for 18 months, the transition from high to low water being slow on account of the great length and depth of the stream; that the chief obstacles were overhanging timber and snags; that transportation up and down its course could be improved at no very great expense; and that seven steamboats were at that time engaged upon the river, three of them being then on their return from a point 650 miles from the mouth.   .

In 1891, nearly 40 years later, Major Chas. J Allen made a preliminary examination of the river from the mouth to Dallas, a distance of 511 miles, in compliance with the Rivers and Harbors Act of 1890.   His report was adverse to the permanent improvement of the river on the ground that in his opinion existing and prospective commerce would not justify the expense. He stated in his report, however, that the Trinity was one of the most important avenues of commerce in Texas before the building of railroads.   More than a hundred steamboats operated on various sections of the Trinity before the advent of the railroads

I have quoted this official testimony to show the injustice of the contentions that the Trinity is without sufficient water, that it is an unimportant creek impossible of navigation, a mere pretense of a river, affording simply a basis for legislative graft

Navigation ceased on the Trinity and other Texas rivers with the coming of the railroads because the shipping stages on the rivers were of irregular occurrence and duration   It became evident that a system of locks and dams would be required to bring about definite periods of navigation on the Trinity and most of the other Texas streams

Recognizing that the highest development of their territory of 265,000 square miles could be effected only through the establishment of waterways, the people of Texas now redoubled their efforts to bring the situation to the attention of Congress.   The result was that the River and Harbor Act of 1899 provided for another survey of the Trinity from its mouth to Dallas, calling for a report as to the cost of low water navigation at depths of 4, 5 and 6 feet, respectively, as to the best methods of improving the river, the report to divide the river into sections with a statement as to the advisability of improvement.   This survey was made by Captain (now Colonel) C S Riché, one of the most gifted members of the U. S Corps of Engineers.   After a careful examination Captain Riché reported that the permanent improvement of the river by locks and dams was not only advisable but urgently necessary   He reported that the local traffic which the improvement would develop in the rich bottom lands of the river and adjacent territory would itself justify the project, in addition to the benefit that would come from the lowering and control of freight rates. It developed that there were millions of acres of valuable timber in the valley of the Trinity, large deposits of coal, iron, clays, and building material, while the counties immediately bordering it from Dallas to the Gulf contained nearly nine million acres of fertile soil Captain Riché divided the river from Dallas to the Gulf into five sections and estimated that 6-foot navigation could be obtained with 37 locks and dams at a cost of $4,500,000.

Captain Riché's report was approved by the Division Engineer, Col. Henry M Robert, who stated that he considered the river worthy of improvement to the extent of six-foot navigation from its mouth to Dallas The Chief of Engineers, in transmitting these reports to the Secretary of War, took no position one way or the other. All these documents were presented to Congress in House Document No 409, 56th Congress, first session. With this document before it, the Rivers and Harbors Committee of the House, of which Mr. Burton was then Chairman, reported a general rivers and harbors bill on January 4, 1901, in which provision was made for beginning the improvement of the Trinity in accordance with the reports before referred to, $750,000 being appropriated and authorized for the inauguration of the work.

In presenting this bill to the House, Mr. Burton had the following to say regarding the Trinity

> "We have not included in the bill any new projects for locks and dams except the Trinity River, in the State of Texas, where we have appropriated or authorized $750,000, part for general improvements and part for the construction of locks and dams. I am frank to say to the Committee that on first examining this project I did not think favorably of it, but I gave it a good deal of consideration The Committee called before them the engineers having the improvement in charge, and it seemed to us that an

expenditure of this amount was justified. The river is easily capable of improvement. It has stable banks, and the construction of locks and dams is a comparatively easy problem. There is a great amount of traffic in prospect both from the source to the mouth and from the mouth toward the source. In this particular it differs from many other rivers, where the bulk of the traffic must necessarily be one way. Great quantities of cotton and grain will be carried toward the mouth, and from the mouth toward the source timber and building material for the large expanse of prairie tributary to Dallas toward the North."

This river and harbor bill failed of passage because it came up in the Senate only a short while before adjournment and was filibustered into its grave by Senator Carter, of Montana. Such was Mr. Burton's enthusiasm at that time for the development of internal waterways that if anyone had suggested to him that twelve years later he would repeat the tactics of Senator Carter in reference to another great river and harbor bill he would have indignantly repudiated the insinuation. Another river and harbor bill was reported by Mr. Burton in 1902 and became a law in that year. This bill authorized the improvement of the Trinity in accordance with the reports of the engineers and from that day till this the Trinity has been recognized in every river and harbor bill as one of the approved projects of the Government. Some years after the official recognition of the Trinity, Mr. Burton visited Dallas and inspected the river for some 50 miles below that city. I am told that he expressed himself as having been favorably impressed, and during the remaining years of his Chairmanship of the House Committee on Rivers and Harbors, appropriations for the Trinity continued. (Applause.)

In his report on the Trinity Captain Riché said that an artificial water supply, by means of storage reservoirs or artesian wells, would give all year round navigation in the upper reaches of the Trinity except in periods of excessive drought. In order to test the upper section a special board of engineers was authorized by the Act of 1902 to determine the possibility of securing

eight months navigation thereon   After studying and observing
the upper section for a year the special board reported that six
locks and dams would give navigation in this section for six
or seven months in the year, making no mention of the need of
an artificial water supply   Thus the question of sufficient water
supply on section one, a section 49 miles long, was disposed of.
There has never been any question as to the supply for the other
four sections, which have a total length of 462 miles   And yet,
whenever the Trinity is mentioned Captain Riché's reference
to artesian wells is invariably thrown into our faces by the opponents of the Trinity   As all-year-round navigation in the upper
reach was not contemplated in Captain Riché's plan his observa-
tion as to artesian wells had no essential relation to the project.

Since 1902 seven locks and dams have been practically completed, and two more have been located but not authorized.   Of
the seven, five have been erected within 50 miles of Dallas, the
other two being located at points 243 and 334 miles below Dallas,
respectively.   The five referred to as being within 50 miles of
Dallas are numbered one, two, four, six, and seven   Locks and
dams numbered three and five have been located but not authorized   Their construction will complete the work on the upper
stretch, the stretch running 50 miles from Dallas, the most difficult section of the river   The entire project must be completed,
however, before through navigation from the Gulf to Dallas will
be practicable, for definite and regular periods   The leading
trunk lines of railroad cross the river at Dallas, and until the
river is navigable from the Gulf to that point it will offer no
serious competition in the matter of local and interstate transportation rates

Let me say here that one of the locks and dams below the
section touching Dallas has been constructed with a lift so large
as to do away with the necessity of the lock and dam originally
planned to be built immediately above it   The project now calls
therefore for 36 locks and dams intead of 37

Early last month I visited Dallas and, accompanied by a party
of thirty or forty of its representative citizens, took a trip down
the Trinity on the *Commodore Duncan,* a 50-ton freight boat
with a draft of more than three feet.   Although there had been

no general rain in that section for five or six months, there was a depth of six feet in the Trinity at Dallas and of eleven feet at Lock and Dam No. 1, 13 miles below Dallas by river. The dam had been closed only a few days and the pool lacked five feet of being at its usual height. Surely this condition at the head of navigation, a point 511 miles from the Gulf, ought to set all doubts as to sufficient water supply at rest. Some two weeks later a committee of the Board of Engineers for Rivers and Harbors, accompanied by Col. Harry Taylor, of the Office of the Chief of Engineers, made the trip in the same boat, going through Lock and Dam No. 1 and to No. 2.

It is true that the locks and dams already constructed have cost about twice the original estimate on account of the enormous increase in the cost of materials, floods and other difficulties. If, however, the final cost should be three times the original estimate, i. e., if the final cost should be $13,500,000, it would average about $26,000 per mile for the distance between the Gulf and Dallas. The report of the British Commission on Canals and Waterways, p. 72, Vol. 6, shows that the average cost of the canalized rivers and canals of Germany is $42,250 per mile, or about twice the cost of the Trinity, even if that cost should be three times higher than the original estimate. (Applause.)

The nine principal canalized rivers of Germany, viz.: the Saar, the Main from the Rhine to Offenbach, the Main and Regnitz, the Fulda, the Saale, the Salle and Unstrut, the Oder from mouth of Neisse to Kosel, the lower Netze from Drago to Nakel, and the Upper Netze from Bromberg Canal to Russian frontier, have a combined length of 425.2 miles, with 78 locks and dams—one lock and dam to nearly every $5\frac{1}{2}$ miles—and an average navigable depth of about $4\frac{1}{2}$ feet.

With 36 locks and dams we will obtain on the Trinity a navigable channel 85 miles longer than the nine principal canalized rivers of Germany combined, with a depth of 6 feet for half the year, and a smaller, but navigable, depth for most of the remainder of the year, at practically half the cost per mile. When we recall that the basis of Germany's phenomenal prosperity, of the efficiency and coordination of her internal energies

—a condition that enabled her to startle the world with her readiness to sustain herself in the greatest war of history—is her system of navigable rivers and canals, we may begin to appreciate the inherent worth of the project for the development of the Trinity. The River Seine, in France, has been improved for a distance of 255 miles from its mouth with 34 locks and dams at a cost of about $88,000 a mile, over three times the cost of the Trinity, even if the Trinity should cost three times the original estimate. The cost of the other canalized rivers and canals of France will show on an average a similar proportion to the cost of the Trinity

Dallas, the head of navigation on the Trinity, has today an estimated population of·130,000, with a wholesale trade of $211,-000,000. The Dallas people contributed $65,000 to one of the first locks and dams on the Trinity and have paid more than $20,000 for the sites of nine locks and dams They have secured 30 acres of land for public wharves on the river front in Dallas having a value of $60,000 or $70,000 They have voted a bond issue of $700,000 for diverting the city sewage from the river in order that sewage disposal may not interfere with navigation. They have subscribed $50,000 for the purchase of boats and barges. The city and county of Dallas have spent in bond issues more than $800,000 for building bridges and viaducts in such manner as not to impede navigation Altogether the people of Dallas and Dallas County have expended, directly and indirectly, on account of the Trinity about $1,800,000, while the Government has expended $1,700,000. (Applause.)

The improvement of the Trinity means the establishment of a navigable waterway 511 miles long, through the very heart of one of the richest sections of one of the most productive States of the Union, the State of Texas. With an area of 265,000 square miles, more than a fourth larger than the German Empire, this State is today practically without interior navigable waterways penetrating its territory more than a short distance from the coast

If waterways mean *anything,* they mean *everything* to the State of Texas If waterways mean anything, the improvement of the Trinity means everything to one of the richest areas of this Republic It is a project that has met every criticism and every requirement. It has been carefully examined and honestly sustained. It may well be doubted whether any other people have ever exhibited a greater willingness to expend their own money, their own enthusiasm, their own energy in behalf of a navigation project, or have shown greater faith in any enterprise, than the people of Dallas and the Trinity Valley in the matter of the improvement of the Trinity. To hurl the words, "graft," "fraud," and "pork barrel" in the faces of such a people and at such a project, is as unjust as it is wicked, the very consummation of absurdity (Applause.)

And I trust that this great Congress, prompted by the sense of justice that has always animated it, the desire to serve the public that has always controlled it, will lend its powerful aid to the vindication of this people, the completion of this project (Applause.)

President Ransdell—Ladies and gentlemen, the Speaker of the House of Representatives of the Greatest Republic on earth needs no introduction to an American audience. (Applause.)

Address—Hon. Champ Clark, M. C., Missouri
Speaker of the House of Representatives

Mr. Chairman, Ladies and Gentlemen·

I am not here to make a speech I preside over the greatest speech-making body on the face of the earth, and I get a sufficiency of it every day I am here simply to testify by my presence to my continued interest in what I consider the greatest problem before the American people (Applause)—the conservation, improvement and development of our natural resources, not only affecting us, but affecting our children to the remotest generations.· There are several of these problems intertwined; irrigation, drainage, improvement of rivers and harbors, prevention of floods, and all the rest of it, all very largely so intertwined.

God Almighty, in His infinite wisdom and goodness, gave us the most magnificent system of waterways that were ever vouchsafed to any people in the history of the world, and we have been more negligent of improving and using them than any other civilized people on the globe

I have two or three reasons for being in favor of river and harbor improvements, and before I undertake to tell them all I want to make a remark or two by way of parenthesis There is not a sensible or patriotic man on the face of the earth that wants to waste a single dollar in river and harbor improvement —waste it; but sensible people and patriotic people believe that we ought to take advantage of the resources that belong to us. (Applause.)

The other day in his address to Congress the President of the United States drew with great delicacy and clearness the distinction between waste and expenditure, because whether you appropriate a million dollars, or a thousand dollars, or one hundred dollars, or one dollar, it does not make any difference how much, that does not mean that you are wasting it. Of course you can waste it, but if you have any sense you will not waste it   (Applause.)

I could not live where I live and not be in favor of river and harbor improvement. My district skirts the Mississippi for 160 miles and straddles the Missouri for 170 miles; and it had in it when I first came to Congress five other rivers navigable by act of Congress, but navigable in no other way. If it had not been for the railroads they would have been left unfinished, every one of them   I had one of them declared non-navigable by act of Congress in order to have a railroad bridge built without a swinging span in it. That is the first time I ever heard of the railroads and the farmers agreeing on any proposition under the shining sun, so I was enthusiastic for it   But still my district is wedged down on that point between those two great rivers, so that as a matter of ordinary selfishness my constituents make me in favor of it.

But that is not all of it   I believe, and have asserted time and again—I am not a tyro in this business, I have been working at it publicly, making speeches about it, for twenty-three years —I have asserted time and again, out of Congress and in Congress, that it would be a profitable investment for the American people to make these rivers navigable in fact if there never was another passenger or a pound of freight carried over them. (Applause.)   They would regulate the freight rates.   I do not believe that they are not going to have passengers carried over them or freights carried over them after they are improved, and I do not think they will hurt the railroads in the long run.

I will tell you what I think will come out of it if we ever make these rivers navigable; here is what will happen: The heavy freights, the stuff that is not perishable immediately, will be carried by the boats, and the perishable freight and the passengers, most of them, will be carried on the railroads.   A man that has traveled around over this country as much as I have in the last twenty years knows this, that one of these two things has got to happen, either the railroads have got to doubletrack their roads or make them four-track roads, or the rivers have got to be made so that they can carry the freight, in order that the freight of this country may be carried.   (Applause.)

I see Judge Bland, of Kansas City, sitting over there, from that live city at the western edge of the State.   He knows, as well as I and everybody else does that knows anything about it, that while there are five or six railroads running from St. Louis to Kansas City, the means of transportation of freights between those two cities is not adequate now.   They have got to doubletrack those roads, or, as the Pennsylvania and some other roads have done, they will have to have four tracks, or the freight will be blockaded.

In the busy season of the year you start from Kansas City to New York, and unless you are on one of those trains that has the absolute right of way, the chances are ten to one that you will be delayed going either way by freight trains.   Down in Missouri I have seen passenger trains sidetracked in order that freight trains might pass, so as to help along commerce.

Now I am not engineer enough, or financier enough—if that is the right way of pronouncing that remarkable word— (Laughter) to know whether or not it is cheaper to improve the rivers than it is to double-track or quadruple-track those railroads; although, as a plain, ordinary citizen, my own judgment about it is that it is cheaper to improve the rivers.   (Applause.)

We are in our infancy in every way. Of course, I would not inject politics into a subject like this, but I like to say a good thing about a Republican when I can find one that deserves it (Laughter)—and it does not take all of my time either James Wilson, of Iowa, was for sixteen years Secretary of Agriculture, the longest time any man was ever in the Cabinet—two others had twelve years each He was a rantankerous Republican, a hard-headed Scotchman, but he did a vast amount of good to the people of the United States. although he was a farmer. He made a speech several years ago from which I would like to quote He said that, if the Mississippi Valley were cultivated for all it is worth, on an average one acre would sustain one human being. I believe that is true. Do you know how many people that would give us? We boast about having 91,000,000 according to the last census; but that would give us 1,250,000,000 of people between the top of the Rockies and the crest of the Alleghanies. (Applause.)

Of course you and I are not going to live to see it, but it is easy to prophesy what is going to happen. We need to increase these methods of locomotion, and we are going to do it. (Applause.)

Three or four years ago one of the magazines gave me two hundred dollars to write an article entitled "When The Mississippi Valley Will Control The Nation " I went to work and I dug it out. It is not more than ten years away from that date now. We intend to improve those rivers in the Mississippi Valley; and while we are at it we are willing to improve the rivers of other parts of the country if they will help us (Applause) But we are tired of being shut out in this great scheme of improvement. There is no earthly reason why the Mississippi River should not be navigable from its mouth to the Falls of St. Anthony; there is no reason why the Missouri should not be navigable from Alton to Fort Benton; and if it belonged to any other nation on earth—if any other nation had ground enough to stretch it out in—(Laughter) it would have been navigable now

Now in regard to this "project" business. I understand that you are in favor of a principle and not a project, but it is well worth while to illustrate the principle with a project.

Now, ladies and gentlemen, I have got to go. The House meets at twelve o'clock. I did not come down here to make a speech; I came down here to give aid, comfort and assistance to my distinguished friend, the Chairman of this Convention. (Applause.) A long time ago I was invited to a Presidential dinner—for the first time, of course. The first dinner is just like the first of anything else. Well, it happened that I had an engagement to lecture that same night down in Pennsylvania for $150.00. I wanted the $150.00, and I wanted the dinner. So I was puzzled. I went to General Grosvenor, who had been here in Congress ever since the Indians were driven out of the country, and I submitted the matter to the General. "Well," he said, "Young man, an invitation from the White House is equivalent to a command." So I got the dinner—and lost $150.00!

Now I have some friends whose requests are equivalent to a command, and the Chairman of this Convention is one of them; because I believe, outside of any personal relations which exist between us—and they are very friendly—that he is engaged in a great, patriotic undertaking.

The Speaker now took his leave, and as he passed outward was saluted with three cheers and a tiger, followed, in recognition of his allusion to President Ransdell, by three cheers and a tiger for President Ransdell.

President Ransdell—Ladies and gentlemen: During my service in the House of Representatives, I had a colleague from New England who always thought seriously on all important matters and never failed to have something to say which carried great weight with his associates. He is now a member of the United States Senate, and his words there carry equal weight.

Allow me to present to you Senator John W. Weeks, of Massachusetts. (Applause.)

Address—Senator John Wingate Weeks, Massachusetts

MR PRESIDENT, LADIES AND GENTLEMEN·

Doubtless you have heard that oratory is no longer found in Washington. If so, you have been disillusionized this morning, because you gentlemen who have heard our friend Senator Sheppard will recognize that he was aptly described by the presiding officer when he referred to him as the "silver-tongued" orator.

Then Mr Speaker Clark has testified that his oratory years ago was worth one hundred and fifty dollars an hour, so that it would appear that those people who say that oratory is in its decadence, are those who are not orators. I want to couple with that declaration the statement that I am not an orator I am here very largely for the reason assigned by Speaker Clark, because I have had, and am having now, the most intimate personal relations with your President, and I have for him such regard that when he asked me to speak here I felt it as a command

Then again, those friends of mine in Massachusetts who are particulary interested in this work have asked me to say a word for that State. I am not going to bore you by making a long address, but shall make a few comments which quite likely have occurred to some of you, or at least to a few.

But I want to say that while I have not been active in the propaganda for which you are standing, I am entirely in sympathy with it I have no sympathy whatever with the tendency to criticize the work of this Association (Applause.) Very few people who have not been in Congress appreciate the duties and demands on the time of a Senator or Congressman Forty thousand bills are introduced at each session of Congress, or each term, and it necessarily follows that any individual member can know but very little of the many enterprises and projects in which the Government itself is engaged

Now, if a member who is devoting all his time to the governmental service is unable to acquire knowledge of all these enterprises, how is it going to be possible for the average citizen, who is devoting his time supposedly to his own affairs, to have any comprehensive knowledge of the great activities in which the Government is engaged? The only way is to have somebody, or some association, furnish that citizen with information; and when he becomes sufficiently informed he will take pains to see that his Congressman or his Senator has that information—and that is what makes public sentiment in this land (Applause)

It took twenty years to pass a pure-food bill which everybody was in favor of. It took fifteen years to pass forestry legislation which almost everybody was in favor of. It took more than twenty years to pass the National Banking Act, which substantially every well-informed man was in favor of, although there were great organizations agitating that subject for years It is not unusual, in fact it is very common, for an association of citizens like this to agitate, and it is necessary that you should be enthusiastic for your cause. You must have some of the qualities of the promoter, or else you are not going to get the ear of the people, and as a result, the ear of Congress (Applause.)

Therefore, I want to say to you that I am in sympathy with your cause and in sympathy with the motives which prompt you; but I want to sound what seems to me a fair note of warning, that your propaganda will be successful as long as it seems to be in the interest of the public welfare and that of the whole country (Applause)

I think you will be treading on dangerous ground whenever you, as an association, attempt to advocate any particular project or any particular piece of development in which you are personally interested If you undertake to do that, in my judgment, you will lose some part of the public confidence which you have today, and which you should have. Get the ear of Congress; get Congress interested in the whole movement, and leave the particular project in which you are interested to others

There was a time when political parties were divided on this question of waterway development, when there were many people who did not think it was constitutional to appropriate money for such projects as the development of rivers and harbors. That time has long since gone There is now a universal sentiment in fa\or of certain projects in which commerce is interested   No one will question the desirability from a country-wide standpoint of making great harbors, like those of Boston, New York, Philadelphia, Baltimore, Galveston, Savannah, or San Francisco, available for the greatest commerce which can come to those ports; because it is not only beneficial to the citizens of those ports but is beneficial to every citizen of the country

Nobody will contend that we ought not to have our harbors improved in order to provide for the coast-wise fleet that is ours today, and which I hope always will be ours.   (Applause.) Nobody will contend that certain canals are not of manifest and vital importance.

Most of you gentlemen are interested in the commercial side of the development of the rivers and harbors; but there is a military side to this question that is quite as important to be given consideration. (Applause.)   Let me call your attention to one or two of the phases of that side of the question.   For example, the Suez Canal was undoubtedly built for commercial reasons; but it was undoubtedly bought by Great Britain not only for the commercial advantages which it afforded, but because it gave Great Britain the shortest, quickest, and best route to her possessions in the East.   It developed her trade enormously, but it has answered as well the military purposes for which its stock was purchased

We have just built the Panama Canal   Very many men in Congress advocated the building of the Panama Canal originally not only because it was to give great commercial facilities to our people, but because it was of immense military importance. Now it costs to maintain a battleship, outside of repairs, something like $600,000 a year, therefore, a battleship fleet of sixteen ships costs something ·like $10,000,000 a year to maintain on the Atlantic, and if we had to maintain another fleet like it on the Pacific—and there has been a strong sentiment in favor of that, and I have no doubt that sentiment would prevail in time if we found it necessary to go around the Horn—it would then cost us another ten million dollars a year to maintain a different fleet in the Pacific; and this sum would represent two and a half per cent on the $400,000,000 which the Canal will cost

As an economic measure, as well as a commercial and military measure, it paid us to build the Panama Canal. (Applause.)

We have just had a canal up in Massachusetts, the Cape Cod Canal, built by private capital. We believe that that will be also valuable in a military way and that, therefore, the Government should be interested in all of these intra-coastal canals.

We do not know yet that the submarine is going to send all of the battleships to the scrap-heap. We do not know what results are going to develop in that line from this war; but we do know that the submarine is going to remain as an important element in naval warfare so that it will be important to be able to get our submarines from one section of our coast to another, because submarines must operate within very narrow limits. Therefore, this intra-coastal canal and this Cape Cod Canal may prove of vital importance to the defense of this country by furnishing the means of enabling the submarines to pass from one section to another without subjecting them to the dangers and discomforts of going to sea. It is certain that submarines cannot go to sea without discomfort; and that is another illustration of the benefits of these canals from a military standpoint, and in this way the canals are of interest to every citizen of the country

Now, whenever we come to the questions of water development, there arise differences of opinion. There is this to consider. There are those who think that it is unwise to develop the rivers of one part of the country unless you can develop them universally, and as was so ably and eloquently advocated by Speaker Clark; and there are those who think that it is wise to develop any of the rivers Now, I want to suggest that river and harbor development should be universally popular instead of substantially universally under suspicion The press of the country is largely to blame for the conditions which exist today They have talked "pork barrel" until suspicion of that sort attaches to every river and harbor bill They have talked graft until people think they are unwise projects Now the Government has not engaged in any work which is of any more vital importance to this country than this very work in which you are interested (Applause); and yet we have to take care that we do not misspend money That can easily be done

I want to make this further suggestion to you, that I am personally opposed to a commission form of government   I favor responsibility which is directly in touch with the people instead of a commission form of government   We are now expending twenty million dollars under the direction of the Corps of Engineers of the Army.   I personally have the greatest confidence in and admiration for the engineers of our army   (Applause)   They have conducted great enterprises of various kinds for the last hundred years, and there has been no taint of graft.   There has been efficiency, economy, and good management in whatever they have had to do.   (Applause.)

In my native State, in my home State of Massachusetts, we appropriate for street improvement purposes, for this street and that street and the other street.   We used to elect aldermen and councilmen from wards; and it used to be said that you could tell with accuracy where an alderman or a councilman lived by the condition of the street in front of his house or in the neighborhood where he lived   And money has been spent in that way, and the best results from the standpoint of the whole city were not thereby obtained.   Now Congress is elected in some such way as that, Congressmen representing their various districts, and necessarily under the methods by which we are elected we are all of us the direct, special representatives of the particular section which is responsible for our coming here, and that section looks to us to obtain for them things which they think are desirable   No man—I do not care how big he is—can fail to recognize the voice of his constituents in such matters   Very often every one of us has been appealed to to vote for this or that bill, many parts of which we approved of, but some parts of which we disapproved, yet we voted for them because of the desire of our constituents to get the things which they wanted done, and it was an omnibus proposition at best

Now it seems to me if the appropriations and the policies were outlined by Congress, a certain amount of money to be spent for harbors, a certain amount for rivers, and a certain amount for canals, the money to be expended under competent direction ---I do not know that I have worked out all the details as to the exact process, but I believe in that way all basis of criticism as to their being "pork barrel" propositions could be eliminated Furthermore, you would get the money spent where it was most desirable it should be spent   Some of the propositions that are included in any general bill we will all admit are of supreme importance immediately   Some of them may be of importance twenty-five years from now, and again some of them may never be important, yet they are all considered in the same general bill   It is pretty nearly impossible to prevent this in the Rivers and Harbors Bill. I want to say that the last one, which was so viciously attacked in Congress, was, in my judgment, as good a bill as any one of those we have had for the last ten or twenty years. (Applause.)

It is pretty nearly impossible to frame any bill in which you will not find some projects which may not be the wisest, and this, of course, may happen through ignorance   Every one of us depends for our reelection on what we are able to do for those who are directly interested in us; you will find that a man who gets his hand literally into the Treasury, the man who gets what his constituents demand of him in general, always has the approval of his constituents   If, therefore, we can be relieved in some degree of responsibility as to where this money shall be expended. in my judgment the criticism against these appropriations will disappear and we will be able to get not only larger appropriations, when it is possible to obtain them out of the available moneys, but we will get these appropriations without any criticism of the kind which now prevails   If it is desirable to spend twenty-five million or fifty million dollars a year, and that money is available, it should be, in my judgment, appropriated as I have suggested

Now, let us say a word about Massachusetts. We have a great State, with four hundred and twenty-one miles of seacoast and one great National port. There are no less than seven cities of importance on our coast and many towns which are benefited by these waterway developments   We have two important rivers in the State, the Connecticut and the Merrimac; and there are four important cities just across the line in New Hampshire which are great manufacturing cities

We have no natural products in Massachusetts Our soil is sterile and not fitted for agriculture. We depend upon commerce and manufactures in our State to make us prosperous We have to have available means of communication in order that we may ship our products to all parts of the country, and it is also necessary to get the raw materials for manufacturing to us as cheaply as possible. Therefore, it is desirable from our standpoint that our rivers and harbors should be fully developed.

Massachusetts has not been backward, and it is not going to cease in this work. The State of Massachusetts has recently appropriated and is spending $9,000,000 in the port of Boston alone, and there has been talk of bringing a line of steamers to this country. A great deal of money has been spent on the port of Boston and in improving our rivers and harbors, and we have a commission to develop all the smaller harbors along the coast. In other words, we have been looking to our own interest In my judgment, the State of Massachusetts has spent more money on its rivers and harbors than the National Government has, and, therefore, we are in a position to say that the project in which our State is interested should be given consideration I believe I speak for every citizen of Massachusetts when I say that we do not want one dollar spent in that State unless it can be demonstrated that it is going to bring a reasonable return on the money expended Unless the great interests of the mills and factories in our State that are sending out such things as textiles, shoes and so forth—unless it can be shown that the whole country will be benefited by the appropriations demanded, we would not ask the Government to make the expenditure We believe that these waterway improvements in our State will cheapen the products of our mills and thus benefit the whole country But I say again that it seems to me that the course of my State in the past justifies the most careful inspection of every project for which we ask support in Massachusetts, because we do not expect the benefit to result alone to ourselves, but to inure to the whole country

I thank you for your attention   (Applause)

President Ransdell—The greatest center of trade in the world is the city of Pittsburgh. (Applause.) We are now to hear from one of its recent Chief Magistrates, Hon. W. A. Magee, former Mayor of the City of Pittsburgh. (Applause.)

A WATERWAY BELT LINE
Address—Hon. W. A. Magee, Pittsburgh, Pa.

Mr. Chairman:

My paper is in support of two canal projects, 500 miles distant from each other. Both are rapidly advancing towards the constructive stage, both have a purely local initiative, both contemplate local public financing, and both so far have been considered almost entirely from the viewpoint of special local benefit, but taken together have a national and international importance.

Pittsburgh pays 55 cents per ton to carry Mesaba ore 900 miles from Duluth to Ashtabula, and 88 cents from there to the center of the Pittsburgh industrial district, 150 miles. Pittsburgh pays 78 cents a ton to carry her twenty-five million tons of coal to the shores of Lake Erie and thence 25, 35 or 45 cents to points of varying distance on the Great Lakes as far as Duluth. Six times the distance at sixty per cent of the rate forms a ratio, in this case, between rail and water carriage of 1 to 10. A canal 12 feet deep over a divide of 300 feet between the Ohio River at the mouth of the Beaver, in Pennsylvania, and a point on Lake Erie near Ashtabula, 103 miles, will conserve the supremacy of the Pittsburgh district in the manufacture of steel for generations. This is the Pittsburgh view of the Lake Erie and Ohio River Canal.

Chicago, seeing rival ports on Lake Michigan rising to power by reason of their less congestion and nearness to markets, is again striving to revive the old canal navigation between the Mississippi River and the Great Lakes via the Illinois River, the Desplaines River and the Drainage Canal, a distance of about 327 miles from Grafton to Chicago. This is the local viewpoint of the second project I mention. An additional expenditure of $3,000,000 on the Illinois and Michigan Canal between La Salle and Joliet to obtain an eight-foot channel is a bagatelle and no doubt this project is assured, subject to legal limitations upon the appropriation of the sum required

One might dilate endlessly upon the details of the advantages to Chicago and Pittsburgh, but such a treatment of the subject would sound petty and narrow   At one time in the silent history of the world, Lake Michigan emptied into the Mississippi. Coincidently the waters of the Allegheny and the Monongahela found their outlet into Lake Erie. As the waters of Lake Michigan changed their ultimate destination from the Gulf of Mexico to the Atlantic, nature, in pursuance of some deep law of compensation, turned the run-off of Western Pennsylvania from the latter to the former. But nature did not fail to leave the evidences of the original condition plainly writ upon her face   The first explorers, La Salle and Marquette, in 1682, recorded their observations and proposed a canal from what is now ´Chicago to the Mississippi via the route mentioned above   George Washington, in 1784, writing to Governor Benjamin Harrison, of Virginia, showed the feasibility of a canal connecting the Ohio and Lake Erie.

And from those days to this day there has never been any very great period of years when the idea of repeating this early feat of nature has not been a tempting, tantalizing field of exploitation to the adventurous mind. The men of imagination from the first, however, have always taken a statesmanlike and not a parochial view of these great works   To link Louisville, Cincinnati, Parkersburg, Marietta, Wheeling, Pittsburgh, Youngstown, Niles, Warren and Ashtabula to Detroit, Toledo, Cleveland. Erie, Buffalo, Toronto, Montreal, Albany and New York; to connect Chicago, Milwaukee. Duluth and the other Lake cities with St. Louis, Memphis, Kansas City and New Orleans by direct and continuous waterways has always been and is their aim   They have always had a larger vision than merely to reduce the cost of Pittsburgh's raw materials or to more surely secure Chicago's commercial hinterland. (Applause)

But, while the discerning have not failed to grasp the underlying significance of these proposed improvements viewed separately, it is a singular circumstance that they have not heretofore been considered jointly. Taking them together they present an additional, a larger aspect In order to comprehend the superlative utility of these two waterway connections we must resort for analogy to the network of railways which covers this country On what is the efficiency of the railways based? You answer immediately, on the mobility of these carriers through the standard gauge of track and the innumerable connections between the various lines An Illinois canal, making possible direct water communication between Chicago and New Orleans, might be compared to a single great railway like the Illinois Central; a slack-watered Ohio and a regularized Mississippi, giving all-the-year-round navigation between Pittsburgh and New Orleans, would be another Pennsylvania Railroad; an Erie Barge Canal in connection with the Great Lakes forms a system rivalling the New York Central and Lake Shore. But these great railroad systems accomplish their maximum of efficiency not through individual operation but by connecting their terminals to each other in the great centers of population, so that a carload or trainload of freight may be consigned over the shortest and most direct routes from any city on the North American Continent to any other city (Applause.)

The economic center of gravity of the United States and Canada lies somewhere within that territory included in the States of Ohio, Indiana and Illinois Around these States from Chicago to Ashtabula there is about 800 miles of Great Lakes; from Ashtabula to Beaver, Pa, it is proposed to construct a canal 103 miles in length, from Beaver to Cairo is the Ohio, about 1,000 miles, now in process of improvement; and from Cairo to Chicago, via the Mississippi, the Illinois, the Desplaines and the Drainage Canal, are about 450 miles of improved river and canal All these together constitute a belt of water 2,400 miles in length Radiating from this belt are great, navigable tributary streams Out from this belt shoot long arms to the sea— one the St. Lawrence, another the Erie Barge Canal and Hudson River and, greatest of all, the lower Mississippi, the Father of Waters, heading straight for the Panama Canal Two other great arteries, the upper Mississippi and the Missouri, extend to the

interior of the continent.   And each of these five trunk lines
has many great tributaries.   ·

These two canals and their connections, therefore, not only
bring the coal fields of the Appalachians into contact with the ore
beds of the Lakes, but they have a scope infinitely larger.   They
bring the grain fields of the Middle West into cheap transportation connection with the industries of the East; they draw
closer that splendid chain of cities which dot the interior of the
United States and Canada; they associate, through the three out-
lets to the sea, all this agriculture and industry with the Atlantic,
the Gulf and the Pacific coasts, which have their own magnificent cities and large navigable streams; and lastly, they bring
directly together the industry and the agriculture of the interior
of the North American Continent and the commerce of all the
world

Nearly every city has a belt line connecting its radiating railroads   It is the last development of railroad transportation
Water carriage will never approximate the mobility of transportation by rail until all the waterways are connected   Our water
commerce must always remain insignificant, our rivers almost
unutilized, until they are made into a unit, a network including
them all into one, so that goods may go long distances without
breaking bulk and without transhipment   The secret of all transportation, whether road, railway or water, is in terminal costs
Railway carriage in the United States amounts now to about
1,200,000,000 net tons.   Between 1899 and 1907, a period of only
nine years, the mile-tonnage increased from 123 to 236 billions
All the waterways of the country can never be adapted to carry
so much, but that amount, as the total tonnage of this country
and Canada, will be tripled and quadrupled in all probability
within the lifetime of people now living.

The waterways are not a lasting menace to the railways
When they shall all have been canalized and connected   into a
single system and connected with the railroads by terminal docks,
wharves and landings, they will only have supplemented the more
mobile system.   There will ensue a natural distribution of the
traffic.   The first shock may be severe but adjustment will follow

and incidentally great good will follow not only to the public but to the railroads themselves   For instance, the immense railway investment contemplated, and estimated a few years ago at $5,000,000,000 or more, will, to a large extent, be avoided. all by the public expenditure of a few hundred millions out of the public funds   And when the two systems have, by economic gravity, been integrated, the one with the other, then every part of the land will have been benefited.

The proposed Ohio and Pennsylvania Canal and the Illinois Canal, therefore, in their essence, should not be considered from the view of two shortsighted cities bent upon local aggrandizement, but as the most important immediate steps toward consolidating all the waterways into one system, thus cheapening the cost of doing business the country over and with the world at large, and indirectly, therefore, as enlarging the opportunities and more easily supplying the wants of mankind.   (Applause)

PRESIDENT RANSDELL.—One of the most serious problems confronting the American people is the control of floods.   The youngest republic on earth, and the most largely populated of all, is the Republic of China, which has, perhaps, a greater flood problem than we have in the United States.   We recently loaned them the assistance of one of the most accomplished engineers that ever honored our Republic; a man whose name will be indelibly connected with that greatest of all engineering waterway feats, the Panama Canal, for he constructed the Gatun dam and locks at Panama.

It is needless to say that I refer to Lieut.-Colonel William L. Sibert, of the U. S. Engineer Corps, late member of the Panama Canal Commission   (Applause and three cheers and a tiger, the audience rising)

A FLOOD PROBLEM IN CHINA

Address—Lieut.-Col. William L. Sibert, U. S. Engineer Corps

MR. CHAIRMAN, LADIES AND GENTLEMEN:

I wish I had the power of oratory that our President has, to express my thanks for the compliment that he has paid me. When I accepted his invitation, given me by telegram a few days ago, to make some talk upon the flood problem in China, I did not appreciate how technical the subject is. I will, therefore, make my talk short, and I hope that the newness of the problem and the distance of the country will assist you in bearing with the technicalities of the subject

The American National Red Cross has been called upon several times in the last decade to render assistance in famine relief in the Huai River Basin in China The people there were suffering from famine brought about by floods, and some of the controlling spirits of the American National Red Cross organization conceived the idea of finding out whether or not it would be feasible to bring permanent relief to that section by preventing or mitigating the floods there. A preliminary examination had been made by them, which seemed sufficiently promising to cause that body, in conjunction with the Republic of China, to decide to send a Board of three engineers there for the purpose of completing surveys, making a study of the situation and preparing a definite project and estimate.

The cost of the work of the Board was to be borne, half by China and half by the Red Cross If the project was found feasible and not too expensive, the American Red Cross agreed with the Republic of China that the Red Cross would exercise its good offices in finding a market for the Chinese bonds necessary to finance this work These bonds were to be secured not only by the faith of the Republic of China but by the value of all lands that would be reclaimed and by the assessment benefits that would result by an additional tax on all cultivated lands benefited by being relieved from floods. It was further understood and agreed that, should this project be financed, all the money advanced by the American Red Cross and the Chinese Government would be refunded from the proceeds of the sale of the bonds.

The Huai River's drainage basin lies in the southern half of the great plain of Eastern China This plain is about four or five hundred miles wide and six or seven hundred miles long—I speak approximately—and is crossed by two great rivers, the Yangtse and the Yellow, with the valley of the Huai intervening, the general course of the Yangtse and the Huai being east and west. The Yangtse is probably the second river in size in the world, being considerably larger than the Mississippi. The Huai, the river that presented the problem that this Board had to consider, is a smaller stream, about the size of the Allegheny or the Coosa, its flood discharge being about 200,-000 cubic feet per second; its low water discharge, about 4,000 cubic feet per second; its fall per mile being about that of the Mississippi at Memphis.

About 130 miles from the sea this river empties into the Hungtse Lake, which has an area of about 700 square miles, and which you can see on the map there. (Pointing.) This Huai River comes from that direction and empties into this lake. Prior to 1324—we get accustomed to antique things in China—the Yellow River made a visit to the Huai River Basin, and that visit lasted for 529 years. During this visit the Yellow River usurped that portion of the bed of the Huai River from the Hungtse Lake to the sea and raised the bed to such a height as to destroy its utility as an outlet for the Huai River floods. In addition this great silt-bearing stream raised the bed of the Hungtse Lake to from 30 to 33 feet above sea level, the water in this lake at low stage being now from one to two feet deep. The Yellow River left there sixty years ago and went back north, and now empties into the sea some 250 miles north from where it did when it visited the Huai River country.

The outlet of the flood waters of this portion of the country was also interfered with by the construction of the Grand Canal across the natural drainage lines of that section. This canal is simply an artificial river, running north and south, with high banks on either side, into which several small rivers were diverted in order to create navigable depths. The history of this canal extends back to more than 600 years B. C. It was completed in its present location from the Yangtse River to Peking in the latter part of the thirteenth century, 1280. So we can appreciate how early the Chinese were trying—sometimes in the wrong way—to solve some of their problems.

The primary object of this canal, which, as you can see, practically parallels the coast, was to carry tribute rice from the country in the vicinity of the Yangtse River and east of the canal, to Peking   The mouth of the Yangtse River has about the same latitude as New Orleans.   Since the construction of the Grand Canal and the visit of the Yellow River, the floods of the Huai have been directed from their natural route and have found an inadequate outlet, through some lakes and marshes to the west of the Grand Canal, into the Yangtse River.   This inadequacy of outlet is the great cause of much of the serious flooding of the valley of the lower Huai, and of the country north of the Hungtse Lake

All that portion of the country lying between the Grand Canal and the Huai River, the great rice-producing section of China, was suffering from floods to a very serious extent, and in order to remedy that situation they built a high stone dike, thirty-five miles long, across this edge of the lake to prevent the water from passing south   The result of that was, of course, that the Huai River had practically no outlet but flooded all the country, until finally the Chinese themselves made five large openings in this dike in the endeavor to give an outlet for that water to the Yangtse River.   So you see that the work of man and the work of nature by the Yellow River has been such as to destroy the value of the Huai River and make of it a peculiar problem in flood prevention.

The problem as it presented itself was to provide a suitable outlet for these flood waters either to the sea or to the Yangtse River   After thorough study it was found that it was cheaper to send all of the waters in one suitable channel to the Yangtse River, and that the waters could be so diverted as to reclaim the entire bed of the Hungtse Lake, which, when drained and irrigated, would make most excellent rice lands and relieve, to a slight extent, the struggle for food in this over-populated country.

This reclamation would make practicable the draining of a large section of the country to the north of the Hungtse Lake, and this, in conjunction with levees on the lower Huai, would materially benefit a large section of country that is frequently flooded. The rains and floods in this part of China come in the summer months, and an inundation of land means destruction of growing or ripening crops   We are fortunate in our country that the floods come in the late winter or early spring and that crops can generally be planted after their subsidence   Our Board decided that it would be cheaper and better to excavate adequate channels through which the flood waters of the Huai could pass through a series of locks to the west of the Grand Canal into the Yangtse River. We saw that by doing that it would be possible to utilize those waters in such a way as to reclaim all the bed of the Huai River and add 600 square miles of territory to the producing area   We were confronted always with the proposition that all the country to the east of the Grand Canal needed irrigation water for its rice   We finally worked out a proposition for turning all the low water flow of the Huai River into the Grand Canal for irrigation purposes, and sending the flood water over to the Yangtse River so as to relieve the situation.

The project as estimated by the Board would cost $30,000,000 and could be completed in six years if funds were available as needed. The value of the reclaimed land was estimated to be at least $27,000,000, and the benefits to specified areas in consequence of flood relief were estimated at some $21,000,000.

While the flood conditions and resultant famines in the lower Huai are most serious, the people of that country having no reserve means, the destruction of one year's crop always meaning a famine, these conditions were materially worse when the Yellow River traversed that section   Consequently the probability of a return visit of this stream, known as "China's Sorrow," was investigated

One of the most interesting propositions that we found in China was the Yellow River. In all my experience I have never known or read of a stream like it   It is the most abnormal and unusual river, I think, in the world   If unconfined it would have excavated a channel upon the plain of China which would simply spread in every direction covering an area of fifteen or twenty miles wide   Geological evidence is to the effect that it is an exceedingly new river in its present location; that it formerly emptied into a series of great lakes in Mongolia, the outlet for which lakes was in the neighborhood of Peking; and that, on account of a recent and extensive change in the earth's surface, the country occupied by these lakes was raised and a great fault about 450 miles long, running north and south between Shansi and Shensi Provinces, was developed; that the Yellow River took this fault as a channel, ran around the end of the fault block and debouched from the mountains in its present location; and that, geologically speaking, a short time thereafter the great plain of Eastern China was lifted from the sea, increasing the length of the Yellow River four or five hundred miles.

This plain was undoubtedly exceedingly flat and the Yellow River commenced immediately the process of building up this plain. The ultimate end of this process, had it been allowed to continue, would have been to give the plain such a slope that the Yellow River could have run in a depressed channel and carried its immense burden of silt to the sea. Before this process could be completed, however, man intervened and tried to hold the river between certain lines by constructing levees to confine it, in order that the land might be cultivated. The result was that the river confined its delta building to the space between the levees and lifted that part of the valley above the surrounding country. After this process was continued for a time the river would often break through the levees, leave its old channel permanently, and wander aimlessly over the surrounding plain, its waters being ten to fifteen miles wide, dealing death and destruction wherever they went.

It has been stated that as many as a million people were drowned when this river changed its channel sixty years ago and entered the Yellow Sea at a point two hundred and fifty miles north of its previous mouth. The people of China have struggled with this monster for probably four thousand years.

Our Board, on studying this problem, concluded that this great plain of China was probably lifted up out of the sea, a perfectly flat expanse, and that the Yellow River found itself upon a plain too flat to carry its sediment to the sea. We could

find no other physical explanation for the conditions that existed
there. So we commenced to study the researches of all the
geologists who had visited China, and we found corroboration,
or practical proof, for the belief that the condition was due
to the causes I have just explained. I do not know whether
you can all see this small map or not showing the course of the
Yellow River within historical times in China, and at various
times geologically speaking I will mark on the map the general
route of the Yellow River now Then it ran in every direction
It has been all over that country, as historical records show. Its
channel now comes out at a point four hundred or five hundred
miles from where it originally ran.

In riding up the Huai River by boat I saw a Buddhist temple
on an apparently inaccessible mountain overlooking the meanderings of the stream, and upon inquiry I learned that this temple
was erected in memory of a great engineer by the name of
Yu, who lived about four thousand years before Christ, and
who, tradition says, fixed the courses of the Yangtse, the Huai
and the Yellow Rivers, by building levees. It is very probable
that he was the first engineer in history that ever attempted
to control floods in great streams by the construction of levees;
and that system has remained from that day to this the only
practicable way of controlling floods in the valleys of great
rivers. (Applause.) Confucius refers to this same man Yu

The Yangtse River has been leveed for centuries; its delta
plain is normal and its bed is well below the surrounding country. Had the Yellow River made its delta in a normal way by
gradually building out into the sea, or had it been given time
to so shape the plain that was raised from the sea that it could
transport its sediment across it, its meanderings would have
·been stopped, or could at least have been controlled. Man's inter-
ference has limited its natural action for short periods to fixed
areas, but it is doubtful if he can ever prevent that stream from
creating, in a large part of the plain of China, its normal delta
slope.

This river found itself, as I said before, in possibly the most
abnormal condition of any river within the world's history; and

I do not know how China could ever prevent that stream from giving that plain such a slope as it would naturally have built, unless they should build levees about fifty miles apart and allow the river to build a valley between them of sufficient slope, the levees being raised as the building progresses; then the stream could probably be kept on top of a ridge so built, and thus preserve the remainder of the plain and allow the river to carry its sediment to the sea No river that normally builds its delta plain can raise its bed. That is against the laws of physics, whether it be leveed or not, unless its length be increased. (Applause.)

As a river increases its length it must maintain the same slope that it had in order to carry its sediment to the sea, because its ability to transport its sediment depends upon its velocity, and that depends upon its slope The relatively sudden increase seaward by four or five hundred miles of the length of the Yellow River is the cause of the abnormal situation there The Mississippi River in extending its delta from Cairo to the Gulf raised its bed 296 feet at Cairo in order to make a slope necessary to carry its sediment to the sea. If such a slope does not exist, sediment will be deposited until it is created This is a physical law—levees or no levees The extension of a normal delta is so slow that the consequent raise of bed is almost imperceptible The Mississippi River will never raise its bed except as it increases its length; and since its length is increased in such small increments, it cannot raise its bed on account of any work of man (Applause)

The Yangtse River is similar to the Mississippi, and caves its banks in the same way, but not so fast or to such an extent, and the valley is protected from overflow by lines that are permanent so long as the banks on which they rest are not caved into the stream All rivers that I noticed in the level part of Japan had levees along their banks to protect the flat country from floods The Yangtse has been leveed for centuries The plain through which it flows is normal It can carry its sediment to the sea, and its bed is well below the surrounding country, in fact, 150 miles from the sea its bed is 45 feet below the level of the sea That illustrates, I think, the general proposition that I have intended to cover.

Now just a remark or two on non-technical lines Travelling under the auspices of the Red Cross in China caused us to receive many courtesies. That organization has certainly established a reputation for altruistic motives. The people in the Huai River area, at least, feel that the Red Cross is one organization that does not want to exploit any of China's resources. So travelling in that way had many advantages and also some disadvantages The people felt that they could trust the Red Cross, that it had no ulterior designs, and we were received royally everywhere

To give you an illustration as we entered a town of probably two hundred thousand or three hundred thousand inhabitants—and there are towns over there of twenty thousand or thirty thousand inhabitants that have not a post office—the magistrate who came to call upon us said that he regretted that he had received instructions from Peking the day before to proceed to the boundary of the province and settle a grasshopper dispute The country was burdened with grasshopers during the year that we were there, and these grasshoppers at that time were not able to fly, they could just hop along, and all the people turned out to drive away the grasshoppers off their property on to somebody else's property. They would keep that up until they reached the boundary line of a province and there they met the population of the adjoining province that was going through the same process (Laughter), so that Peking had summoned this magistrate to proceed to the boundary and settle this dispute. But this magistrate, before he left, sent us a train of thirty-one servants to help wait on us while he was gone We already had all the servants we needed; but we understood that the courtesies of the country required us to accept all these hospitable attentions so we, of course, had to feed and pay these thirty-one men while the magistrate was settling the grasshopper dispute

We were called upon by the natives who thought that we could cure disease, thinking that that was one of the things that the Red Cross generally does when it goes abroad We dodged that issue as much as we could, but we had one man who came in from a distance and wanted relief for some trouble with his scalp The man he applied to in our party did not have anything to give him but some peroxide of hydrogen, and he handed that to him, with a sponge to apply it, and he applied is assiduously. His scalp did not heal, but he developed the most beautiful strawberry blond hair I think I ever saw! (Laughter)

We had many other ludicrous experiences like that, but the time is too short, and I must refrain.

I thank you for your attention. (Applause.)

PRESIDENT RANSDELL—We have just heard a very interesting account of the floods in China. but although we sympathize with conditions there, we sympathize more with the troubles of our countrymen in the United States along similar lines

I am now going to present to you the man who is better qualified than any man I know of to talk about floods on the Mississippi River. He is the President of the Mississippi River Levee Association You will think, when he gets through, that he knows his subject and how to handle it Allow me to present Mr A. S. Caldwell, of Memphis, Tenn (Applause)

THE MISSISSIPPI RIVER
Address—A. S. Caldwell, Memphis, Tenn.
President Mississippi River Levee Association

MR PRESIDENT AND GENTLEMEN OF THE NATIONAL RIVERS AND HARBORS CONGRESS:

Our Government has done many big things recently The Panama Canal has been built; the tariff has been revised; a new banking system has been inaugurated; the railroads have been regulated; and general business has had considerable attention from Congress. but there is one thing. as big as any of these. which has not been done It has been the subject of national investigation and discussion for over half a century; nearly all of our Presidents from Lincoln to Wilson and our great statesmen, from Calhoun and Clay to those of today, have declared its doing to be a national duty; and for nearly as long a period our political parties have pledged themselves to it—and yet it remains undone Many other projects, much less National in scope, after brief consideration, have been undertaken and completed by the Government, but this great work has not yet been provided for in a comprehensive way, though Congress has salved its conscience by giving it some financial aid. That its doing is not only a matter of simple justice to a large number of our fellow citizens, but will also prove a benefit to the whole country, can only be denied by those who are so blind they will not see. (Applause)

Let me first bring the matter before you by a question If, without firing a shot, and without the loss of a single human life, the United States could add to its productive area a territory adjacent to it, almost as large as Belgium and Holland combined and more fertile than either, and at a cost of sixty millions of dollars—would this be bad business? Only sixty millions of dollars to make productive a territory as large as the States of Vermont, New Jersey and Massachusetts combined! Remember—we did not hesitate to sacrifice many American lives and to spend over two hundred millions of dollars to take Cuba from Spain and to give it to—well, not to ourselves. And Cuba has not as large a productive area as the territory to which I refer.

And if, without further cost, another and contiguous part of our country—somewhat larger than the State of Connecticut—would be protected from periodical disasters nearly as great as those which now befall unfortunate Belgium, would that not be an additional inducement to make the expenditure?

Gentlemen, such a principality lies in our very midst and sixty millions of dollars of Government funds, added to moneys raised in the region itself, will make it more productive than any similar-sized territory in the whole world It is the Delta of the Mississippi River, embracing about twenty million acres, of which only about 3,500,000 acres are now productive, and a large part of this three and a half million acres is not productive in years of flood The other sixteen and a half million acres is not, as many people think, low swamp-land, unhealthy and unfit for the homes of men. Freed from floods, nearly all of it is susceptible to cultivation and its fertile soil will support an immense population.

In addition to the reclamation and protection of this vast area, the expenditure of this same sixty millions of dollars will also materially improve the navigation of the largest river of our country, so that this great artery of commerce will be maintained not only as a means for transportation of commodities, but also, and equally important, as a controller of freight rates. Scientific authority is practically unanimous that all work done in the protection of the Delta from overflow will result in improvement of navigation. While this is an important matter and one undoubtedly of great interest to the whole Nation, I intend to address my remarks to those features of the case with which you may not be so familiar, and to tell you why it is but simple justice for the Government to prevent overflows of the Mississippi River and why flood prevention and the making productive another sixteen and a half million acres will be a benefit to the whole country.

These floods are not local. The drainage basin of the Mississippi River constitutes 41 per cent of the area of the United States and thirty-one States of the Union pour their waters down upon the helpless people of the Delta. These waters come from a territory bounded by Canada on the north, by the Appalachian and Alleghany Mountains on the east, and by the Rocky Mountains on the west. Isn't this portion of the United States, in which arises the causes of disaster to the alluvial valley of the Mississippi River, large enough to make it a National matter? Ought not the 1,250,000 square miles from which the waters come help the 29,000 square miles which suffer from them? It has been rightly said: "The process by which the country above is relieved, is the process by which the country below is ruined."

The last National Democratic platform declared "The control of the Mississippi River is a National problem; the building of the levees to prevent overflow of the land * * * and the enormous loss of life and property, impose an obligation

which alone can be discharged by the General Government."
Has the present Democratic Congress paid any attention to this
party pledge? The last Republican platform called the Mississippi River "the Nation's drainage ditch" and stated that "the
States unaided cannot cope with this giant problem, hence we
believe the Federal Government should assume a fair proportion
of the burden of its control so as to prevent the disasters from
recurring floods." Has the Republican minority in Congress
made itself conspicuous by its efforts to live up to this statement? The last Progressive platform declared. "It is a National
obligation to develop our rivers and especially the Mississippi
River, without delay, under a comprehensive general plan. Under
such a plan the destructive floods of the Mississippi would be
controlled and lands sufficient to support millions of people will
be reclaimed." Have you heard the voice of the small, but
militant, Progressive Party in Congress demanding that the
Government control these destructive floods "without delay?"
What does the present overwhelming majority in Congress think
of these words from the last Democratic platform: "Our pledges
are made to be kept when in office as well as relied upon during
the campaign?" Again I ask, has this all-powerful majority
kept its party pledge about the Mississippi River—and has it
any intention of doing so?

If Congress acts on the principle that it will only help those
who help themselves, then this work should long ago have been
completed, because, up to this time, the inhabitants of the over-
flowed districts have spent over twice as much money as the
Government for flood prevention I venture to say that no
other section of the United States has ever contributed so large
a proportion of the cost of work done jointly by it and the
General Government But even if justice to a sorely stricken
part of our country shall still fail to induce politicians to keep
party pledges when in office, the enormous benefit which will
accrue to the whole country by the prevention of floods of the
Mississippi River, ought to make them eager to adopt a comprehensive plan for that purpose   (Applause.)

The losses caused by these periodically recurring disasters amount to many millions of dollars at each flood and these losses do not fall solely on the people of the Delta, but are shared by many merchants and manufacturers outside of it. A Maryland merchant told me his concern had lost over $200,000 by the Mississippi River floods of 1912 and 1913, and a Pennsylvania manufacturer told me he had suffered great losses from the same floods.

Ex-President Roosevelt, who is well acquainted with the Delta, clearly points out the far-reaching effects of great floods. He says:

> "It cannot be too strongly impressed upon the people that a damage to part of them is in some degree a damage to all. A crushing disaster to the planters along the lower regions of the Mississippi Valley is also a disaster to the whole country. It means just so much of a waste of capital and loss of production for the nation at large and the nation must realize that fact We, the Nation, must build the levees and build them better and more scientifically than ever before."

But the prevention of these losses is only one of the many national benefits which will result from the reclamation of this section.

In 1879, the Mississippi River Commission was created and hope was held out that the National Government intended to actively assist in preventing floods. Buoyed up by this hope, the people of the Delta strained their resources and their credit to inaugurate a system of flood prevention approved by the Corps of Engineers of the United States Army, and between 1880 and 1910 great things happened in the Delta The cultivated area was doubled; land values increased over three times; farm personalty values increased four times; railroad mileage increased over six times. Leaving out the cities of Memphis and Vicksburg, which are not in the Delta there was, in 1880, only one bank in the alluvial territory on both sides of the Mississippi River from Cairo to New Orleans. This had a capital of $20,000 and no published statement of deposits. In 1910, there were 246 banks, with a combined capital and surplus of over fifteen millions of dollars and with over $43,000,000 of deposits. (Applause)

During this thirty years the contributions of the Government to the work of flood prevention were by no means commensurate with the hope inspired by the act creating the Mississippi River Commission and the cost of the work was largely borne by the affected territory. Yet, in spite of this, the remarkable progress I have mentioned was made. Protected from floods, similar progress will be made in the now unproductive sixteen and a half million acres, resulting in an enormous addition to the National wealth. Merchants and manufacturers in various parts of the country will be benefited by the opening up of this new and immense trade territory, the richness of whose soil guarantees a large and profitable interstate commerce.

The addition of sixteen and a half million acres to our cotton-producing area will perpetuate the cotton supremacy of the United States   Even in these war times I venture to say that if the opportunity came to them, either England or Germany would find a way to give many times sixty millions of dollars for this territory so long neglected by our own Nation   While the present European war has disarranged the cotton trade, this is only temporary and the time is near at hand when the world will need much more cotton than is now produced and without increased crops there will be increased prices   It is to the interest of the whole country to foster the production of cotton in order to keep the cost to our own people within bounds   No other of our crops goes so far toward maintaining the balance of trade in our favor as the cotton crop   This is fully known to our great bankers and is a matter of vital importance to the Nation. Merely from a money point of view, the revenue receipts from a productive territory as large as the States of Vermont, New Jersey and Massachusetts, will certainly result in at least part of the sixty millions finding its way back into the National treasury.

I shall not take up your time in a discussion of the various proposed plans for flood prevention, because it is certain no method will be adopted which does not meet with scientific approval That it is feasible to control floods of the Mississippi River at a reasonable cost has been definitely determined by the Corps of Engineers of the United States Army and by every civil engineer who has studied the question The Mississippi River Levee Association has advocated, and is now advocating, the passage of what is known as the Ransdell-Humphreys Bill Under this bill the Government is not required to pay the whole cost of the work, but the sections affected must contribute that portion of the cost, which, added to their past expenditures for flood prevention, will make the total cost of the completed work fall equally upon the Government and the Delta. Doesn't this seem to you to be a fair division?

There has been some objection to the Ransdell-Humphreys Bill because it seems to provide only one method of flood prevention I am sure Senator Ransdell and Congressman Humphreys will have no objection to its being amended to provide that the work shall be done by the United States Corps of Engineers in any way it sees fit; or by the Mississippi River Commission under its own plans; or by a new Commission, provided such new Commission is composed of men scientifically trained in the matters they are to handle and provided further it is authorized to proceed with the work without delay The important and pressing matter is not the method of flood prevention but flood prevention itself, and the fact that everybody cannot agree on the same method is no excuse for sidetracking the whole project Members of Congress did not know how to build the Panama Canal but they left it to engineers who did Why should they not do the same with the Mississippi River? (Applause.)

The people of the Delta ought not be compelled to wait another fifty years while politicians continue to make pledges during the campaign which they do not keep when in office The people of the Delta strongly resent being called dippers into the "pork barrel" and any public print which stamps the project of flood prevention of the Mississippi River with this label as a term of opprobrium, is either seeking cheap notoriety or is not acquainted with the facts I have given you. The people of the Delta are not asking for something the Nation is ignorant of, but, on the contrary, a thing which has been approved by the best thought of the country for over half a century and which I have no doubt, if submitted to popular vote, would carry by an overwhelming majority

These long-suffering people have a right to demand that members of Congress keep their party pledges and "Adopt a comprehensive plan of flood control of the Lower Mississippi River without delay." (Applause)

President Ransdell—Owing to the lateness of the hour. we will defer the closing number of the program We hope you will all be present promptly at two o'clock this afternoon We have a very interesting program, and I would like to have as many present to hear the speakers as possible. We will now stand recessed until two o'clock this P.M.

Adjourned accordingly.

FIFTH SESSION
Thursday Afternoon, December 10

The Convention met pursuant to recess, President Ransdell in the chair.

PRESIDENT RANSDELL—Ladies and Gentlemen: We are to hear an address this afternoon on the subject of "Waterways a Necessity," by a gentleman who has been to every Convention of this organization for many years. He is one of the closest students of waterways in the country, and one of the best informed men. You can rely absolutely on his statements. I now present to you Mr. Perry A. Randall, of Fort Wayne, Ind. (Applause.)

WATERWAYS A NECESSITY
Address—Perry A. Randall, Fort Wayne, Ind.
President Erie and Michigan Deep Waterway Association

MR. PRESIDENT, LADIES AND GENTLEMEN:

I was converted to the necessity of waterway improvements in 1907. I had always and have always regarded waterways as needful for reducing the cost of transportation and as freight regulators. I was convinced in 1907 that they were a necessity, whether they reduced the cost of transportation or not.

I was in business during the years 1905, 1906 and 1907 that forced me to know how inefficient our railroads were to do the business of the country. I waited weeks and months to get in shipments of material. I was from two weeks to six weeks in getting carloads of lumber and logs switched out of the Pennsylvania yards, at Fort Wayne, to the Wabash track, a few blocks away. I had cars of lumber three months on the road, going a distance of 300 miles, and cars of lumber thirty days on the road, on a direct line, going a distance of 190 miles. I had a carload of lumber and shingles from eight to ten months on the road, coming from the State of Washington to Fort Wayne. Barley had grown on the car and gone to seed and a second crop was ready to harvest, when it arrived.   (Laughter.)

My neighbors, in the grain and hay business, waited from two to five months to get cars to ship hay and grain.   Their cars were often so long in transit that the corn became what is called "mahogany" and had to be dumped out as worthless Nearly one-half of the grain and hay merchants in Indiana went into bankruptcy during these years because they could not get their products to market to fill their contracts of sale.   Grain merchants, as a rule, sell their products to arrive, and when they don't arrive the purchaser buys to fill the order and charges the seller with the excess price.

Mr. Chas. S. Bash, of Fort Wayne, Chairman of the Committee on Legislation for the Grain and Hay Dealers of Indiana at that time, tells me that he audited the claims for damages of the grain and hay shippers of Indiana against the railroads. and the damages for one year, for corn, oats and hay, as filed, were far in excess of five million dollars He says that the loss to this class of men during those three years was in excess of thirty million dollars This thirty million dollars was the loss to one class of business It is safe to say the entire loss of the State of Indiana, to all classes of our people, due to insufficient shipping facilities, was more than fifty million dollars.   And Indiana was not alone in these losses; they were general throughout the Nation, as every shipper and business man will readily recall.   It has been estimated that the country at large lost during those three years, on account of inadequate shipping facilities, from one and one-half to two billion dollars—more than twice as much as our Nation has spent on her rivers and harbors.

The cause for this breakdown in transportation was explained at the time by Mr James J. Hill He said that while the transportation business of this country had doubled for every decade, prior to the one ending in 1907, the facilities for doing it had always kept pace with the business but for the decade ending with 1907 freight business increased one hundred and fifty-one per cent and passenger business one hundred and twenty-one per cent, while the facilities for doing this business had increased but twenty-three per cent. He said then that it would require five billion dollars to put the railroads in position to do the business of the country as it was in 1906 and 1907; he also said that if the business of 1907 was doubled it would necessitate the duplication of every railway terminal in the country.

In the winter of 1908, a Chicago statistician, writing on this subject, said that there are twenty-two hundred miles of railroad in Chicago. The ground they stand on is appraised at three hundred million dollars, but should it be duplicated it would cost ten times that sum, or three billion dollars. He said he had no data for New York, but in his opinion it would undoubtedly cost twice as much to duplicate the terminals in New York as in Chicago, or about six billion dollars. He said there are twenty-eight other large cities in the country and that to duplicate the terminals in all of them, including New York and Chicago, would cost more than was then represented by the face value of all the stocks and bonds of the railroads, which at that time exceeded fifteen billion dollars.

Mr. Theodore P. Shonts, in a speech at Chicago, in 1908, after discussing the difficulty of the railways in getting terminals, said: "The fact is this problem has attained such magnitude that some profound students of transportation affairs are discussing the feasibility of having the Government provide the terminal facilities for the railroads of the country, in order to save American commerce." He suggested as a solution of the problem that the country should go at once to waterways, as Government ownership of railways was not a desirable thing.

In the spring of 1908 I had a talk with a wealthy gentleman who told me he had been a member of a syndicate that had for its object the building of a trunk line railroad from New York to Chicago; he said that after spending a year's time and a large sum of money, they found that the terminals in New York alone would cost at least twice as much as it would to build and equip the road between New York and Chicago. The project was dropped because the cost of the terminals was prohibitive. He said: "There will never be another railroad built between New York and Chicago.

Mr. James J. Hill said, in a speech in New York two years ago this month, that there is no use of building more railroads or increasing, to any extent, the capacity of those we have, unless we can also furnish additional terminals for them. There is no use, he said, of increasing the size of the bottle unless you can enlarge the neck. He further said in this speech that he very much doubted if the railroads would be able to get money sufficient to increase their terminals so as to take care of the present capacity of the roads, and that unless railroad rates were very much increased they would not be able to do the business of the country in normal times. He said that if the railroads are to meet the requirements of the Government in providing safety devices, steel cars and sufficient terminals, railroad rates would have to be doubled.

The fact is the one unsurmountable problem the railroads have to face is that of terminals. The nature of railroads makes this so. The car is rigid, the track it stands on is rigid, and often miles of cars must be moved to get out one car that is needed. The president of a railroad in New York says that it costs his road often sixty dollars to spot a single car in that city. The ever-increasing cost of real estate in large cities is the main difficulty. Much of the ground that single cars stand on in New York is worth over one hundred thousand dollars. Railroads must have this property for their terminals, no matter what the cost.

I talked with a man last January who said he formerly held an official position with the Pennsylvania Railroad and that he thought it the best managed railroad in the world. He said he retired from all business six years ago, and at the time invested his surplus cash in the stock of the Pennsylvania and New York Central Railroads; that he paid for the Pennsylvania $144.00. and for the New York Central $114.00, per share. He said he had just sold all of these stocks, the Pennsylvania for $111.00 and the New York Central for $92.00. "I believe," he said. "these stocks are bound to go much lower. I would not be surprised to see them both in the hands of receivers. They have invested so much money in terminals, and are bound to invest so much more, that they will not be able to pay dividends upon it." I think he said the New York Central would be there now if it were not for the earnings of the Lake Shore Road, which is a wonderful money maker. I do not vouch for what this man said, but I know he was sincere and believed what he said was the truth.

It is in line with what every railroad man of importance tells us. Mr. Hill wrote recently, in *Forward St. Louis:* "Now these are the facts with which the railroads of the country are soon to confront the abnormal conditions that will follow the close of the great European war. Seven years ago a conservative calculation showed that they needed a new investment of five billion dollars, not to provide for future growth, but merely to do the business that was then offered to them. The need of such investment, and the amount of it required to raise the facilities of railroads to the level of the demands made upon them by the public, have grown each year since then."

"With the new stimulus which our people reasonably expect after peace is established, the new markets to be satisfied, the new demands filled, all involving additional demands upon the carrier, his machine will break down hopelessly unless it can be made more adequate. That can be done only by securing the investment of enough capital. It could not be done today if the supply of capital and the demand for it stood relatively as they did six months ago. To imagine that it can be done when there is such a poverty of available capital as there will be for ten, twenty, possibly more, years to come, is absurd."

The one place where there exists the greatest danger of a breakdown is in the transportation business between New York and Chicago. Here is the greatest stream of traffic in the country. There is no place where traffic is so congested today, and no place where it is increasing by such leaps and bounds. Even today there is an embargo on hay on the Erie and New York Central lines. The terminals of all the eastern roads are clogged with cars. There are 4,500 carloads of wheat at Baltimore. Most of them have been there for a month. There are double that number in New York, and the Toledo shipments have been delayed for more than a month, and this in not even normal times of shipping There must be adequate shipping facilities between New York and Chicago. Chicago is the greatest inland distributing center in the world. Over thirty trunk line railroads have their terminals there It is the heart of the Middle West. A thousand miles to the east is New York City, the greatest ocean port in the world, with a population of eight million people within a radius of twenty-five miles They are all busy people If the people of New York live they must have the products from the rich land of the Middle West If they live, then the West must take their products as well There are eleven trunk line railroads connecting these cities, which are now, in any normal times, working to their full capacity You cannot add another railroad to this list

The only relief that can be had for this stream of traffic between these cities is a waterway This waterway must be a through waterway, one that does not compel the breaking of bulk in transit. Such a waterway can be furnished by extending the Erie Canal through to Chicago This can be done by connecting the head waters of Lake Erie with the head waters of Lake Michigan by a waterway that will cost from thirty to forty million dollars Such a waterway would be the spinal column for the business between the East and the West. This waterway will be known as the New York and Chicago Barge Canal. The extension will correspond, at first. in size and capacity with the Erie Canal, but the Army Engineers who have made the survey say that all plans should be made now to increase the size to a thirty-foot canal from Chicago clear through to New York City within a period of twenty-five years. Other waterways are perhaps as important, but unless this waterway is built there will be a complete breakdown of the business between the East and the West. and that very soon. One cannot conceive of a more important project. It will be worth infinitely more to the people of this Nation than is the Panama Canal.

We have not had a normal year of railroad business since 1907. We have had for a few months each year, during the past four or five years, a swinging back into the normal, but for the most of the time there have been plenty of empties to accom-

modate the shipper. The conditions we have had for the past
seven years will not continue forever. Everybody is looking forward to, and hoping for, bumper business We expect it to
come upon us at the close of this present war The next ten
years after the close of the European war ought to be the fattest
years for business this country has ever had They will be,
too, unless our transportation system breaks down, as it did
seven years ago. There is nothing to prevent these years being
golden with opportunities for us, if we have transportation facilities for taking advantage of them   (Applause.)

We 'should at once turn our attention to this question. We
should study the needs of our railroads and give them every
help within our power. Above all things, give them such increase in rates that they can pay liberal dividends and thus attract money for their needs In addition we must improve our
waterways, not in a niggardly way, but in a munificent way.
We should do, in the next five years, more for our waterways
than we have done in the last twenty We know that the railroads, unaided by waterways, cannot do the business of this
country on the large scale in which it will come to us To depend upon them alone will be inviting bankruptcy and ruin to
every class of our citizens.

Waterways will not hurt the railroads; they will aid them.
They will take from them the heavy and bulky freight that clogs
their terminals and makes them no money. Waterways will
leave to them the quick freight, the passenger business, the express and mail   Their terminals will be sufficient to do this
business and they will make out of it more than they do now
by trying to do it all   There are certain things business men do
because they have to, not by choice but by compulsion   A large
retail grocer said recently, "I sell thousands of tons of sugar
every year, and lose money on every pound of it   I am compelled to sell sugar or quit the grocery business." The railroads
of today are in the same shape as to heavy and bulky freight.
They are better off by far without it

We ought, as business men and legislators, to study what
France and Germany have done, and what Canada has done
and is doing with her waterways If we had spent as much

money on our waterways as Canada, in proportion to our population, we would have spent to the present time five billion dollars instead of seven hundred million dollars. If we had spent as much on transportation as Canada has, in proportion to our population, we would have spent at this time twelve billion dollars. (Applause.)

We have heretofore spent seventy per cent of all our national revenue, outside of our postal receipts, for wars, past, present and to come, and five to seven per cent for commerce. These proportions must be reversed. When this terrible war is ended, big armies and big armaments and big gunboats will be ended as well. Murderous war between civilized nations will never be again. The future contests between civilized nations will henceforth and forever hereafter be commercial, and those nations will win, in these contests, that have the best and completest transportation facilities. (Applause.)

President Ransdell—During the sharp criticisms of the rivers and harbors bill recently pending before Congress, one project, which its friends are pleased to designate as a very great one, was subjected to unsparing and ruthless criticism. That project was the Chesapeake and Delaware Canal. It was ably defended on the floor of the Senate by the junior Senator from Delaware, who is going to tell you something about it today, and to show you why it was very improperly and wrongly criticised —Senator Willard Saulsbury, of Delaware. (Applause.)

THE CHESAPEAKE AND DELAWARE CANAL
Address—Senator Willard Saulsbury, Delaware

Mr. Chairman, Ladies and Gentlemen:

I am trying to get my colleagues in the Senate and House of Representatives to invest for the Government about $7.500,000 so they will get a net annual return of at least 18% to 20% for ten to fifteen millions of our people, and a war risk insurance on many billions of dollars' worth of property as well as save the Government several millions of dollars each year in naval expenses.

The net profits per year may increase to 50%. Ten human lives will be saved each year which are now sacrificed; our

Capital City, two of the great cities and many of the smaller cities of the country will be doubly protected; our chances of victory in any future war with a naval nation will be tremendously increased, and in peace we will draw our dividends of at least 18% regularly and reduce the cost of living, increase the means of livelihood and generally benefit millions of our people That sort of a proposition would look pretty good to an ordinary business man but the initiation of this investment was possibly prevented at the last session of Congress by the physical ability of one Senator to vocalize for a week or so and to do this at a critical time for twenty-four hours at a stretch.

The statement I have made is not an exaggeration. I have practiced law and advised clients in their business affairs, sometimes of considerable importance, during a period of over thirty years. I have gone into this question, of the acquisition by the Government of the Chesapeake and Delaware Canal, as I would examine the most important law case I ever had, where clients of mine might become interested to the extent of millions of dollars. I have acted, so far as I could volunteer my services in this examination, as the counsel of the Government and every word I have said I believe would be approved by any open-minded man who will exhaustively examine the reports of Government engineers, of commissions and of committees of Congress They are many in number and extend over a period of 42 years, beginning in 1872 and ending last April.

Let me give you as briefly as I can some of the undisputed facts about the Chesapeake and Delaware Canal It is a little less than 14 miles long, from the entrance at Delaware City to the outlet at Chesapeake City The distance from Philadelphia to Delaware City by water is 42 miles, from Chesapeake City to Baltimore 56 miles, making a total distance between these two great cities by water of 112 miles The canal will pass vessels 220 feet long, having 9 feet draft and 24 feet beam. The distance between Baltimore and Philadelphia is 96 miles by rail against 112 by water. Freight delivered in Philadelphia at 5 00 o'clock in the afternoon to the small boats plying through the canal is landed in Baltimore at 7 00 o'clock the next morning, while the average time for freight deliveries by rail is something like two or three days   (Applause.)

The gross earnings of the canal from tolls on vessels passing through it for the past ten years have averaged about $175,000 annually; its cost of operation has averaged $65,000, leaving a net annual income from operation of $110,000   The interest on its bonded indebtedness of $2,602,950 at 4% is $104,118, leaving a net annual income above all charges of about $6,000. The interest on its bonds was some years ago decreased from 5% to 4% and has been earned and paid. Its average annual gross earnings between the years 1864 and 1874 approximated $400,-000, and during the same period its average annual operating cost was about $130,000, leaving $270,000 for charges and dividends

There are 10,000 boats engaged in the commerce of Chesapeake and Delaware Bays and their tributaries, which have a shore line of 2,500 miles. The combined traffic on these two bays, as shown by the report of the Chief of Engineers, exceeds 50,000,000 tons annually; and if to this the undocumented and unregistered tonnage is added, which includes the vast amount handled daily by thousands of local trading boats, the total tonnage is estimated to exceed 100,000,000 tons. As I compile it from the Engineers' Report, the tonnage of Delaware Bay and River and tributaries for 1912 was 26,267,335 short tons   On Chesapeake Bay and tributaries the aggregate is 36,333,489 tons, although I am not sure these figures are as accurate as the others

Last year (1913) 5,778 boats passed through the canal carrying 908,589 tons of freight, an average of less than 200 tons to each vessel, boat or barge   This is not a small traffic, but the Government engineers have estimated, declaring their estimates to be conservative, that this tonnage on a 12-foot canal such as now recommended would be 2,537,000 tons, and the annual saving to commerce, as estimated by the Board of Engineers, if the Government shall take over the canal, widen it to 90 feet and deepen it to 12 feet, will be $1,414,000   The cost, including the acquisition of the canal at a reasonable figure, will be between seven and eight millions of dollars, which provides for a purchase price of the canal of $2,514,000   It is believed that the canal can be condemned for this figure, although the various Boards of Engineers have estimated that the Government, to duplicate the canal, would have to expend $3,700,000 Government engineers have consistently and uniformly recommended its purchase for $2,514,000

The approaches to the canal at its Delaware end are defended by the forts on the Delaware and New Jersey shores as well as an old fortification in midstream, and the Chesapeake end is above the important defences of the whole of the Chesapeake Bay There are no difficulties in the deepening and enlargement of the canal, no rock work being necessary

When I was urging this matter in the Senate one of my colleagues asked me what the Atlantic Ocean was there for, if not to sail boats on. I told him that ten lives is the average annual death toll taken by the sea on the rough outside passage between the Delaware and Virginia Capes I proved this by official reports, and then showed him that this canal would shorten the water passage between Baltimore and Philadelphia by 308 miles, and between Baltimore and New York, by going out the Delaware Capes instead of the Virginia Capes, by 180 miles Indeed, it will materially shorten the distance from Baltimore to Europe

The facts I have given are all contained in official reports printed in public documents. It may interest you to know some of the men who, as Government Engineers, have made these reports The list is too long to give the names of all of them, but I select from this list of distinguished engineers the following: Gen Thomas L. Casey, Colonel Craighill, General Bixby, Admiral Dewey, Major Raymond, Colonel Black, Colonel Flagler, Colonel Rossell, Captain Turtle, General Humphreys. Benj H Latrobe I can hardly think a finer, abler lot of engineers could be found anywhere than that, nor could any business man hesitate to accept their conclusions or follow their advice

On the Delaware Bay and its tributaries is carried annually fifty million tons of freight On Chesapeake Bay and its tributaries that much and more Only a narrow isthmus of less than 14 miles stops the free exchange between millions of people of a hundred million tons of freight.

We are almost a hundred years behind our time, for in 1829, nearly one hundred years ago, the people of that day, only one-eighth as numerous as they are now, built a canal sufficient for their commercial needs across this fourteen miles and brought together the two greatest commerce-bearing estuaries of the Atlantic seaboard. They had seen in the War of 1812 how their inability to concentrate the land and naval forces of the United States in this region had led to the capture and destruction of this Capital City. They could understand what the exchange of the then relatively small commerce of these two great bays and their tributaries meant in the way of increased business and comfort to the people of the whole section, and they dug a canal ten feet in depth which satisfactorily carried the water traffic of the section for many years

It proved of use to the Federal Government during the war between the States Indeed, that was the greatest time of its prosperity Some have said its use prevented this Capital City from falling into the hands of the Confederacy. The railroad bridges had all been burned and at one time troops and supplies from the North could only be sent here by boats which were hastily brought through this small canal It then proved its military value, and, if properly enlarged and deepened, it can and may again The great shipyards of the Delaware and Chesapeake, the oil refineries and pipe lines at Marcus Hook, the great coal traffic of these bays, and the cities of Philadelphia, Baltimore, Wilmington, Chester, Camden and Trenton deserve and should have the protection a modern canal here would afford

In 1886 Colonel Craighill, of the United States Engineer Corps, reported

> "No argument is necessary to show the great value in time of war with a maritime power of such an interior line of communication between the great Chesapeake and Delaware Bays and their tributary streams as this canal would be "

The Committee on Railways and Canals of the House in that year said·

"Its entire feasibility has been definitely determined by three Government surveys ordered by Congress."

And President Arthur, in forwarding the report of the Secretary of the Navy, invited the attention of Congress to his recommendations, in which the Secretary said:

"To secure the combined commercial and military advantages which these avenues for merchant and naval vessels would afford, the work should be immediately begun and deliberately and economically prosecuted, and not left to be done hastily and expensively in an emergency."

The committee of the House in 1886 recommended the appropriation of $1,000,000 to begin the work on this canal, and in its report quoted from the report of Captain Turtle, made to the Forty-Second Congress, second session, as follows:

"It will be doubted by no one that a deep-water connection between the two bays would be of vast importance in the contingency of war with a maritime nation. Such a connection would provide a means of concentrating the floating defenses of the two bays, and, besides, would render more secure the communication between the naval stations at Philadelphia, Norfolk and Washington. Vessels defending ports have two offices to perform, the one being to assist in the direct defense, or to prevent capture or occupation by a hostile force, the other being the prevention or breaking up of the blockades.

"Without a canal a blockade at the Capes of the Delaware would close the port of Philadelphia, or the blockade at the Capes of Virginia would close the outward commerce of Baltimore and the other ports of the Chesapeake. With the canal built where communication would be secure, neither the ports of Philadelphia nor of Baltimore would be closed, unless an effectual blockade were established both at the Delaware and Virginia Capes. It may be assumed that if a war with one of the great naval powers should arise, and the mere appropriation of the money could provide such a channel of communication between the bays, the amount would be at once provided without hesitation. That would, however, be too late "

Every Board of Engineers which has had this Chesapeake and Delaware Canal under consideration has recommended its purchase, and there have been so many boards, so many investigations, that it is an immense task to go through the reports made to Congress from time to time concerning it, but every board which has reported on the subject has declared its great usefulness for military purposes and as a means of defense, should our country be attacked I venture to predict that if, because of the failure of the Government to provide for the passage of its vessels between these two great bays, we should suffer a naval disaster due to inability to concentrate our fleet, our torpedo boats and our submarines at the point of danger, those who have actively endeavored to prevent the building of a proper canal between the Delaware and Chesapeake Bays by the Government would be as earnest in disavowing their responsibility for such unpatriotic efforts as the European nations are now in endeavoring to escape responsibility for bringing on the present war. (Applause.)

Not a transport, supply ship, hospital ship, destroyer, monitor or third-class cruiser in our Navy could get through this canal to assist in a naval battle in one bay or the other if Norfolk, Baltimore or Philadelphia were being attacked. There is not even a gunboat in the American Navy, if we except those on the Asiatic Station, that could use this canal About one-half of the converted yachts could get through it and not one-half of the Government tugs could pass, for the dimensions of the lock do not permit any vessel of over 24 foot beam, 9 feet draft, or 220 feet length to use the canal

When I speak of beam and draft of vessels, I wonder if some of these critics of water transportation understand what

I mean. From the intelligence displayed in the speeches they
make and the articles they write, I sometimes doubt whether they
could tell, if they saw them, the difference between a capstan
and a binnacle, a cook's galley or a mizzenmast. (Laughter.)

Somehow or other, those of us who have lived where we
have the smell of the sea in our nostrils love a ship and shipping.
The sea to us promises romance and adventure; tales of the sea
have come down to us from grandfather and great-grandfather.
We have seen the ships come and go between our ports and the
distant places of the earth, our old sea captains and our naval
men have told us tales, which charmed our boyhood days, of
different races of men and of adventures throughout the world.

The acquisition of this canal by the Government will be in
accord with the last two platforms of the now dominant party
in this country. In its platform at Denver, in 1908, the Democratic Party declared:

> Water furnishes the cheaper means of transporta-
> tion, and the National Government, having control of
> navigable waters, should improve them to their full-
> est capacity. * * * We favor, when practicable,
> the connection * * * of the navigable rivers with
> each other, by artificial canals, with a view of perfect-
> ing a system of inland waterways to be navigated
> by vessels of standard draft.

At Baltimore, in 1912, its declaration was as follows:

> We favor the adoption of a liberal and comprehen-
> sive plan for the development and improvement of our
> inland waterways with economy and efficiency, so as to
> permit their navigation by vessels of standard draft.

We believe our country is a great one, we believe our flag
should again be seen on every sea and in every port, and yet,
when we try to increase our commerce, when we try to build
up our water transportation, we feel the sordid combination of
the selfish interests which are working against the cheaper trans-

portation of our commodities and the expansion of our commerce. We don't like it when, after years of labor, we bring matters to a point where we think progress is possible, that instead of argument, instead of convincing figures being offered to combat us, all else failing, resort is had to filibustering tactics when men are worn out beyond the possibility of further endurance

It seems strange that this little canal has managed somehow or other to keep out of the clutches of the railroads, yet there is a good explanation for it. The canal company was never able to get from the State Legislatures of Delaware and Maryland the right itself to transport freight and passengers and, for that reason, because it had to allow every one owning a boat to use the canal on equal terms, it could not, itself, furnish active competition with the railroad lines which have so industriously acquired and put out of use nearly all the canals on the Atlantic Seaboard The Chesapeake and Delaware Canal has been preserved from railroad ownership only because it has no powers as a transportation company. It is a toll proposition entirely, and, since its owner must allow everyone's boat to pass through on the same terms, the attractive monopolistic feature, so useful for capitalization purposes, is absent

In my humble judgment, this canal may have been preserved that the people of this country may have an object lesson in a square deal for water transportation as against railroad transportation I do not believe that our very useful Interstate Commerce Commission could bring about greater good, in the field of transportation, than by letting us have a square deal on the canal transportation problem by separating the old canals from the railroads Let us have the beginnings of a square deal in water transportation by separating the canals, the landings, the wharves and the boats that must use them, from railroad ownership. (Applause.)

If the Government can expend money in public work which will greatly assist in the defense of our Atlantic Seaboard and at the same time save to our commerce 18% on the cost of such work—it looks like a good public investment. The Panama Canal equipment will possibly be largely available for the actual work. I believe that the old idea of commerce by canal will be magnificently proved or irretrievably condemned by the success or failure which will attend the Government's purchase, improvement and operation as a free waterway of this comparatively little channel between the Delaware and Chesapeake Bays.

It goes without saying that I believe the proposal will be magnificently vindicated in practice or I should not think for a moment of advocating its purchase and enlargement by the Government with public money. You gentlemen who are familiar with conditions of water transportation elsewhere may get small appropriations here and there for some little canal in a less thickly settled portion of the country and in a small way you may demonstrate the wisdom of such expenditures, but if you wish to prove the availability of canals for modern commerce there is no place in the whole country like this narrow neck of land between the two great bays, separating the great commerce they carry, to get quick proof of this and demonstrate what a great benefit water transportation can be to communities which can use it.

Believing as I do in the great utility this canal would be to the commerce of the country, with even the small improvement its deepening to 12 feet would make; believing as I do that a demonstration of this canal at that depth will prove absolutely to the Government the great desirability that it should be made a ship canal through which our warships may be concentrated for the defense of our country in time of war, I feel that I would be unpatriotic if I did not urge that this work should be taken up by the Government. I believe it is now in a position where we will soon have the last word on this project so far as the able engineers of the Army and Navy can say that word.

When, after the most careful study and consideration of all the reports which have been made on this project by skilled engineers of the Army engaged in work on waterways, by committees of both Houses of Congress, and by commissions, in the membership of which civilians were included, one has become convinced that there cannot be two opinions on a proposition by men who have sufficient intelligence and industry to learn the facts, one is inclined to be somewhat impatient with the trifling and almost unintelligent criticism or questions raised concerning it.

When it became impossible in the last Congress to start this great project by an appropriation, feeling absolutely confident that no capable engineer could make unfavorable reports on this project, I offered and secured the passage in the Senate of a resolution directing the Secretary of War to secure, prepare and report to the Senate, summaries of the reports of the Government commissions, officers and engineers heretofore made, and such facts, information and opinions of boards or officers of the Army and Navy as he may deem proper or pertinent as to the advantages or disadvantages, commercial, naval or military, of the acquisition of the Chesapeake and Delaware Canal by the United States, with such information as he can secure as to the price at which the property can be purchased.

In my judgment, gentlemen, when the Secretary responds to that resolution in a report setting out the facts known to the Government regarding the canal, its great possibilities for good to commerce and the National defense, there will be no popular criticism or objection to the action of the Government in taking over this property and making it available, in the broadest sense and in the biggest way, for commercial, naval and military purposes.

I believe in this great work. I believe its greatness will be demonstrated and its benefits certified to by the best engineers and the highest officials in this branch of the Government service and on the report which will be made pursuant to that resolution I pin my faith that there will be a start made by this Government in the development of that waterway for commerce and defense. I believe this waterway will come to be used by the great ships of the United States; I believe its usefulness will be so proven that the Government will soon proceed, after its practical development has shown the people of this country its great advantages, to extend northward a canal which may be similarly used between deep water in the Delaware River and New York Bay.

I do not believe that anyone should advocate this latter work until the smaller and less expensive work is done and demonstrates its usefulness and success, but when the two are completed, then the enormous advantages to this country will be self-evident. The whole fleet of the United States, without knowledge of an attacking force, could be concentrated anywhere on our Atlantic Seaboard, from Narragansett Bay to the Virginia Capes. Should such concentration ever be needed for defense, the value of such a passageway would be incalculable. Can anyone today compute the value to the German Empire, either in money or for defense, of the great, but less important, military canal at Kiel?

Our greatest warships last only a few years. At the end of ten years they go into the second line of defense, I believe, because they have become partially obsolete and outclassed. For less than the cost of one warship, this great propect may be demonstrated. For the cost of a few warships, the whole great project may be accomplished, with a saving to the commerce of the country of 20% on this investment and a thousand per cent advantage for the military and naval defense of this country over that of Germany's great military canal at Kiel.

I shall try to be patient, I shall try to convince my colleagues of the desirability of this great work, even if they hesitate at the expenditure and question the certainty of its result. But if I can be in any way instrumental in forcing along the accomplishment of this project, of bringing the people of the country to see how, along peaceful lines, we can double, quadruple, possibly quintuple, the effectiveness of our naval forces for defense of the Atlantic Seaboard and at the same time secure almost inestimable facilities for the free interchange of products of the whole East, I shall not feel that my time has been ill-spent, no matter what labor or loss of energy it may entail. (Applause.)

· APPENDIX

By joint resolution of Congress (public resolution No 37, 1906) the President was authorized to appoint a commission to examine and appraise the value and works and franchises of the Delaware and Chesapeake Canal, and an appropriation made for that purpose This caused the appointment of the so-called Agnus Commission, which consisted of Gen. Felix Agnus, of Baltimore, as chairman; Maj C A F. Flagler, now Colonel Flagler, of the United States Army, who appeared before the Committee on Coast and Insular Survey at its recent investigation, and Mr F. T. Chambers, civil engineer, of the United States Navy The commission reported January 1, 1907 (S. Doc No 215, 59th Cong, 2d sess)

This commission obtained and brought together a vast amount of information and reported in favor 'of acquiring the Chesapeake and Delaware Canal at an early date, if practicable, and if it can be done at a cost not to exceed $2,514,289 70," which sum was reached by appraisement of the works and franchises of the canal. The canal company valued its property at $5,348,071 The commission, basing its estimate on cost of reproduction valued the property at $3,708,186. The itemized estimate of values is as follows

Dry excavation, 15,000,000 cubic yards, at 16 cents	$2,400,000
Dredging, 1,435,760 cubic yards, at 14 cents	200,996
Revetment, 80,000 linear feet	70,000
Masonry, 44,000 perches, at $3	132,000
Lock at Delaware City	120,000
Lock at St. Georges	118,220
Lock at Chesapeake City	147,970
Land holdings, 8,000 acres, at $50	400,000
Summit level supply	5,000
Bridges	31,000
Houses, offices. etc.	30,000
Tools, machinery, etc	1,000
Telephone line	2,000

Total "cost of reproduction," 1907	$3,708,186

PRESIDENT RANSDELL——When the attacks on the Rivers and Harbors Bill last summer had reached the point where patience had ceased to be a virtue, a ringing address was made in the Senate which was echoed and re-echoed throughout the entire Union and brought to its author encomiums of the strongest and most sincere character from every friend of waterways in the country.

That address was delivered by Senator William Alden Smith, of Michigan, who will now address you. (Applause.) The Senator is so modest that I find it hard to get him on the platform.

Address—Senator William Alden Smith, Michigan

MR. PRESIDENT AND GENTLEMEN:

Lest some of my colleagues who happen to be here should fail to recognize the new virtue ascribed to me, I desire to say to my honored friend who presides over this gathering that it was not wholly modesty that prompted me to remain in the audience, but rather a feeling of unpreparedness and inability to add anything to what has been said in any special line.

I had no thought of being here today, although I got a very peremptory request from your President, who admonished me of the fate that was in store for the lady traveler who, for the first time in many years, started on a journey from an interior western State to New York. Unlike her lady friends, she was rather inclined to be somewhat talkative on the journey, and engaged almost every one within sound of her voice in conversation upon almost every question of interest to her. Finally, when all of her surroundings were exhausted, a new complement of passengers boarded the train at Syracuse, among them a tall, raw-boned Irishman, who sat down near her; and with that thoroughness which had characterized her journey thus far, she ventured to ask him whether he thought that train would stop when it reached the Grand Central Station in New York; and he said, "I think it will, Mom; if it don't you will get the domdest bump you've iver had!" (Laughter.)

I was not looking for any bump Really, I am not looking
for an appropriation—strange as that may seem   (Applause.)
I do not want you to get too enthusiastic about that, because
the time may come when I shall change my mental attitude
toward the Treasury; but the only reason why I am not looking
for any special appropriation is because all the rivers and all
the harbors that are worthy of improvement in the State of
Michigan have already been completed   (PRESIDENT RANSDELL:
Through your efforts.)   At least in a measure, thanks to the
genius of our Corps of Engineers, who have seen merit in most
of our appropriations   (PRESIDENT RANSDELL You have forgotten to mention your own efforts)   Well, I have not done
much.   I find myself rather modest, compared with some others.

I think that the defeat of the last River and Harbor Bill,
or a river and harbor bill, was psychological   (Laughter.) It
seemed to be coincident with a diminished revenue, and the di-
minishing revenue seemed to be coincident with public affairs
However, I see no special merit in hanging out of the window
the red flag of the auctioneer.   The country has not yet struck
the rocks   The sources of our monetary supply are as great as
they ever have been.   The riches that have flowed like madden-
ing rivers into our Federal treasury have responded only to the
natural demands which our country has a right to make upon
them, and to neglect to put in great public works because of this
psychological situation is to admit that the policy of the Government in the past has been unworthy of our championship—
and I decline to subscribe to that idea   (Applause)

I look into the face of the Mayor of New Orleans over
there, and I see men who live along the Mississippi Valley, who
have been patient and long suffering.   But, as yet, with all due
respect, no scheme commensurate with the importance of that
improvement has been developed, and those who should take
the responsibility for what nature may some day do to bring
before the eyes of our countrymen and of the world the position occupied by the people of that Valley may take that responsibility, but for myself I shall never subscribe to that policy
of the Government which exposes millions of my countrymen to

unfair disadvantage as compared with the balance of the people of our land. (Applause.)

I am glad that you have this organization, that you meet annually to infect others with your warmth and glow. Those who are familiar with the Gulf Stream know that although but about three hundred miles wide, extending from the tropics to the Bay of Biscay, it warms all the superincumbent atmosphere, and makes habitable parts of the world that would otherwise be as desolate as the Arctic. People of the Southland who enjoy this soft moisture that is blown on to the mainland by the southeast breezes know full well their great advantage in the variety of their products, in the diversity of their employments, in the wealth of their productions is due, in great part, to causes attributable directly to this warm, pulsating current that sweeps from the tropics to the far North. And I think to the internal waterways of our country this organization is the Gulf Stream from which our country may receive the moisture in early spring and the soft and refulgent and palpitating glow of your oratory and enthusiasm and of encouragement in our great struggle to do justice to the waterways of our country. (Applause.)

Slander, vituperation and vilification come from the arsenal of self-conceit. (Applause.) The traveler on the middle Rhine, as he travels down the river and passes the Drachenfels' rounded crown, smiles as he reads the story of myth and romance that clusters around those rugged sides. His reason tells him that those stories have no place where ancient tradition has located them. But as he journeys on, long after vine and valley and ruin have passed from view, the grand old features of the landmark stand out against the sky as if a perpetual monument to the Creator. So slander, vituperation and abuse, the petty tyranny that is exercised to delay and harass a just cause, will not triumph; and long after such carping criticism and the voices that uttered it have ceased to be, the grand old features of that landmark stand out against the sky, and over river and over harbor they are beacon lights of honor and glory to those who have had any part in setting them there. (Applause.)

Now I have not any especial project to speak about—not one. The only project in my State not yet completed that is on my heart particularly, I could this afternoon, if I felt disposed to do it, pass a hat in a generous convention like this and raise money enough in fifteen minutes to take care of   (Applause.) So I am not speaking selfishly; but I do want to see something done.   I want to see it done prudently, wisely, tactfully, courteously—but I want to see it done.   I do not want to see the great work that now engages the thought and attention of the people of almost every State slumber, as though it had taken a perpetual anæsthetic.   I have no desire whatever to awaken unkind thoughts, but being one of the men who helped make a river and harbor bill, being one of the men who expect to help make the next one, I want this Convention to know that I shall be guided in the performance of my proper duty by what I regard as the interest of the entire Nation; and that it will be done considerately and with a view to such fair and just economies as must commend themselves to the fair and unbiased judgment of our fellow citizens   (Applause)   Having done that, I think we may safely leave the approval of our work with those who have given us temporary commissions to represent them in this Government

For twenty years I have buffeted the billows of public life in this Capitol; but never yet have I felt called upon to make any apology for anything I ever did here in a public way.   And if the work that falls to our hands shall be done with care, with thoroughness, with painstaking detail, with a desire to see that no money is unwisely expended, but with the desire to see that all that is necessary to do the appropriate thing is done, I think we may go back to our countrymen with every feeling that our course will be sustained and the reputation of the Republic will not have suffered through our profligacy or disregard. (Applause)

President Ransdell—You do not wonder now, my friends, that Senator Smith thrilled the Senate and the Nation

I will now introduce to you a man who will also thrill you He is from another section of the country.   He is going to tell you something about a project which was also very much assailed in the recent rivers and harbors bill, the Sacramento and Feather Rivers, away out on the Pacific Coast, thousands of miles from here. This gentlemen is the Hon. John E. Raker, Member of Congress from California. (Applause.)

THE SACRAMENTO AND FEATHER RIVERS
Address—John E. Raker, M. C., California.

MR. PRESIDENT AND GENTLEMEN:

In the Rivers and Harbors Bill (H. R. 13,811, 63d Congress, 2d Session), was this item: "Improving Sacramento and Feather Rivers, California, in accordance with the report submitted in Rivers and Harbors Committee Document No. 5, 63d Congress, 1st Session, and subject to the conditions set forth in said document, $200,000."

This is one of the items which was so severely criticised by Senator Burton in the United States Senate when that bill was under consideration by that body in August, September and October of this year. The real Rivers and Harbors Bill was defeated and a lump sum appropriation of $20,000,000 was made.

The Committee on Rivers and Harbors, after fully considering the matter, reported to the House as follows:

> "The project for the improvement of the Sacramento and Feather Rivers is also one which the committee regarded as worthy and of great importance. The whole work is to cost something above $33,000,- 000, but as a greater part of the work is for the purpose of preventing overflows from floods, and of protecting and reclaiming lands in the valley of the Sacramento and Feather Rivers, the State of California and local interests are to contribute all money necessary for the work except $5,800,000, which is recommended by the engineers as the amount the Government should expend in the interest of navigation. The plans and the report indicate that the project has received the most thorough consideration

engineering skill could bring to bear, and that nothing has been left indefinite that it was possible to make certain."

When the bill was considered by the House this item was unanimously approved

The Commerce Committee of the Senate also gave the matter full consideration and recommended that the item as passed by the House should be adopted.   The only objection to this project in the Commerce Committee was made by Senator Burton, who submitted a minority report in which he said:

"The comparatively modest appropriation of $200,-000 is made for this improvement   The fact is that the total cost will be $5,860,000   While navigation is incidentally affected, the main object of this great expenditure of money is for the reclamation of lands It is a matter of common experience that the insistence upon improvements of this character, the degree in which they are urged upon Congress and the individual Members, is far greater than that for legitimate river and harbor improvements, and the tendency to increase this class of projects, of very doubtful benefit to the general public, deserves immediate attention "

The reasons for action on this subject are based upon the conditions of the Sacramento and Feather Rivers as they existed prior to the prosecution of hydraulic mining in California, as compared with the conditions produced by the filling of the channels from that cause.   Prior to 1860 the channels of these rivers were in excellent condition for navigation, having sufficient depth of water to accommodate any vessels that now attempt to navigate those streams   Under license of Congressional legislation hydraulic mining was prosecuted upon the public lands in California, whereby vast quantities of clay, sand and gravel were precipitated into the mountain streams leading to the Sacramento River.   The spring freshets carried this debris into the channels and filled them to such an extent as to destroy navigation in some portions and to greatly imperil navigation in all portions of these streams.

The report of the California Debris Commission (House Executive Document No. 81, 62d Congress, 1st Session), makes the following statement:

> "The channel of the Sacramento River from the Feather River to Suisun Bay contains large deposits of mining debris brought down by the Feather and American Rivers. The accummulations of mining debris in the channel of the Sacramento River have raised the bed about five feet and reduced its capacity about five or ten per cent. In the lower reaches of the Feather, Yuba, Bear and American Rivers there still remain at least three hundred million cubic yards of material which must in time enter the Sacramento."

The report of the Board of Engineers for Rivers and Harbors, dated October 10, 1908, states that the river has a navigable low water depth of seven feet below Sacramento, and of four feet from Sacramento to the mouth of the Feather River. The Feather River throughout its entire course has been filled to such an extent that navigation is impossible and is not even attempted.

In 1893 the Federal Government, in recognition of its obligation to navigation and its duty relative to removing the effects of the hydraulic mining which had been permitted by the inattention of the Government, passed what is known as the Caminetti Act, creating the California Debris Commission. Section 4 of that act reads as follows:

> "That it shall be the duty of said Commission to mature and adopt such plan or plans, from examinations and surveys already made and from such additional examinations and surveys as it may deem necessary, as will improve the navigability of all the rivers comprising said systems, deepen their channels and

protect their banks   Such plan or plans shall be matured with a view of making the same effective as against the encroachment of and damage from debris resulting from mining operations, natural erosion or other causes, with a view of restoring, as near as practicable and the necessities of commerce and navigation demand, the navigability of said rivers to the conditions existing in eighteen hundred and sixty"

We claim that under this act Congress especially recognized its obligation to restore these rivers to their former state of navigability   Section 24 of the act reads as follows:

"That for the purpose of securing harmony of execution and economy in expenditures in the work to be done by the United States and the State of California respectively, the former in its plans for the improvement and protection of the navigable streams and to prevent the depositing of mining debris or other materials within the same, and the latter in its plans authorized by law for the reclamation and drainage and protection of these lands or relating to the work of hydraulic mines, the said Commission is empowered to consult thereon with a Commission of Engineers of said State for said purpose, the result of such conference to be reported to the Chief of Engineers of the United States Army, and if by him approved shall be followed by said Commission"

Under this provision it is evident that Congress made overtures to the State of California relative to the joint prosecution of the work rendered necessary by the filling of the rivers with debris from the hydraulic mines. Up to and including 1913, the State of California has appropriated for such improvement the sum of $2,120,000. and in all particulars the State and Federal Governments have acted in harmony and have divided the cost of the work thus far performed.

Many years ago it became evident that some general plan would have to be adopted, inasmuch as the floods were of such volume that the channels of the rivers were insufficient to carry the water at extreme flood stages, while at the low stages they did not carry sufficient water to produce a scouring effect The State of California procured the services of eminent engineers, forming what is known as the Dabney Commission, who made examinations and recommended a plan for this work The California Debris Commission also made constant examinations and investigations with a view to formulating a practical and comprehensive scheme to reach the result contemplated by the Caminetti Act.

On June 30, 1907, the California Debris Commission made a report which recommends the improvement of the Sacramento and Feather Rivers to the extent directed by the Caminetti Act, from the mouth of the Sacramento to Chico Landing. The plan contained in this report in all its general features is identical with House Document No 81 Congress adopted the recommendations of this report in 1910 by appropriating $400,000 for the construction and operation of two hydraulic dredges, conditioned upon the State of California making a similar appropriation and upon the donation of the rights of way necessary for that portion of the work then contemplated

The State of California promptly met the proposal of Congress by making an appropriation of $400,000 and depositing it in the Treasury of the United States. The private interests as promptly donated the rights of way at a cost of over $200,-000, of which $75,000 was contributed by the city of Sacramento, the balance being provided by private subscription

By this action Congress (if it had not previously committed itself to the general problem of improvement of the Sacramento and Feather Rivers) finally and conclusively recognized and adopted the project: and, in view of such Congressional action, the State of California made its appropriation and the citizens of California provided the funds required by that Act to purchase the rights of way

In 1910, still pursuing the directions contained in the Cammetti Act, and in further consummation of the avowed purpose of the Commission contained in its report of 1907, the California Debris Commission made a final report upon the perfected plans for accomplishing the purposes prescribed in that act This report adopts all that was contained in the report of 1907 and supplements that report by a detailed plan involving the improvement of the river channels and, as a necessary adjunct thereto, the control of the flood waters of those rivers

This report, however, adopts a different basis for the division of the expense Previously the cost had been equally borne, but, considering the interests that would be benefited by the control of the river floods, the California Debris Commission decided that an equitable division would be that the National Government should provide one-third and the State two-thirds of the money needed, to complete the work

A misconception has arisen in the minds of some persons who have glanced at this report, to the effect that this work does not involve any improvement or promotion of the interest of navigation. This misconception is due to the language of Col. Wm T Rossell in his communication transmitting the report of the California Debris Commission to the Board of Engineers for Rivers and Harbors This error can be easily removed by the explanations of the War Department and is entirely removed by a careful reading of the report of the Commission itself All that was intended by Colonel Rossell was to indicate that the interest of navigation could be cared for without the adoption of a larger plan.

With five feet of debris in the bottom of the Sacramento River and with three hundred million cubic yards of debris yet to reach the river, it would be difficult to imagine a more serious menace to navigation than exists upon those streams. Conditions have been greatly aggravated since those reports were made. In 1910 and 1911 the Sacramento was not passable with ordinary river craft as far as the city of Sacramento The river boats were compelled to unload, or lighten their loads, below the city and even the smaller vessels were unable to reach the city without great difficulty and delay.

We have the plain declaration of the Board of Engineers for Rivers and Harbors that a nine-foot channel is required in the interest of existing navigation, the expressed declaration, both of that Board and of the California Debris Commission, that seven feet is the present depth of low water, and we can afford abundant evidence that since those reports were made the depth of the channel has decreased and has reached a stage below six feet during certain periods of 1910 and 1911.

THE RELATION OF THE STATE OF CALIFORNIA

When the report of the California Debris Commission was transmitted to the Speaker of the House of Representatives, the Governor of California called an extra session of the Legislature At this session an act was passed which approved and committed the State to the plans and recommendations of the California Debris Commission, as set forth in House Document No. 81; created a board to be known as a Reclamation Board, to be appointed by the Governor; empowered such board to pass upon and approve all plans of reclamation and construction of levees; directed the State Engineer of California to procure data and make surveys and examinations of the project and to report thereon to the Board of Reclamation; and made an appropriation to pay the expenses of carrying out the provisions of the act

It will be observed that $800,000 was placed in the Treasury of the United States, one-half of which was appropriated by the State of California, for the purpose of prosecuting this project This money has been applied to the construction of two large dredges which are used for the improvement of the Sacramento and Feather Rivers The people of California also have acquired, at an expense of nearly one-quarter of a million dollars, the right of way and properties needed for the construction of the first unit of this work Unless this project is carried out as a whole it cannot be made beneficial to any degree The expenditure of $800,-000 in the construction and operation of dredges would be an idle waste of money unless the plan should be consummated in full

Congress, when it appropriated the $400,000, the State of California, when it made a similar appropriation, and the private citizens, when they purchased and paid for the rights of way, understood that the report of 1907 was the basis of those appropriations and expenditures and that this was intended only as part of a continuing project. This was as well understood by Congress as it was by California, because the Act of Congress making the appropriation adopts the report of 1907 and makes the appropriation for the purpose of carrying out the plan embodied in that report. It was clearly understood that this appropriation was only one step in carrying out the express policy declared in the Caminetti Act, and that the recommendation of the report of 1907 was to be supplemented by a perfected plan. This plan has been perfected and is embodied in House Document No. 81, which has been adopted and approved by the State of California, and by the War Department, as the consummation of the directions of the Caminetti Act and subsequent Acts of Congress, and in furtherance of the cooperation that has been understood and acted upon by the United States and the State of California from 1893 to the present time.

It is very manifest that unless Congress adopts this plan, it will repudiate the policy of the Caminetti Act and render ineffective the appropriations that have been made; and, more than this, it will have accepted the money of the State of California and the contribution of its citizens under circumstances that would render its inaction at the present time inequitable, if not plainly violative of its expressed declarations contained in the various Acts of Congress hereinbefore referred to.

At the 1913 session of the Legislature an act was passed known as Senate Bill 1218. This act, which was prepared under the direction of the Flood Control Committee, received unanimous support from the Legislature, as well as from the people whose lands are to be taxed for an enormous expenditure, provides that the construction of levees, the purchase of by-passes and rights of way—all of the plan except the rectification and enlargement of channels and construction of weirs to regulate the flow in the river, so as to encourage the removal of accumulated mining debris by scouring—should be carried out at private expense.

The California Debris Commission kindly assumed the burden of separating, as far as possible, the portion of the plan which related to reclamation and which did not relate directly to navigation, although it has always been understood that a complete separation of these elements is impossible.

As an illustration we call attention to the fact that private interests construct all of the levees along the streams, whereby the water is confined to the channels, promoting scouring and aiding navigation. For this part of the work Congress is not called upon to contribute any sum whatever, although it involves an expense of $7,838,975, as estimated by the Debris Commission.

In many instances in other States, Congress has made appropriations for levee construction where flood control has been the primary object and reclamation the primary purpose. We do not ask this. While we are doing so much for navigation, is it unreasonable for us to request some participation by the Government?

The purchase of rights of way for channel enlargement and rectification by the drainage district, created by the Act of 1913, clearly affects and assists navigation, and this burden is cast upon the district; there is no logical way to separate the two elements. Channel enlargement, in the interests of navigation, also has a resultant influence on the flow of the streams, and, of course, benefits reclamation to some degree.

A supplemental report has been submitted by the California Debris Commission, embodying its conclusions and rearranging the estimates upon a basis considered by it to be fair to the United States. This report has been approved by the Board of Engineers for Rivers and Harbors (see House Doc. No. 5, 63d Congress, 1st session) and by the Chief of Engineers (ib. p. 1).

The estimate of cost by the report of 1910 was $33,000,-000, one-third of which, or $11,000,000, was apportioned to the United States. The supplemental report segregates all except $12,517,000, from which is to be deducted $800,000 already appropriated, leaving $11,717,000 to be borne by the State and Federal Government, $5,858,000 each. This leaves over $20,000,000 of the original estimates to be provided by taxing the land of private owners which would be benefited by the work A considerable portion of these estimates has already been paid by the reclamation of large tracts at private expense. under direction of the State Reclamation Board, which is guided by the Debris Commission

The purpose in urging an approval of the supplemental report and recommendation is that it will harmonize the work in the future, and secure from Congress such action as will clothe the California Debris Commission with jurisdiction over the entire subject In the past the State has carefully complied with the plans and recommendations of the Debris Commission, but it is doubtful if the Commission has jurisdiction over subjects not closely connected with channel improvement and flood control as identified with navigation. It is necessary that there should be a primary head to an enterprise as great as this. The State of California has recognized the Debris Commission as the proper governing influence, and has enacted laws to bind the State to follow this theory Congress, however, has not adopted the plan, and empowered the Debris Commission to execute it, except in part.

The supplemental report now strongly recommends a definite policy, as follows·

First. That the Federal Government should not relinquish control over the entire plan, for the reason that control is necessary to prevent anything being done in one part of the work that affects the general plan, particularly in limiting flood heights

Second. The adoption by Congress of the plan would confer on the Commission power to exercise control over the work done on other elements of the plan than those participated in by the Federal Government It also appears that the plan, as supplemented by the present report, is necessary in the interests of navigation, and apparently the best method of securing reasonable and permanent navigation. It is upon these recommendations that the State of California requests specific, definite approval by Congress of such legislation as will fulfill the requirements for successful execution of the plan. The necessity for Congressional action is urgent and immediate. Of course, one of the objects of the plan is the preservation of life and property, as well as the reclamation of a vast territory of rich land that must be dependent upon the execution of this plan for any kind of cultivation or profit.

There are about 400,000 acres in a comparative state of reclamation, but it will never be safe until the plan is executed. In 1907 millions of dollars' damage was done and nearly all of the reclamation districts were flooded. There are about 300,000 acres more in process of reclamation, because of the expectation that the plan will be carried out, but no one would expect these reclamations to be effective to any degree unless the plan should be executed. It must be borne in mind that all of this reclamation is being made at private expense, and that all of the plan, excepting the river channel improvement and control, is to be paid for by the owners of the land.

NAVIGATION

The interests of navigation are very much involved in the carrying out of this plan. Among the special instances in which navigation is affected we can mention the following:

First. By maintaining a uniform flow of water in the river at its greatest capacity the debris now in the stream, and that which will in due course find its way into the stream, will be carried away by the scouring process and the channel permanently deepened.

Second. The erection of levees along the river by land owners will form part of the reclaiming works to effect a constant flow of water and improve navigation; and these levees should be standardized and controlled by the Debris

Commission, to the end that the channel improvement and rectification shall not be abortive or interrupted by breaks in levees.

Third.   The by-passes, which are to carry the excess water escaping at flood periods, must be controlled so that the flood elevation in the by-passes will not exceed that in the river, and thereby endanger the restraining levees and render the weirs ineffective.

The Board of Engineers for Rivers and Harbors reports

First.   That the execution of the plan as now presented by the Debris Commission is the most economical method by which permanent and practical navigation can be attained and preserved in the Sacramento and Feather Rivers

Second.   That Congress should enact legislation approving the plan, and such modifications thereof as may hereafter be recommended by the proper engineering department of the United States, and giving jurisdiction and control over the plan to the California Debris Commission.

Third.   That the recommendation of the Debris Commission appertaining to the expense is fair and just to the United States.

Fourth   Recommending appropriations from time to time as the work progresses to meet the expenses in accord with the supplemental report of the Debris Commission.

We want an appropriation for the initiation of work on the weirs that are intended to regulate the flood discharge from the river, to the end that the scouring capacity may be maintained to the most practical extent.   The estimate for the whole of this work, including fifteen per cent for contingencies, is $1,860,194.

An initial expense in the purchase of the land required for the weirs must be borne by the land owners, as the title must be turned over to the Government.   This expense will probably reach a sum in excess of $1,000,000.   It would be unwise for the land owners to incur so large an expense, unless Congress manifests some intent of joining the State in constructing the weirs   The drainage district has already begun purchasing lands for by-passes

Any appropriation would be contingent upon acquisition of title to the necessary land, and an equal appropriation by the State. Such action would encourage an advanced movement in the execution of the problem, under the stimulus of an interest displayed by Congress. The drainage district would purchase the by-pass lands, at a cost exceeding $4,000,-000, and pay for them by assessments upon private property. It would be an act of folly for the district to purchase these lands without some indication that the plan will be executed.

It is impossible to measure the importance of a friendly attitude on the part of Congress in establishing a confidence that will result in the complete and early execution of that part of the plan which falls to the share of the people of California.

The immediate construction of one weir, at least, the Sacramento weir, is necessary in the interests of navigation, because. under existing conditions and with all its tributaries in extreme flood at the same time, there would be poured into the Sacramento River 600,000 second-feet of water, while the maximum capacity of the channel, from Sacramento City to Rio Vesta, a distance of about 50 miles, is 100,000 second-feet. The inevitable result would be breaks in the river levees, a pouring of the flood into adjoining basins, and the deposit below each break of mining debris and creation of sand bars which would interfere with navigation until the bars were dredged out at heavy expense.

The Sacramento weir is designed to relieve the Sacramento River of the American river floods (pouring in just above Sacramento City and estimated to have reached in 1861-2 to 180,000 second-feet), and of the excess from the Upper Sacramento and Feather Rivers which will not run into the Yolo Basin. A condition of this kind has not been created within the past three years only because there have been three dry seasons.

These points we desire to press to your attention, in connection with the Sacramento River flood control project:

1. Congress is asked to appropriate no money save in the direct interest of navigation. Expenditures are specifi-

cally confined to (a) deepening and widening the mouth of the river; (b) dredging and rectifying the channel; (c) constructing four weirs over which excess flood waters can be diverted, under control, out of the channel This diversion will prevent the injury to channel and impairment to navigation which has persistently accompanied floods by the depositing of mining debris in great shoals below each break or crevasse.

2.   Of the expense of such portion of this work as is entirely in the interests of navigation, Congress is asked to pay one-half, the State of California paying the other half—$5,800,000 being the share of each

3.   All other expenses of the project, including the erection and maintenance of 503 miles of river levees and 186 miles of by-pass levees, the securing of rights of way for weirs, by-passes and overflow channels (about 85,000 acres) are to be paid by private land owners under assessment to be levied by the State Reclamation Board. This expense, under the original report, 1910, was estimated at $22,000,000, or two-thirds of the entire cost It will very much exceed that amount, because of the higher standard of levees adopted and the evident necessity for bank revetment because of wave wash, due, in the river channel, to passenger boat traffic, and in by-passes, to wind action .

4.   A large portion of the work to be thus done, entirely at private expense and in the interest of reclamation, is also necessary for the preservation of navigation—notably the construction of river levees which preserve the river channel and which, in some other projects, are maintained at Government expense

5   The Government engineers report (see House Document No 81, Sixty-Second Congress, First Session, page 4) that "The interests of navigation, debris control and flood control in the case of this river are so inseparably connected that they should be considered under one great project." They report also (House Document No 5, Sixty-Third Congress, First Session, page 9) that they "know of no way of maintaining navigability with certainty and permanence

except under a plan which is part of a plan for flood and debris control."

It was for these reasons that the original report, in 1910, suggested that Congress pay one-third and California two-thirds of the total estimated expense, $33,000,000   To meet the objections that Congress would thus be appropriating money partly for reclamation work, the subsequent report, February 8, 1913, segregated the elements of the project and assigned to the Federal Government and California, jointly, certain portions manifestly in the interests of navigation, the balance to be paid for by the land owners. The estimated expense to Congress was thus reduced from $11,000,000 to $5,800,000, which is considerably less than one-sixth of the present estimated total expense.

6. The Government engineers agree, after seventeen years' investigation and experiment, that this is the only plan, economically practicable, which will restore and maintain the navigability of the Sacramento River.

The impression that the engineers had reported that this project was not necessary in the interests of navigation was created by the closing sentence of the report of the Board of Engineers for Rivers and Harbors, December 27, 1910 (Document 81), approving this project as recommended by the California Debris Commission. That sentence has been the subject of so much question that in the California Debris Commission report, February 8, 1913, approved by the Board of Engineers for Harbors and Rivers, June 17, 1913 (House Document No 5, before referred to), the conditions are thus clearly set forth (page 9):

> "It is thought that the Board of Engineers for Rivers and Harbors, in stating that the execution of the original plan was not necessary in the interests of navigation, meant to imply that a sufficient degree of navigability could be maintained at less cost. This Commission knows of no way of maintaining navigability with certainty and permanence except under a plan which is part of a

plan for flood and debris control, nor does it seem possible to estimate with certainty the cost of maintaining navigability apart from flood and debris control.

"Should nothing be done to control floods, there is every probability that from time to time navigability will be temporarily destroyed 'To the cost of restoring navigability should then be added the damage done to navigation interests during the periods of non-navigability."

7 While the Sacramento has been charged with all amounts expended on its channel and tributaries, such appropriations have, to a certain extent, benefited the San Joaquin as well. The two rivers are connected in their deltas by various sloughs and waterways; and crevasses or breaks in the east levee of the Sacramento below Sacramento City carry flood and deposits across to the San Joaquin. Navigation in the San Joaquin is largely dependent upon the maintenance of the integrity of the lower Sacramento.

Large amounts have been expended on the Sacramento River by Congress and still should be in pursuance of the policy recognized in the Congressional Act of 1893, creating the California Debris Commission. Because the United States Government, claiming the exclusive right to control the Sacramento as a navigable stream, had failed for years to prevent the pouring therein of debris from hydraulic mines, the navigability was practically destroyed. The act referred to made it the duty of the Debris Commission of Federal Engineers to find some plan which would restore the river to the degree of navigability it possessed in 1860, before the damage was created.

It was in attempting to restore the navigability whose destruction it had permitted, that the Government expended most of the appropriations on this river. And it must be remembered, too, that the State of California expended an equal amount for the purpose The State appropriated from 1897 to 1911 almost $2,000,000 for river improvement in the interests of navigation. These expenditures were necessitated by the failure of the United States to PROTECT the river from injury through hydraulic mining.

8. It is hardly fair, in the case of the Sacramento to gauge the amount of appropriation by the amount of tonnage now shown   The reason is that the tonnage cannot be shown until the necessary measure of navigability is restored   The river would probably have had today a tonnage commensurate with its length and the rich country it traverses if, through neglect of the Government, its navigability had not been allowed to be seriously injured.   The extent and richness of the valley tapped by the river is the measure of the tonnage it will carry if properly improved, and should, it seems, be the measure of appropriation which would be justified in making the necessary improvement.   This, of course, is entirely aside from considerations of equity which might well govern Congress in securing the restoration of the Sacramento to its original condition of navigability.   And yet, notwithstanding grave handicaps, a large and increasing tonnage is shown.

9. Not only is navigation dependent upon the speedy completion of the flood control project, but there is involved also the safety of the Sacramento Valley and the lower portion of the San Joaquin   There is in the districts indicated, including the cities of Sacramento and Stockton, property valued at several hundred million dollars, which will suffer very material injury if big floods come before the project is well advanced.   The danger constantly increases under existing conditions, because, in the absence of waste ways and with the closing of the basin reservoirs through reclamation, the flood plane steadily rises.   California and the property owners are willing and anxious to do their share, and, as a matter of fact, the work under control of the State Reclamation Board is already in advance of that in charge of the Federal Engineers and to be paid for jointly by State and Nation.

The success of the project is dependent upon co-ordinating the work upon its various units, and the California Debris

Commission, in a supplemental report to the Board of Engineers, made in the early part of 1914, calls attention to the necessity for speedy prosecution of the Government's share' of the work In House Document 5, at page 8, the Engineers call attention to the extreme urgency of increasing the channel capacity of the river below Cache Slough, and the rapidity with which reclamation interests are prosecuting their portion of the project.

10. Remembering that the United States Engineers' report that in the problem of the Sacramento the interests of navigation, reclamation, flood control and debris control are so inseparably connected that they cannot be practically and economically served save under one comprehensive project, it is certain that private reclamation has bound itself to pay at least its fair share of the expense, and probably much more. It seems fair to say, too, that in a project absolutely indispensable in the interests of navigation, no other State has made so generous a proposition as has California in this matter, since Congress is called upon to pay much less than one-sixth of the entire cost and less than one-half of the expense directly chargeable to navigation, and this notwithstanding the part of the United States Government in permitting the growth of conditions which created in large part the necessity for the present expensive project. Contrast with other projects will make this point clear.

Never has a State, and never has a population upon any river approached Congress in the same liberal spirit with which California and its people present this problem States and communities are constantly asking donations for flood control, but in no instance within our knowledge have they offered to share so large a proportion of the expense, if any at all. We are asking for less than one-sixth of the whole. We are undertaking a work in which the whole Nation is interested, and one that has always been recognized as one of the burdens of the general Government.

We are contributing one-half of the money applicable to the interests of navigation, and, in addition, we are expending millions of dollars in the construction of restraining levees which directly benefit navigation by keeping the waters within the channels.

We are building up and creating an industrial commonwealth which makes an immediate demand for better navigation to carry the augmented product, and we are presenting to the United States an opportunity to assist in creating a condition which, within a few years, will bring the combined Sacramento and San Joaquin Rivers to the front in commercial importance; they are now occupying the fifth position.

Above all, we are creating homes where useless swamps exist and presenting to the people one of the most productive tracts of land in America. The United States is already proud of California, and by some slight encouragement there will be further cause for congratulating the whole Nation because of the unique and desirable territory that is being developed.

The extent of land to be protected is 1,750,000 acres. The product from this land is now too great to depend upon present navigable capacity of the rivers. We need better navigation, and the commerce of the United States demands that all reasonable improvements be made

The dredging of the mouth of the river will relieve the condition which has been produced by the narrowing of the channel at that point, causing it to become crooked and tortuous. When this choke has been removed, the water will find a free, uniform passage and the debris in the channel above will escape. Control of the water in the upper reaches of the river will prevent deposits and keep the channel clear for navigation.

Caring for these features is purely a function of the Federal Government, the expense of which is usually provided for by Congress alone. When this work has been completed, the problem of navigation on the Sacramento River will be forever settled. It must be remembered that the burden of maintenance of these works, after completion, falls upon the State of California, and that the Federal Government is to be relieved.

Does it not appear to you that California should not ask in vain for friendly consideration?   (Applause.)

President Ransdell—The chair recognizes for one minute Hon. Charles F. MacLean, of New York City.   .

Hon. Charles F. MacLean, Ex-Judge Supreme Court New York City

Mr. President

I desire to read the following resolution:

"In view of the appalling lessons of the European War, through the sudden devastation, by bombardment, of a great seaport city, with consequent destruction of a nation's foreign commerce, be it

"*Resolved,* That this Congress request the Secretary of War to give, in plans for improvement of harbors, special consideration to providing adequate facilities for protection, by our Navy, of the cities immediately upon our seaboard, destruction of any one of which by a foreign fleet would bring commercial ruin to an important section of the Union, destruction of three of which would paralyze the country's commerce for a generation to come."

I ask that this resolution be referred under the rules, Mr President, and that I be permitted to present it to the Committee on Resolutions so soon as we have heard my distinguished friend Mr Cresson.

President Ransdell—Under the rules all resolutions must go before the Resolutions Committee, so this will be referred there.

The chair will now call for a number on our program that we were obliged to omit this morning   Our beloved and very efficient Secretary, Mr S A Thompson, will talk to you briefly on "Our Objects and Methods."

He needs no introduction—Mr Thompson   (Applause.)

OUR OBJECTS AND METHODS

Address—S. A. Thompson, Washington, D. C.
Secretary National Rivers and Harbors Congress

MR PRESIDENT, LADIES AND GENTLEMEN

In so far as you are advocates of waterways—and no doubt
all of you are—if half the things that have been said on the
floor of Congress, if half the things that have been published
by a portion of the press of the country, are justified, the proper
way for me to address you is "Fellow Criminals!"

No doubt the philosophical attitude of mind is the correct
one, but is is sometimes a little difficult to avoid feeling vexed
when those who are devoting their lives to a movement which
they believe is of vital importance to the development of this
great country of ours are vilified and misrepresented, and, not
to put too fine a point upon it, that is what has been done. It
is sometimes hard, at least for me, to stand with patience the
accusations of men who have taken no trouble to ascertain the
facts, even when the facts are right at hand

As an instance—which is important only as showing the
extreme devotion of the man who made it to truth and accuracy
—take the statement made by a Member of the House of Representatives: "I have investigated this National Rivers and
Harbors Congress; it occupies one entire floor in one of the
greatest office buildings in Washington " Now I am unable
to see that there would be anything in the slightest degree improper in our occupying an entire floor, or an entire building for
that matter; but those of you who have been in our offices know
that we have three modest little rooms in the extreme rear of
the eighth floor of the Colorado Building The point is that
the Colorado Building is only a mile from the Capitol and the
Member of Congress referred to could have learned the facts in
less than forty minutes by personal inspection, or in forty seconds by telephone (Applause.) And at that there was a great
deal more truth in his statement about our offices than in many
others that he made.

One of our newspaper critics is not only inaccurate, but, what is even worse from a journalistic standpoint, utterly behind the times This Chicago publication, which claims to be the greatest newspaper on earth, in a recent editorial upon this organization, its officers and its work, speaks about "The National Rivers and Harbors Congress, of which Hon. Joseph E Ransdell, a Representative from Louisiana, is the President," and it inveighs against a provision of our Constitution, which it says it does not believe the members of the organization know is there, or would approve of it if they did know, this provision being one urging that not less than $50,000,000 a year be expended on the waterways of the United States.

"The Greatest Newspaper on Earth" has not yet learned that the former Representative from Louisiana took the oath of office as Senator on the 4th of March, 1913, or that the provision referred to no longer appears in our Constitution, having been dropped at our Convention two years ago. Fifty million dollars a year for the waterways of the United States, let me add, is not too much but too little. With the opportunities we have, with the wealth at our command, with the demonstrated benefits that would follow from such expenditures, if we were a clear-minded, foresighted business people we would be spending, not $50,000,000, but $100,000,000 a year on the waterways of the United States. It is my deliberate judgment that if under the wise control of the Engineers of the Army we should spend a hundred million dollars a year for the next ten years, we would thereafter receive benefits greater than a billion dollars every year as a result

When I note that Germany, which is one of the great nations of the world, either in peace or war, but with an area so small that it could be lost in our State of Texas, had in 1913 a foreign commerce $818,000,000 greater than that of the United States; when I think of Holland and Belgium, two little countries which together are about as large as West Virginia, having a foreign commerce greater by $515,000,000 than that of the United States, and then recall the fact that these countries have the finest system of waterways on earth, I wonder why we cannot see the point and put ourselves in position to compete with them by improving our own waterways

There has been placed in your hands, and will be included in the proceedings of this Convention, a general statement showing our receipts and the objects for which expenditures have been made. None of the members of the organization have inquired as to how many lead pencils we have bought, how many sheets of paper we have used up, or as to details of that kind, but the records are complete and the books are open at any time to you or to anyone who desires to inspect them

There is a letter which I wish to read, but before turning to that I want to say to you that our records are clean and our consciences are clear I am ready at any time to defend my acts as an officer of this organization before any tribunal on earth, but if, as has been proposed, an investigation of the National Rivers and Harbors Congress is ordered, I want that at the same time there shall be ordered another investigation, one which will show what are the influences, sinister or otherwise, that are behind the vituperative attacks that have been made upon us (Applause); the influences, whether sinister or otherwise, that have brought about the amazing result that papers published in cities whose future prosperity, in some cases almost their physical existence, depends upon work that is being done, are calling the rivers and harbors bill a "pork barrel" and a steal, and criticising the National Rivers and Harbors Congress for trying to secure appropriations for the improvement of waterways.

Possibly we ought to feel complimented when a member of the House of Representatives declares that we have conducted "the greatest lobby in all history, compared with which the puny efforts of Mulhall and the National Association of Manufacturers sink into utter insignificance"

In reply to this charge which is as base as it is baseless, let me say to you that, unless the true meaning of that word is utterly different from anything you can find in the dictionary, nothing has ever been done by this organization or by its officers which can be called lobbying without a distortion of the truth.

From the date of the organization of this Congress down to
the present minute, we have loyally lived up to our motto, "Not
a Project but a Policy."   As the officer directly in control of all
the detail work of the organization, I desire to say to you that
I have never gone before a committee of Congress regarding
either a project or a policy   I never by voice, pen, typewriter,
telephone, telegraph or telepathy have ever approached a member of the Senate or House of Representatives· concerning any
item of a river and harbor bill, or concerning a river and harbor bill as a whole, with the single exception of asking at various
times some such question as "Do you think you will be able to
get to the bill this week or next?"   (Applause)

What have we done?   We have carried on a continuous,
nation-wide campaign of education   We have presented to the
people of the country facts and arguments based thereon showing the benefits produced by improved waterways, striving
thereby to create that intelligent, concentrated. forceful public
opinion which is at once the absolutely legitimate and supremely
effective method of influencing the action of the Federal Congress.   (Applause.)

Even if it shall occupy all the rest of my time, I think I
will read one of the letters sent out, from which you can see
the character of the work that has been done.   I may say in
passing that the total sheets in the letters sent out from our
offices during the past year to the newspapers, commercial organizations, mayors of cities, members of this Congress, etc , is no
less than 386,999.   Here is a sample of the kind of letters that
has been sent·

A Sample Letter

———

Washington, D. C.
July —, 1914

Dear Sir.

One of the most violent attacks, if not the most violent. that
has ever been made upon the policy of improving our national
waterways has for some time been in progress in the Senate

of the United States, supported by a portion of the daily press and certain periodicals of wide circulation

Since 1910, when the policy of annual, instead of triennial, River and Harbor bills was adopted, the estimates submitted by the Army Engineers call only for the amount which can probably be expended during the succeeding fiscal year To provide for continuous work on projects already under way, the pending bill should have been passed before July 1st, and already, because of exhaustion of funds, work has been suspended on a number of improvements, and, with every day of delay in the passage of the bill, the number of suspensions will increase.

But that is not the worst of the situation. For many reasons Senators are anxious to get away from Washington; other legislation of great importance, and concerning which there is a wide difference of opinion, is yet to be considered; the River and Harbor bill has had no right of way—it has received only brief and occasional consideration and has now been definitely displaced by the Trust Regulation bills and can receive no further consideration until these have been finally disposed of; the rules of the Senate allow any Senator to speak on any subject to the limit of his endurance—in 1901 Senator Carter, unaided, talked a River and Harbor bill to death; several Senators are cooperating in the present attack; some of them have stated directly that they consider the bill so bad that it ought to be defeated; and the tactics which have been pursued thus far look very much like a filibuster.

Out of about 350 waterway projects only fifteen are under the continuing contract system. On all the rest, if the pending bill fails of passage, work must be stopped for at least a year —costly machinery will rust in idleness, efficient working forces, built up during the past four years, will be disorganized and scattered; uncompleted work will be damaged or destroyed; investments in terminals will be rendered unproductive; the movement, well under way in many parts of the country, for the restoration of navigation on our inland waterways, will receive a serious check, the deepening of our ocean harbors will be delayed while our foreign competitors take the cream of the benefits of the Panama Canal; and the railways will retain their monopoly of transportation for at least another year, meantime redoubling their efforts to retain it for all time by preventing the completion of a national system of connected waterways and harbors

Along with the charge that this bill is "the most vicious and vulnerable" that has ever been framed, must be considered the statement of General Kingman, the Chief of Engineers, "My judgment is that there is less than one-half of one per cent of 'pork' in the River and Harbor bill now pending in the Senate," and the assertions of Senators Simmons, Smith (of Michigan), and Ransdell—all members of the Commerce Committee and of the sub-committee which devoted weeks of conscientious study to the framing of the bill—who have stated on the floor of the Senate that it does not include a single item which is not fully justified and that there is not one cent's worth of "pork" in it.

One of the enemies of the bill has intimated that it is highly improper for the people of a community to seek to promote the improvement of the waterways or harbors in which they are particularly interested, or for a national organization, with an office in Washington, to request that any letters or telegrams shall be sent to Senators or Representatives regarding pending legislation

Nevertheless, I consider it my duty to inform you that, unless the friends of waterways bestir themselves, the bill is likely to fail because, after a month or more of debate on the Trust Regulation bills through the heat of a Washington summer, Senators will be so worn out that it will be very hard to keep a quorum present to consider other legislation, no matter how important it may be.

In the opinion of the writer the failure of the River and Harbor bill would be nothing short of a national disaster. Whether you will take any steps to avert this threatened disaster is a matter which must be left for you to decide.

Very truly yours,

S A THOMPSON, *Secretary*

If there be anyone anywhere who considers a letter of that kind improper, I am totally unable to agree with him. It is my deliberate judgment, Mr. President—and for this statement no one is responsible but myself—that no man has any business to remain in public life in the United States who does not recognize the right of the people to know what legislation is proposed and to express their opinions and their desires regarding that legislation to their duly elected Senators and Representatives, because in this country the people are the supreme power Senator Burton himself once said that the only despotism in the United States is the despotism of public opinion, and I wish to emphasize the statement that the public acts and the public utterances of any American public man are legitimate subjects of discussion and of criticism by any American citizen.

Senator Burton, because he was for so long Chairman of the Rivers and Harbors Committee of the House of Representatives, later was Chairman of the Inland Waterways Commission. and still later Chairman of the National Waterways Commission, came to be recognized as an authority on waterway subjects, and his words, therefore, carry great weight and have great influence. During the twenty-seven days and one whole night in which he spoke on the rivers and harbors bill, he mentioned many projects, but to me the significant thing in Senator Burton's remarks was not his criticism of individual projects, but his statement that water transportation is obsolete and no longer of public benefit; that there are other cheaper and more efficient methods of carrying the products of farm and factory to market; that it is an idle dream and a chimera to think that the traffic which has been taken by the railway can ever be restored to the waterway; and that it would be a waste, a folly and an extravagance to make further expenditures for the improvement of waterways

This means, if it means anything—and no one has ever accused him of ignorance of the English language—that Senator Burton has reached the conclusion that the railway is a better method of transportation than the waterway Whether it be his purpose to bring this about, I do not know, but the one, the only, the necessary, the inevitable result of the course of action, which he advocates would be to give to the railways of the United States an absolute monopoly of inland transportation.

With all due respect to Senator Burton, I deny that water transportation is obsolete, and for proof point you again to Germany, which, even in the midst of the greatest war in all history, is not only maintaining and operating the waterways she already has, but is actually building more. When I look at the waterways of this country and think of its marvelous resources, the development of which has scarcely been begun, I look forward to a time—which perhaps may not come until long after my voice has been silenced forever—when we shall have a great, connected system of waterways in the United States, extending from Boston down the Atlantic Coast to Key West, across the peninsula of Florida and along the Gulf Coast to Brownsville, in Texas, and connecting the Great Lakes both with the Atlantic and the Mississippi and its tributaries, so that a barge-load of goods may be started from any point and sent to any other point on all this great waterway system without breaking bulk When that time comes, and it is sure to come, all the past growth of the United States, wonderful as that has been, will be but as the prologue to the mightiest drama of national development that the world has ever seen. (Applause.) And yet those who are striving to bring this about are called criminals seeking to loot the public treasury for private ends!

If Senator Chamberlain, of Oregon, is right, we may expect a continuation of that kind of talk, and even more of it than we have yet had. He said to me some time ago that as long as the railroads were free to use any kind of cut-throat competition which they chose to kill off water transportation, they paid no attention to the waterway movement or to the National Rivers and Harbors Congress, but now that Section 11 of the Panama Canal Act has been passed—and I am proud to say that this organization had an honorable share in securing its passage—and signs of the restoration of water traffic are appearing in all parts of the country, they are paying a great deal of attention to us

In this connection, let me emphasize the fact that the friends of waterways are not opposed to railways, and that the development of transportation by water will not injure but will greatly benefit the interests of the railways In a study of the subject covering nearly thirty years, I have never been able to find a single instance anywhere, in any country, or at any time, in which the improvement of an existing waterway or the creation of a new one has done anything else than increase the business and the dividends of a railroad running alongside. (Applause.) The prosperity of the railroads depends upon the prosperity of the people, and no other one thing so powerfully promotes the prosperity of cities, states or nations as the cheap transportation furnished by waterways.

The credit—or the blame, according to the way you look at it—for defeating the River and Harbor Bill of 1914, or of compelling its passage in a diminished and mutilated form, belongs more to Senator Burton than to anyone else It is much easier to defeat a river and harbor bill, or any other bill, at the short session of Congress than at the long one, and according to press reports, he has announced his intention to prevent the passage of a river and harbor bill at the coming short session of Congress. If he shall do so, the distinguished senior Senator from Ohio can carry with him, when he leaves public life on the fourth day of March, next, the consciousness, whether it be satisfactory or otherwise, that he has done more to delay the development of this country than any other man who was ever elevated to public position in the United States.

But the President admonishes me that my time is up. Let me repeat that any committee of Congress, any tribunal, any one of you or any man off the street is free to come to my office at any time. I will open every book that I have; I will show him everything that has been done, and if he be a man who is sane and fair-minded, I have no question as to the result.

As my last word, I want to say that if working for the development of this great country of ours through the improvement of its waterways constitutes a man a criminal, as has been charged, then here is one criminal, at least, who is not only unrepentant—but defiant   (Applause)

PRESIDENT RANSDELL—We are now to hear from the Atlantic Coast A very interesting question, "New Jersey's Relation to the Port of New York," will be discussed by Mr. B F Cresson, Jr, Chief Engineer, New Jersey Harbor Commission—Mr Cresson   (Applause.)

NEW JERSEY'S RELATION TO THE PORT OF NEW YORK

Address—B. F. Cresson, Jr., Jersey City, N. J.
Chief Engineer New Jersey Harbor Commission

MR. PRESIDENT, LADIES AND GENTLEMEN:

The development of the Port of New York should be of as much interest to the people of this country as any other waterway or port question. It is well known that at the present time New York is handling more foreign commerce than all other ports of the United States combined. Statistics show that, before the outbreak of the European war, New York was handling about 47% of the total foreign commerce of the country, and this percentage at the present time is largely increased It, therefore, is to the interest of the industries of the country that the Port of New York shall develop along economic lines and that the facilities there should be such as to make the passage of commerce as easy, as cheap and as rapid as possible

The speaker was invited by Commissioner Henry Byrne, of Jersey City, to present a paper which would bring before this very important Congress the opportunities, as well as the needs, of New Jersey. It is, of course, impossible in a brief paper to more than touch on these questions Only last year the New Jersey Harbor Commission presented to the Legislature a report under this same title containing more than 200 pages, and it did not begin to exhaust the subject.

New Jersey is to the Port of New York a good deal as the Port of New York is to the United States. It has been stated above that a large part of the foreign commerce of the country passes through this port, and this commerce must be received from and distributed throughout the country largely by the great railroad systems; with the exception of the New York Central Railroad and the New Haven Railroad, all of the great systems terminating at the Port of New York have their tidewater terminals in the New Jersey portion of the harbor, and New Jersey is the medium through which this distribution of commerce takes place. New Jersey, therefore, has been used at important points in the Port of New York largely for the transshipment of freight and her valuable frontage has been taken up with railroad facilities. Great stretches of waterfront which might be devoted to factories and warehousing are now used as railroad yards for the handling of commerce passing through the port. There is probably no port in the world where desirable locations are in such demand; New York receives enormous rentals for piers on the North River and New Jersey could do likewise if it could devote its North River frontage to other than railroad purposes Railroads are generally a benefit to a community, but, in the case of the waterfront of Jersey City on the North River, they have been a positive detriment and hindrance.

The establishment of a uniform railroad rate throughout the greater part of the harbor has made it possible for factories and industries to locate in parts of the harbor where railroad connections do not exist, and the railroads must deliver freight to them and to shipping in other parts of the harbor at the same rate that they do to the rail terminals in New Jersey, even though lighterage enters into the former service.

It cannot be denied that New York has been far more progressive in developing its industries and its waterfront; New Jersey has lacked control over its waterfront and this has, therefore, been used to a great extent to serve the better organized and administered parts of the harbor in New York

It is logical to bring ships with cargoes for transshipment by rail alongside of railroad tracks, and this is done almost everywhere except in the Port of New York. Here the steamship terminals are massed in the New York portion of the harbor, the railroad terminals are massed in the New Jersey portion of the harbor, and an enormous amount of lighterage of freight is therefore necessary There are more than sixty steamship lines with regular sailings to foreign ports docking at piers in the New York portion of the harbor, and not one of these piers has a direct rail connection with the great transcontinental railroad systems of the country. New Jersey has magnificent steamship terminals in Hoboken from which the German and Dutch and Scandinavian lines —six in number—have their sailings, but even at these piers, owing to the lack of any general terminal railroad organization, the advantage of rail sidings on the piers is not fully utilized.

There has been too much of rivalry between the railroads and too much of individual development There is no joint railroad system in the harbor in the full meaning of the word, and owing to this, and to the establishment of free lighterage, the harbor waters have been employed as the joint transportation system about the harbor, free for the use of all the carriers

Costs are increasing in railroad operation, the terminal costs are now excessive, and it seems logical to believe that the extensive individual railroad terminal systems and operations will give way to a joint operation under which costs may be reduced and better and quicker service rendered. A large amount of duplication of service could be eliminated by the railroads pooling their interests instead of each trying to operate its own terminal system; and a big, well-organized system can unquestionably be operated with less unit costs than a number of small systems

New Jersey is vastly interested in having a general railroad terminal system adopted at the Port of New York. Without it, and with the necessities of the individual railroad companies, New Jersey can scarcely hope to release its waterfront on the Hudson River from railroad yards With a general joint railroad system, there would come the opportunity to substitute for railroad yards, steamship piers and behind them warehouses and factories, which could do business with the railroads directly on their sidings, and not experience the delays and drawbacks incident to the lighterage of freight

Such great companies as the Bush Terminal Company and the New York Dock Company located in Brooklyn— the former alone bringing a population of some 50,000 to its district and paying taxes in excess of $1,000 a day—show the possibilities about New York harbor. With a joint railroad system in New Jersey, similar terminal companies could locate in New Jersey directly on railroad sidings, which would not be dependent upon lighterage for every pound of their railroad freight, as is the case with the companies above referred to

New Jersey has now a commission—the New Jersey Harbor Commission—with power to act in the interests of the State where before none existed. It is ready and anxious to cooperate with New York in all questions of port organization New York has so far not been able to adopt any general port plan, but many plans have been advanced in the past, and the Board of Estimate and Apportionment of New York City is now considering a plan for a general terminal railroad system

New York needs a railroad reorganization very badly in order to make better and more economic use of its waterfront But New York cannot accomplish a reorganization by itself; it must consider the condition in New Jersey and the two States must work together. Rivalries and jealousies must be eliminated, for that which can be accomplished by a general terminal system will be vastly beneficial to the interests in both States; New Jersey is now ready and willing to cooperate

In addition to creating a State Harbor Commission, New Jersey has enacted laws whereby municipalities can develop their waterfronts Newark is at work, as is Trenton;

Camden and Jersey City have municipal piers, and the whole State seems to be awakening to its commercial possibilities.

Jersey City, through its local government, is planning a model industrial city on its Hackensack River frontage, in a locality where that river can lead shipping to and from the New York harbor proper, and where a joint terminal railroad can immediately be built tying in to three of the great railroad systems, with ample room on what is now undeveloped property to lay out industries and to provide for the population which will come by reason of industries   This is within easy riding and trucking distance of all the activities in the great metropolitan district.

Elizabeth, Bayonne, and Perth Amboy, as well as the communities on the Hudson River, are all alive to the advantages which their location brings them.

When the New Jersey Ship Canal, making an inland waterway between the Delaware and Hudson Rivers, shall be constructed, great opportunities will be created at Perth Amboy, at Camden, Trenton, and all along its route.   In the opinion of many there is no more important link in the entire Intracoastal Waterway project than the New Jersey Ship Canal   There will be required Federal appropriations for construction of the canal itself, for dredging in the Raritan Bay and in the Delaware River.   In connection with this project the Government should make an appropriation to examine into the feasibility of rendering the Delaware River navigable, at least as far north as the cities of Easton and Phillipsburg.

Dredging is needed, however, along the New Jersey waterfronts and in its rivers   Camden needs a greater depth of water; Perth Amboy needs it; Newark Bay needs it; and particularly is it needed on the New Jersey frontage of the Hudson River   There is probably no river in the world which carries so great a tonnage as this river—the lighterage adding greatly to it—and on its shores dock the finest and largest ocean liners built.   Liverpool, London, Havre, Antwerp, Glasgow, Rotterdam, Bremen, Hamburg and Genoa are some of the ports in Europe which have been sending their best and largest ships to New York and docking them in the Hudson River. There should be sufficient depth of water in the Hudson River from pierhead line to pierhead line for the largest vessels built to manœuvre in and to find dockage on either shore. Some of the Jersey City frontage on the Hudson River now lacks enough water by fifteen feet to float the *Vaterland* and much difficulty was experienced on the maiden trip of this ship in docking her, which would probably not have occurred if there had not been shoal water in the river immediately south of her pier in Hoboken

The Federal Government has been most solicitous in regard to keeping the Hudson River from being unduly narrowed, and properly so, but it has permitted the river to remain, opposite Jersey City at least, with only about half of its width available for deep draft vessels. It is true that a thirty-foot channel 800 feet wide along this frontage has been authorized, but this will not accommodate the largest types of vessels using this port. The lack of deep water on the Jersey City frontage was emphasized recently when one of the great steamship companies sought to obtain dockage for its large ships on the New Jersey side of the Hudson River, but was prevented from completing its negotiations because of insufficient depth of water.

The New York portion of the Hudson River frontage is badly congested, but, by railroad reorganization and a deepening of the river, New Jersey can help accommodate the growing commerce, and can do it economically, by opening up industrial opportunities it can relieve the New York portion of the harbor of industries which can be better accommodated where there is room to spread out and where they can have the benefit of direct rail connection.

The New Jersey frontage in the Upper Bay needs a channel; at the present time much of the shore front in Bayonne is as much as 12,000 feet from the channel as it now exists, and pierhead and bulkhead lines must be established and channels dredged in order to bring this most valuable frontage into service. These things will add to the facilities at the Port of New York, and in doing so will play an important part in aiding the commerce of the Nation passing through this port; and at the same time will be of benefit to the State of New Jersey by increasing its industries and through this its rateables and its population   (Applause.)

This concludes my paper on "New Jersey's Relation to the Port of New York," but there is another matter which I would like to bring before this Convention very briefly I wish I could paint a word picture of the scenes I have witnessed on the New Jersey coast during this week's great storm On Monday I went down to Long Branch and for an hour or two walked along the boardwalk, as best I could, watching the assault of the waves upon the bulkheads and jetties   It was a wonderful sight, the wind was blowing full sixty miles an hour, and the sea was tremendous. The bulkheads there were standing up mostly in good shape, but at many places they were being weakened by the force of the waves.

On Tuesday, with one of the officials of the New Jersey State Chamber of Commerce, I went down to Seabright, where the storm had done the most damage   We had to drive from Red Bank, as the railroad was out of commission The situation at Seabright can almost be regarded as desperate   Scores of houses had been undermined and had collapsed, and bulkheads, well designed and built, had been battered to pieces.   About last Christmas a great storm visited Seabright, and another last January, but the municipality and the citizens got together and spent thousands of dollars to rebuild and strengthen the bulkheads. The work they then did seems to have been of no avail for the wreck caused by this week's storm is greater than any previous storm has caused   The Mayor of Seabright said to me, "I think Seabright is done for; I don't believe the people will rebuild unless we can get help to effectively guard against disasters like this."

It is not that Seabright has encroached upon the ocean and is suffering on that account. Formerly the beach extended considerably outshore from where the houses are now located, but there is a general northerly shift of the sands and the beaches have been eroded. The whole north Jersey beach front stands in danger from the movement of the sand It is not a local problem. The New Jersey coast serves a wide area as a health resort and a summer recreation ground, and the danger that threatens it is of national consequence. This week's storm is said to have caused more than $1,000,000 damage

Next Wednesday, at the Capitol in Trenton, a hearing will be held under the auspices of the New Jersey State Chamber of Commerce. The New Jersey Harbor Commission has been asked to sit at the hearing, as have also the United States District Army Engineers. Governor Fielder will preside Citizens, civic organizations, municipal officials and private interests will be asked to lay before the meeting all available information and to make recommendations as to the methods to pursue An effort will be made to have the whole subject studied and to devise means whereby the citizens, the private interests, the municipalities, the counties and the State may cooperate and to urge the Federal Government to also lend its aid Would it be proper for this Convention to adopt resolutions directing the attention of the Federal Government to this situation and urging that at least it receive Federal investigation and study? (Applause.)

PRESIDENT RANSDELL—The next on our program is an address, "The Merrimac River," by Mr. Andrew B Sutherland, a member of the Massachusetts Merrimac Valley Waterway Commission.

I wish to say that this gentleman headed a large delegation, seventy-five in number, if I mistake not, who came here on their own special train this afternoon to present their views before the Rivers and Harbors Committee—Mr Sutherland (Applause.)

THE MERRIMAC RIVER

Address—Andrew B. Sutherland, Lawrence, Mass.
Member State Merrimac Valley Waterway Commission

MR PRESIDENT, LADIES AND GENTLEMEN:

You have heard about rivers in the South and in the West, but we have a river in New England, not as large as some of your rivers throughout this great country, but one of the most important rivers industrially that there is in the United States. Two years ago I was appointed on a State Commission to investigate the Merrimac River, and we who live there in the Merrimac Valley realize what an important position in the industrial world the Merrimac Valley occupies and the important character of its industries

The Merrimac is a river only 110 miles long, fifty miles of which is in the State of Massachusetts and which we propose to develop. On that fifty miles of the Merrimac River we have 307,000 people, and we have there built up some of the greatest industries not only of this country but of the world In the Massachusetts part of this valley are the prosperous manufacturing cities of Lowell, Lawrence, Haverhill and Newburyport

We bring into that valley annually $116,000,000 worth of raw materials. that is only on the Massachusetts section of the river There are three other industrial cities further up the river in the State of New Hampshire. From this valley we send out annually over $196,500,000 worth of finished product. Add this to the raw materials, and you have an aggregate of $313,500,000.

Now. gentlemen, when you trip those figures quickly off your tongue they may not carry a great deal of force; but when you compare them with statistics elsewhere do you realize that that sum amounts to seven and one-half per cent of the entire foreign trade of the United States? (Applause.) It amounts to more than twelve and a half per cent of the entire foreign trade of France: it is more than thirty per cent of the entire foreign trade of Canada Do you know that Canada has spent over $360,000,000 in improving her rivers. harbors and canals in order to develop her foreign commerce? It amounts to twenty-five per cent of the entire imports and exports of Austria-Hungary or of the Russian Empire Just imagine— in that little space up there in the Merrimac Valley, in Massachusetts, our trade is equal to twenty-five per cent of the foreign commerce of that great Russian Empire which extends almost from the Atlantic to the Pacific and across Europe and Asia, and then, when you pass over further to the Orient, our trade is almost fifty per cent of the entire foreign trade of China, and over fifty per cent of the foreign trade of Japan

Now how do we compare with other places in this country? Why, these figures represent a larger commerce than any of the seaports in the United States, with the exception of the single port of New York. They represent a greater commerce than that of any of the seaports in the western hemisphere, with the exception of New York and Buenos Aires They are greater than the foreign commerce of any country on this western hemisphere, with the exception of the United States, Canada, Brazil, and the Argentine Republic.

It exceeds the foreign trade of Galveston, our second seaport, by over $24,000,000 It exceeds the foreign trade of New Orleans, our third seaport, by $61,000,000. It exceeds the foreign trade of Boston, our fourth seaport, by $97,000,000. It exceeds the foreign trade of Manchester, England, where almost $100,000,000 have been spent in constructing a thirty-six mile canal with a magnificent system of docks, by $37,000,000 It exceeds the foreign trade of Glasgow, Scotland, where $50,000,000 have been spent in dredging and dock construction, by $66,000,000

We clothe the people of this country from the Merrimac Valley. We manufacture all kinds of textiles in Lawrence and Lowell When you gentlemen go to your tailor, to buy a suit or an overcoat, the tailor shows you his best pieces of cloth which he calls best English or Scotch goods, but in all probability the goods were made in Lawrence by the American Woolen Company, or some other of our high grade woolen or worsted manufacturers

Let me digress here to say that this RIVERS AND HARBORS CONGRESS is a splendid organization and has accomplished great and lasting good for this country, but I would like to see another organization equally as representative as this of all the States in the Union with its rallying cry, "American Made Goods for the American People." (Applause)

Our cotton and woolen fabrics manufactured in Lawrence and Lowell are the best in the world. I want the word to go out through this country that American Goods are the best in the world (Applause). We will clothe you from head to foot We have textiles in Lowell, textiles in Lawrence and boot and shoe factories in Haverhill We have three of the most important cities in New England, industrially speaking, right there on the banks of the Merrimac

Now, gentlemen, the United States Engineers have examined the possibilities for development of that river, and the State of Massachusetts is so much interested in the development of this splendid proposition that last year the Massachusetts Legislature made an appropriation of $1,000,000 towards this work and we feel that the United States ought to adopt the project and complete the work

This project means an expenditure of $7,250,000 The State of Massachusetts has appropriated $1,000,000 already in order to show that it is in earnest in this undertaking That bill passed by a tremendous majority Out of about three hundred representatives only fourteen opposed it—and they were from away in the back woods country where they never heard of the Merrimac River. (Laughter)

There has been a lot of talk here about economy Why we can pay for that expenditure in a few years, for the raw materials alone that come in would effect a saving of $1,600,000 a year in freight charges We handle in the valley over 6,000,000 tons of freight The $1,600,000 is based on the saving on inward freight only and basing our figures on the figures of a German writer, and the Germans are perhaps the most reliable we can find when it comes to statistical problems, we estimate that from one-fifth to one-quarter can be saved in exports, and that would bring our savings up to almost $2,000,000 We ask the United States Government to put in

$6,250,000 in order to effect benefits that will save that sum in three years (Applause)

You have a number of very important waterway propositions throughout the country, but there is not any that is in the class with the Merrimac River. It is in a class by itself (Applause), because we have got the tonnage, we have got the freights and we have the mills. Why, we have one mill in Lawrence that you can start to walk around and walk for a mile and a quarter before you get back to where you started We have similarly large factories in Lowell and in Lawrence. so that we are one of the most important sections not only in Massachusetts but in all this great country. We believe that this is the best project for development that has been brought to the attention of this Congress.

Ladies and gentlemen, I thank you for your attention. (Applause.)

PRESIDENT RANSDELL—We are now about to hear from one of our Directors, who is one of the biggest business men in the Mississippi Valley. He has some very valuable thoughts to give to us

Allow me to present to you Mr. J W. Cooper. St. Paul, Minn. (Applause) You notice his marked resemblance to a great man, Mr James J. Hill, who spoke before you some years ago on different lines and in reference to a different branch of business.

Address—J. W. Cooper, St. Paul, Minn.

Director National Rivers and Harbors Congress

MR. PRESIDENT AND GENTLEMEN·

Seldom, if ever, in the commercial history of our country, has prophecy been so quickly fulfilled as that made only a year ago at your last meeting.

It was then predicted that the opening of the Panama Canal would change the entire existing systems of freight rates. as well as revolutionize the old methods employed in making and maintaining said rates The over twenty-five millions of people of the greater Mississippi Valley—about one-quarter of our entire population—are awakening to an entirely new situation They now find that instead of adjusting freight rates to apply to the entire country—both terminals and intermediate points—on the general basis that all should be dealt with alike, the Interstate Commerce Commission is now adjusting, or trying to fix. rates and freight regulations to apply to communities. This has created such changed conditions that, taken in connection with the opening of the Panama Canal, something must be done to protect the interests and conserve the welfare of the great Mississippi Valley.

Here are a very few concrete examples of the changed conditions. Rates on certain products from California and Washington State to New York are twenty-five cents per hundred. Now on these same products, the rate from New York to Mississippi Valley points, plus the Panama Canal rate for these products makes the rate much lower than the all rail rate now in existence. It therefore follows that certain commodities may be shipped via the Panama Canal to New York by water, then by rail to the Mississippi Valley, at a less rate than the all rail rates now being paid

The freight on salmon from Seattle clear across the continent is seventy cents per hundred, and that is a blanket rate or supposed to be But the Interstate Commerce Commission has established a salmon rate of sixty cents to Chicago and fifty-five cents to Pittsburgh, leaving the seventy cent rate intact to all intermediate points These rates were made solely because the Panama Canal rate from Seattle to New York, plus the rate to the point of destination is lower than the all rail rates—another illustration of how the Canal is going to change the entire shipping traffic

The same conditions exist in regard to all rail rates from New Orleans to water terminals on the Atlantic Coast There is a lower rate to these points than to the intermediate cities and towns. All rates from Chicago to South Atlantic Coast points do not apply to intermediate points A zone rate, so-called. is being put into operation, which is a graduated raise in freight rates of seven per cent over the rates in operation at the interior points. If this system is insisted on it is self-evident that it will destroy the shipping business of the West, and demoralize the producing capacity of a rich and populous section of the country. Starting from Chicago, this zone rate strikes at most of the prosperous cities of the Mississippi Valley.

Now the Mississippi Valley people cannot stand for such a condition. What is the remedy? We must have these existing all-rail rates lowered so that competition will be equal and opportunities the same in the Mississippi Valley as in other sections, or else we must resort to a tremendous shipping movement on the Mississippi River from New Orleans to all the up-river country. (Applause.) I believe, and it is susceptible of demonstration, that thousands of tons of freight can be sent from the Pacific Coast to New Orleans for less than the water rates from the Pacific Coast to New York, and I have heard some mighty strong arguments by experts to prove that it would be impossible for an all-rail rate to be made low enough to meet this New Orleans competition.

What is the remedy again? We propose to put boats on the broad waters of the Mississippi River, and then see to it that water transportation shall be protected, and that the Interstate Commerce Commission shall put into practical operation the following provision of the Hepburn Bill:

> "Whenever a carrier by railroad shall, in competition with a water route or routes, reduce the rates on the carriage of any species of freight to or from competitive points, it shall not be permitted to increase such rates unless, after hearing by the Interstate Commerce Commission, it shall be found that such proposed increase rests upon changed conditions other than the elimination of water competition."

It is said that river terminals are difficult upon the river because of their use and control by the railroads and that an effort ought to be made for all cities to have river terminals that will protect them in the use of river traffic. In the Northwest there are five million people tributary to the Twin Cities. We are the wheat-growing country and with the adjustment of rates

the Mississippi River would make the product of the farmer
more valuable and carry it to countries from New Orleans
equally as well as from any other point.

I believe that all California products would come via New
Orleans. I believe that our coffee from Brazil would come
through New Orleans. I believe that our foreign goods would
come through New Orleans I believe that every pound of cane
sugar used in our market would come from New Orleans and
we would get rid of the present condition in the sale of sugar,
which makes the rate from New York practically apply to all
points.

In the sale of glucose, made from the grains grown in the
West, we are forced to purchase at the Chicago price and freight
to the point of sale, regardless of the point of manufacture. So
that the farmer, in the sale of his product made into glucose, is
obliged to buy the product back at a much higher price than
had the laws of trade in their sale been established

In the article of cereals, we can say that their distribution
has been injurious to the railroads carrying them, expensive to
the consumer and destructive to the merchant handling them.
They are carried upon the grain rate of which they are made;
they are put into packages of different kinds and usually sold
from Portland, Maine, to Portland, Oregon, at the uniform
price established by the manufacturer, so that the users of these
products pay a much higher price for them than they should
if the ordinary trade conditions pertain in their manufacture
and sale It is expected that the laws recently enacted will, in
a certain degree, correct evils of this character and make it
possible for all parts of our country to manufacture the things
that they consume, upon a basis that will be satisfactory to
those who produce the Nation's wealth upon our farms The
great Mississippi Valley offers wonderful opportunities for the
production of all kinds of materials used by them and, with
the development of the water powers along the stream. I can
see no reason why the great Mississippi Valley should not be
independent along these lines

I am of the opinion that the railroad rates might be adjusted,
so that there will be no difficulty in financing the railroads of

the country. We cannot expect that money would be invested in railroads unless their income provided a fair return upon the money invested and, if the great change takes place that is predicted, these adjustments should be made to protect them in the change of traffic that this will bring about.

I say that the people residing in the Mississippi Valley and its tributaries should say to Congress: "We ask that you appropriate money enough to make these rivers equally available; and, if we have not sufficient laws to protect money invested in boats upon the river, by reason of the rail rates that might be made in opposition to them, that such laws shall be provided." (Applause.)

I believe this is a fair business proposition and should have the attention of our Members of Congress, because the acts of Congress in reference to protecting the men upon our soils will be carried out if the Mississippi River and its tributaries are made available for river transportation. This will add to the value of every bushel of grain carried; it will decrease the cost of material that they use; it will add to the manufacturing industries along the river and create a district that will be the pride of our Nation; and will carry out, as far as I can see, what is the wish of Congress concerning its citizens (Applause)

PRESIDENT RANSDELL—The New York Barge Canal system is one of the greatest in the world and in connection with it Hon. James S Parker, Member of Congress from New York, now wishes to say a few words about the Hudson River (Applause)

Address—James S. Parker, M. C., New York

MR. CHAIRMAN AND GENTLEMEN ·

I only want to take up a few minutes of your time, because I know the hour is getting late and you have heard many very instructive papers read. I am not prepared to make a set speech; but, when I listen to the other gentlemen from different parts of the country describing their propositions, I realize that this is the occasion when we all get together, and this is the time that we must stand together for river and harbor improvements throughout the United States (Applause.)

Each one of us comes here with a pet proposition in which our own communities or localities are particularly interested; I think, without any fear of contradiction, with due respect to the gentleman who advocated the Merrimac River, that we of the State of New York come here with a proposition that is the most important of any in the United States. (Applause)

You know in many communities you have to stimulate the interest of the people in waterways, but you do not have to do that in the State of New York   The fact that we have appropriated $120,000,000 ourselves for our Barge Canal is sufficient proof that we do not need any enlightenment on that subject   (Applause.)   You do not have to come up there to educate us in that respect; but we do want the United States Government to carry forward the improvement of the Hudson River so that our Barge Canal will be effective

The gentleman from New Jersey spoke regarding the congested facilities in the harbor of New York. That is quite true, and we wish, with him, that a speedy remedy might be found for those congested conditions in the harbor of New York, because they affect the efficiency of the Barge Canal   It is expensive to handle, transport and transfer freight to and from ocean steamers and coastwise steamers and barges, and it is especially onerous when you have to pay the exorbitant charges that are paid in New York.

We believe that the United States Government should consider it not unreasonable when we suggest to it that the thing to do is to build a channel 400 feet wide and thirty-five feet deep to the dam at Troy. How much will it cost? $15,000,000. We of New York have already spent $120,000,-000; and that, gentlemen, was not a partisan movement, it was not a scheme to take money out of the pockets of the people. It was carried by a majority vote of all the people after being submitted to referendum, and they decided that they wanted the Barge Canal, and they have got it.

Now all that we ask is that you gentlemen stand with us. We are with you The State of New York pays one-fifth of all of your taxes. We are for your proposition, whether it be for the especial benefit of California or whether it be for the benefit of New Hampshire, or wherever it may be. We do not care where it is, because what benefits one benefits all. We believe that you have got more votes in the Senate than ever, and we think in all fairness that you should stand behind us and enable us to complete what we have begun and carried forward as far as we could.

Some gentlemen have said that the Government will let us go on and improve the Hudson River. That is a mistake; the Government will not do that. If the Government would allows us to do that we would do it; but I doubt if it would agree to that. The United States Government would not allow us to go on and improve the harbor of New York. If it would allow us, we would do all this work with reference to the Hudson River, but the United States Government says, "No, you cannot do it, it is a navigable stream and subject to Federal control." I believe you stand for what is right. I believe you exercise a tremendous force and influence. We ask you to stand behind us, and see that the State of New York and the Hudson River gets a good, fair and square deal.

If it were possible, and in order, I would offer a resolution to this effect, but I understand that it is not in order. I have a resolution here, I will not offer it, but I believe and hope that you will unitedly stand behind us and see that the Barge Canal, which affects about one-third of the people of the United States, is made increasingly efficient through the improvement of the Hudson We do not charge the people who grow the grain on the Great Lakes anything to send it through our canal. It is ours; we built it; we paid for it; but we do not charge you a cent on the tonnage going through that canal. It is free. You are reaping just as much benefit as we are, but we do ask you that you stand behind us and complete what we have commenced and have paid for.

Gentlemen, I thank you for your attention. (Applause.)

President Ransdell—The last address of the afternoon will be made by a man whom we have all heard before, and many of us have read with pleasure his addresses on river and harbor topics. For years he has been a very eminent engineer, and he has now concluded his active career as Chief Engineer of the United States Army.. He has spoken at many of our Conventions and has always given us the best advice.

Ladies and gentlemen, rise and join with me in honoring Gen. William H. Bixby, Ex-Chief of Engineers, U. S. A., who wishes to say a few words to you. (Applause, the audience rising in honor of General Bixby.)

Address—Gen. William H. Bixby, Washington, D. C.
Late Chief of Engineers, U. S. Army

Mr. President, Fellow Members of the National Rivers and Harbors Congress, Ladies and Gentlemen:

It is hard, probably, for you to realize what a great pleasure it is to me to come back here once a year, now that I am out of an executive position and have no official relation with river and harbor improvement, and hear you all discuss the work of this development of the waterways. And it seems to me, after listening to what has been said yesterday and what has been said today, that perhaps I am in a better position to make a few suggestions to you in this work than would be even the Engineers who are in active service, or Members of Congress, or Senators, or even the officers of this association; because I am in a position now where my recommendations do not affect me individually. Everybody in Washington that knows anything about my present conditions knows that I must naturally be now quite unbiased in my views.

There are two or three thoughts that come to me today which it seems to me I might properly suggest to you. It is very pleasant for me to meet you gentlemen and ladies once a year, bringing projects here from various parts of the country, discussing them, framing your resolutions, and adopting them. All such work is valuable to you; and it is, moreover, exceedingly valuable to your representatives in Congress, because this is a representative country, because ours is a representative Government, and Congressmen here depend on what the people at home say, in order that when they get up on the floor of Congress to talk, they can do so much better if they know that the people are with them.

Whatever the people in this country really want, they are going to get, providing they make their ideas clear enough to their representatives in Congress and give them good solid facts and reasons therefor. One of the necessary and most valuable things that you can do is to collect good solid facts and reasons and present them to your representatives both here and at home, and see that your representatives on the floor of Congress have sufficient ammunition in readiness to defend their actions in your interests, so that, if any one at any time attempts to raise a word of objection to the improvement of the waterways, they can give him solid facts and reasons that will convince him of the error of his ways. Everyone of you can do such work, and everyone of you will benefit if you do it when you get home.

Then there is another way in which you ought to use your personal influence at home, and that is with the local press. The press, all over the United States, is bound to talk about all things of public interest which are up before Congress. The newspaper men do not always know what is right, but they have to say something. One of them said to me once in Chicago, when he came around to talk to me, "Did you see that interview with you that I used last night?" I said, "Yes, and I have been wondering whether I had got to talking in my sleep." He said, "Well, I had to write up something, and I couldn't get you at your house and so I had to go ahead and write an interview the best I could. I hope it was right, but if it was not right I will be glad to

write another article correcting it if you will tell me how to
do it." (Laughter.)

That is the way with press writers all over the country.
They have to say something. You come here and you hear
all these discussions and you get better posted on waterways
than your local newspaper men at home. You will find that
often things get into the papers that are not true, or, at least,
not correct, but they are more often incorrect through ignorance than through any intention to tell an untruth. When
you see incorrect statements, write your newspaper man a
letter, tell him the facts, tell him the real situation, and the
chances are that he will come around to your views and back
you up. (Applause.)

I know once in my own experience a prominent New
York paper had published an article reflecting not only
against the Army Engineers, but against the views of the
Ｎational Ｒivers and Ｈarbors Ｃongress. I sat down and
wrote a page letter to the editor, and marked it "Personal and
not to be printed;" just a little note saying that it was for the
information of the editor the next time he printed anything on
that subject, which, in this particular case, happened to be a certain improvement on the South Atlantic Coast. The result was
that the editor sent members of his staff down to the South.
Atlantic Coast to examine the situation, and inside of three
months he came out with a statement in his paper which stopped
forever its attacks against waterway improvement, and changed
its waterway policy permanently. Its subsequent printed views
were different from what they had been before. My request
had a quieting effect, which was just as good as if I had taken
a much more violent course. Now you can make real friends
of the representatives of the press, every one of you, in the
same way by quietly and courteously bringing to their attention the solid facts within your own personal knowledge.

Now here are one or two things that I think you could do
very nicely. Some of the papers recently have talked about
the waterways not being as good or not being as useful as the
railroads. Now the waterways constitute one-third of the
transportation facilities of the country, which consist of the

ordinary highways, or roads, railroads and waterways. The
waterway is a tool of transportation Without actual tools
you cannot do much of anything useful A farmer who has
not proper farming tools would hardly make a success of
agriculture A merchant, if he did not advertise and equip
himself with a good office force, with the necessary clerks,
stenographers and typewriters and various other assistants,
could not do much business Neither can you carry on transportation advantageously unless you have the tools, and
waterways are prominent among these tools. The time to get
your tools together and your instrumentalities together is
before you need them, not five or six years afterwards
(Applause)

We are getting ready to develop this country much more
fully than ever before, and to do that we must carry freight
at a sufficiently low cost When people tell you that the railroads can carry goods cheaper than waterways, tell them that
they must not compare the fully developed railroad systems
with undeveloped waterways, but they must credit the waterways with what they can do when they are improved, when they
are provided with proper terminal facilities, and when you can
ship your freight on through bills of lading over trunk waterway lines and over connecting waterways through to destination and deliver them at terminals owned or controlled by the
waterways. Then our waterway transportation will be able
to tell a different story than in the past (Applause.) Then
you will be able to get the goods onto the boat, transfer them
to other boats, and deliver them at destination without excessive cost.

We can carry goods on the Great Lakes for example, for
about one-half of a mill, or one-twentieth of a cent per ton
mile The railroads cannot meet that rate directly; but when
that boat gets to the shore it, in most cases, has to land its
goods at a railroad wharf and pay whatever the railroad charges
The policy of the railroads in the past has been to make its
charges all that the traffic will stand; in other words, to find
out what rate can be charged without entirely losing the business The waterways must have proper facilities at their

wharves to unload onto railroad cars or they cannot handle freight in transfer as readily as the railroads can, and when they have such facilities then the waterways will come into their own. In many cases in the past the railroads have been utterly unable to handle their traffic, and they are hampered by the congestion which results. When the waterways are at work relieving this congestion, it does not mean that they are taking anything away from the railroads, it simply means that the country has more transportation than it had before and more than can be efficiently handled by either the railroads or the waterways alone.

I have been around New York for a good many years, and I have never seen the time, for the last thirty years, when the elevated railroads and the subways of New York City had sufficient facilities to carry all the passengers offered during the rush hours. They have put in more tracks, have doubled their existing tracks, they have put new tracks above and below, and still the cars are overcrowded and the people cannot be accommodated at certain times of the day. It is the same today with freight transportation. There is but little danger of having more lines of transportation in this country than we can use advantageously if properly handled. (Applause.)

The waterways are automatic rate regulators. Some newspapers say that the creation of new water routes is not the proper way to control rates, that nowadays you can control rates better by proper methods of legislation. All you need to do is to point to the Panama Canal and say that since the Panama Canal has been operated not only have the new boat routes nearly cut in two the railroad rates from the Atlantic Coast to the Pacific, but that the new situation has developed a whole lot of commerce in grain that nobody ever calculated would go through the Canal. We already have more commerce in sight than both our railroads and our waterways can take care of.

The waterway is a great developer of the country. When I was on duty on the South Atlantic Coast from 1884 to 1891, there were some twelve or fifteen little rivers down there that were being improved, and some of the newspapers attempted to ridicule many of these rivers by calling them creeks. We took out their snags and sunken trees so that the boats could ascend these little rivers freely in spring time when the farmers wanted to bring fertilizer up into the country, and in the fall when the farmers wanted to get their goods to market. At the time we started that improvement there had been very little farming and town development in that part of the country. When the water-way improvement was ended there it was found that for every thousand dollars that Uncle Sam had expended on these streams there was a new development of $20,000 worth of goods annually carried on those streams for every $1,000 once spent upon them. The new commerce thus developed was commerce between that country and northern coast cities, extending also to Milwaukee, Chicago, Duluth, St. Louis, and even to towns in Iowa; and all these cities and towns and the surrounding country were benefited by the opening up of those little waterways. The annual profits on this new tonnage of manufactured and transported articles, was one hundred per cent of the total cost of the water-way improvements. Wherever the United States can make one hundred per cent a year for ten years by taking hold of such improvements, as was secured in this particular case, I hold that we are idiots if we do not find some way of getting the money to carry them on. (Applause.)

This new development did not take a pound of freight away from the railroad, because the nearest railroad was then forty miles away, and the railroad could not afford to deliver or collect the tonnage at the farmers' doors. In such cases water-ways tend to develop railroads and bring them more business, rather than to injure them. Railroads cannot always find money to build double tracks. Down where those particular waterway improvements were made, land that was worth five dollars an acre twenty years ago is now selling readily for fifty dollars an acre, and the population is now about twenty or thirty times as dense as it was twenty years ago. In that case, a new section was opened to civilization, settlement and business; and the development brought back to the United States, as a whole, an ample revenue in return for its expenditures.

During this last month I saw a book with the title "Graphical Methods of Representation," and one of the illustrations in that book caught my eye.   It was a map showing a strip of New York State along the line of the Erie Canal from Buffalo to Albany and down to New York, the country for five miles on each side of the Canal being shown in dark shading.   I immediately thought of the difficulties encountered by Governor Clinton years ago, when he was endeavoring to persuade the people of New York to build the original Canal.   At that time many of the people said that he was foolish, that the State never would get its money back, and all that sort of thing; but the Erie Canal went through and became an established fact all the way down the line from Buffalo to Albany, connecting with the river from Albany down the Hudson to New York.   It built up an enormous business.   Within that strip only ten miles wide, as shown on that map, from Buffalo to Albany and down to New York Harbor, inclusive, it has been stated that there is today ninety per cent of the wealth and eighty per cent of the population of the whole State of New York.   But without the Erie Canal such developments would have taken fifty more years; and even then, probably, would not have been anywhere near as great as they have been, because of the existence of that Canal.   It never hurt the railroads a bit to have the Erie Canal built.   Today the railroads have at least six tracks along the whole route, and even then cannot handle all the transportation offered, the waterway doing a lot of it.

Some of the newspapers have recently been saying that we must be more economical, cut down our expenses, etc.   You heard yesterday the remarks of Speaker Clark, that there was quite a great distinction between economy and lessened expenditures, and that it is not always economical to reduce expenses. Sometimes you can cut down by economy so much that you kill everything.   You, of course, remember the old story of the farmer who said that when he had got his horse's rations so reduced that he was merely eating shavings, then the blamed old horse died.   You can be just that economical if you want to, but I do not advise it.   There is a great difference between watching the spigot and watching the bung of a water barrel. The fellows that are trying to be very economical are sometimes only saving at the spigot, while great leakage is going on at the bung. (Applause.)

Our development in population and commerce throughout the entire country is large and growing; and the way to develop it best is to spend money properly. Do not economize to excess; just expend all you can get and all you can borrow just as long as you can see a good liberal percentage of return for the money invested. If you can get one hundred per cent profit a year for ten years, as in the case on the South Atlantic above described, it is economy to levy on all your friends, and even put a lien on your real property for the sake of getting money to finance the development.

Some of the papers at present say that there is no commerce on some of these streams, and that, therefore, it is not worth while to spend any money on their improvement. That is not very logical, my friends, because I never saw any building, or storeroom, or factory that was ever rented advantageously until its construction was completed. (Applause.) More than that, you could not rent it until it had good sidewalks and a good road in front of it, so that the public could get to it and you could get your goods out to the public. No waterway improvement is completed until you have the snags, sunken trees and other obstructions removed and gotten out of the way, nor until you have given your boats a fair chance to do good work by providing suitable wharves, with tracks running out to the various parts of the city, nor until you have your terminals developed; and when that time comes I do not think there will be anybody in the United States who will be able to say that our waterways have no commerce on them. (Applause.)

That brings up another point on which all of you can talk to your people at home. You can talk to your townsmen, to your county, city and State, about the advantage that will accrue to them in getting good city terminals free to the public, so that anybody that wants to take his goods to a boat can get them there cheaply. When it comes to the question of terminal facilities people who have recently been designing port terminals for the Atlantic Coast, have told me that the difference between the taking of goods out of a boat by hand, by the old-fashioned longshore method, hauling them up the bank by carts, and then hauling them to the town, is very great as compared with efficient modern methods, using improved machinery and overhead trolleys; the difference being so great that if there were a town on the lower Mississippi, or on the Hudson River, without improved terminal facilities, and there was another one three to six hundred miles away, with good terminal facilities, it would be cheaper to the public to send their goods by boat to the town having the improved terminal facilities, and then ship them back by rail to destination. Consequently, it is money in your pocket to see that at your own town you have the best terminal facilities that can be obtained.

New Orleans has done that. They are not only getting their goods hoisted to the wharf cheaply, but they are getting their goods hauled now by a Municipal Belt Line Railway from the wharf to the various parts of the city for about one-quarter of what they used to have to pay. That is the difference between good transportation and poor transportation. Tell your people that they must consider not the waterway alone, but the waterway when it is improved and provided with proper terminals, completed and ready to handle the business in an up to date manner.

A good many people say that we should not start new works until we finish up all of the old ones by the aid of continuing appropriations; and that we should not make any appropriations which are not continuing. That is all very well so far as concerns the getting of continuing appropriations, and the completing of work which is in progress. That is all right for the fortunate few already partly provided for; but it is hardly fair to say that sections that are without transportation ought not to have any at all, until you have completed the few big improvements. Give all sections of the country a chance to improve and develop. Some times it pays better to develop sections that are less able to help themselves, than it does to develop sections that are prosperous and can easily afford to help themselves. (Applause.) Adopt the optimist's motto,

"Boost, don't knock; don't tear down, build up," as the best thing for all sections of this country. (Applause.)

One of the large papers recently syndicated an article referring to the river and harbor developments proposition, in which it was said that the Missouri River in its upper portion was full of snags, and in which there was a picture of a view taken at low water stage, the article saying that such was the kind of streams which we are trying to improve, and adding that it is a waste of money to improve such a river as that. Why, I had the pleasure and the honor of being with the National Waterways Commission about five years ago when they went all through Europe inspecting a whole lot of European streams, the majority of which did not carry as much water as the upper Missouri, although they carried a great deal more commerce than the upper Missouri. But the National Waterways Commission did not see, in its whole trip, a single snag in any stream carrying one-tenth of the water carried by the Missouri River. From my point of view, that syndicated article showing the Missouri River to be full of snags is an excellent argument that the United States ought to be ashamed of itself for not appropriating money for river and harbor improvement, just as long as there exists in the United States any waterway full of snags, logs, and sunken timber, to such extent as to obstruct or endanger navigation by any sort of craft that can float thereon, even if it does not carry as much as two hundred tons. (Applause.)

A two hundred ton light draft boat can do a great deal of business when it is allowed to. There are several of these small boats now plying on the Missouri River, gasoline launches of light draft running to and from railroad crossings, that could, if they wished, go all the way up the Missouri River to the mouth of the Yellowstone River, every day of the year. They do not do it regularly at present, because there is not much encouragement just now; the population is not big enough, and the shipments are not big enough; but the Missouri River up above Sioux City is not one-tenth as well supplied with transportation as are similar rivers in Europe.

We have got to wake up and to see that our country is developed as fully as it ought to be developed, or we will not come into our own at the earliest possible date.

Now, some papers have said that one reason the river and harbor bills have been so big, is that Engineer Officers have been too liberal in their favorable recommendations for waterway improvement, because they were affected by fear of losing their jobs or their promotion. Now you can just tell those newspapers that ever since 1812, or thereabouts, ever since the Engineer Corps came into existence, there has not been a single man who has ever lost his job because of his recommendation, either for or against anything that came up for his action (Applause); and he is not afraid of losing it now. Again, how can he lose his promotion or his rank, when the United States law for the last hundred years has always been to the effect that after a man graduates at West Point his promotion in the Engineer Corps is by seniority, and not for any other reason or cause? And every officer knows well enough that as long as he is still alive, and able to do the work, he will get his regular promotion whenever his regular time comes. There never has been the slightest attempt by Congress, or anybody else, to stop such promotion. Tell everybody that those newspaper stories were overdrawn, and that if the newspaper authorities will look up the Army regulations and the laws of the country, they will know better. As I told the reporter, in Chicago, when he wrote up that fake interview to which I referred a few minutes ago, "Any man in the town that knows anything about waterways knows what a fool you have made of yourself" (Applause). You can safely tell any newspaper man that, if he goes on writing such yarns as that, everybody will know that he is making a fool of himself; at least, the people will who know anything about the Army Engineers, and that he had better wait until he gets real facts and real solid, logical arguments to write up, and that then he will be in favor of waterway improvement and not against it. (Applause.)

And so I say to you, in closing my remarks, that one part of your duty as members of this association is, when you get home, to collect all the facts and arguments about waterway improvement work, furnish them to your Representatives, and tell them how waterway improvements will benefit your business, and that of the entire country. Send those facts to your Members of Congress to be used on the floor of the House or Senate. Send them also to the editor of your local paper, and then tell every editor that the thing for him to do is to print the truth, the whole truth, and nothing but what is really the truth in this matter.

I thank you gentlemen. (Applause.)

PRESIDENT RANSDELL—I think all of us owe a vote of thanks to General Bixby for his words of wisdom. I know we all return our thanks to him, and I tender them in the name of the assembly.

We are going to have a very interesting evening session. This is to be "Ladies Night." We do not intend to excuse a single man from coming. I know that the ladies are going to be here, and every delegate of this Congress who does not come is going to incur my serious displeasure. I want all of you here at eight o'clock. We stand in recess until then.

The Convention recessed accordingly.

SIXTH SESSION

Thursday Evening, December 10

The Convention met pursuant to recess, President Ransdell
in the chair.

The major portion of the program for the evening was
devoted to the ladies, and previous to addresses by distinguished
ladies, a reception was held at eight o'clock P.M., the following
being in the receiving line · President Ransdell and Mrs. Rans-
dell; Mrs Sarah Willard Strout, President Woman's National
Rivers and Harbors Congress; Mrs William Cumming Story,
President-General D A. R ; Mrs John Dickinson Sherman.
Chairman Conservation Department, General Federation of
Women's Clubs; Mrs. Thomas M Rees, Pittsburgh, Pa ; Mrs
W. B Rodgers, Pittsburgh, Pa.; Mrs J. F. Ellison, Mrs Albert
Bettinger, Cincinnati, O.; Mrs J H. McCready, Pittsburgh,
Pa ; Mrs Elmer G. Laurence, Corresponding Secretary and
Treasurer, Woman's National Rivers and Harbors Congress;
Mrs. Oscar Barrett, Cincinnati, O.; Mrs S A. Thompson,
Washington, D C ; Mrs C H. Rolf, Philadelphia, Pa., Miss
Davidson. La ; Miss Powell, La.

Following the reception the program of the evening was
ushered in by President Ransdell who then turned over the
conduct of proceedings to Mrs. Strout.

President Ransdell said

LADIES AND GENTLEMEN

We are very highly honored this evening to have as our
presiding officer the President of the Woman's National Rivers
and Harbors Congress, who will now give us a talk from the
woman's viewpoint in regard to rivers and harbors Permit
me to present Mrs Strout (Applause)

WHY WOMEN ARE INTERESTED IN WATERWAYS

Address—Mrs. Sarah Willard Strout, Portland, Me.

President Woman's National Rivers and Harbors Congress

This subject is found embodied in several reasons.

First, Is it not a fact women's sphere knows no limit?

Second, If we are to rely upon the good judgment of a statement, which many times has been repeated, about "the feather's weight of worth without a woman in it," we have truisms furnishing splendid reasons why women are interested in waterways. Then, should you desire another proof quite as good, we refer you to that organized force among women, seeking the improvement and sanitation of waterways, which adds greatly to woman's power and opportunity, when public action is the object desired.

We see prejudice which for years bound woman to the past give way to a spirit of cooperation. In fact, the change has been so great that now almost every constructive measure seeks woman's influence in the shaping of public opinion. Why? Because women do things for humanity that men do not. The woman influence gives a touch to activities affecting not men alone, but women and children.

Meanwhile the thinking woman acting on the side of large issues—in striving to improve conditions—gains a broadened viewpoint of life. In this connection we cannot call her "a clinging vine," as she was once pictured; for today she is alert, accepting the situation or offering suggestions, as the case may be, even if she may not lay claim to a vote or a voter. Moreover, have we not been told, time and time again, that, if we as a Nation are to rise to a nobler civilization, woman must take her place in all great movements for community betterment?

As water is one of the essentials to the maintenance of life, does it not create of itself one of the vital problems of the day?

Why call for a better reason why women are interested in waterways?

Women and Economics

In transportation by waterways we have an economic question for solution. However, you may be asking: What have women to do with economy, women who have been held responsible for much of the waste and frivolity of the time, women who have been slow to consider themselves a part of the economic question? "All things are changing," saith the prophet. Why not women? Do we not, at the present time, allow the female contingent to become an important factor in our industrial life? Do we not find them learning monetary values conjointly with their brothers, as well as seeking information on the commercial aspect of questions governing supply and demand and legislation covering many topics?

No sign could be more hopeful of a successful outcome than the desire on their part to study and apply the conservation principle to matters closely concerned with the pocket book. More and more women are making the family purchases, hence the greater amount of knowledge they can obtain governing values and cost the more creditable will be their service to home and country.

Classified facts assure us that, from the economic standpoint, the purchasing public is greatly benefited when commodities used in every home are shipped by a water route. This makes a lower freight rate one step nearer lower living rates. The casual observer takes the matter of the carrying charge into almost no account when ordering the family dinner and little appreciates the extent to which his interests are affected. Besides, every human being is a consumer and pays his pro rata tax on all articles moved for his benefit.

Can you not see in this one item a logical reason why everyone should be interested in waterways?

The significance of European and American waterways cannot be passed by without notice; nor how the Panama Canal and its commercial possibilities have caused a world-wide awakening to the enormous asset we have in nature's gift— "water"—contains valuable data. Surely the women of the land have not overlooked these points.

So much of activity centers around the word "waterways" that when we become analytical then it is we find how much we depend upon them for daily comforts.

BEGINNING THE STUDY OF WATER

The complex situation resulting from cause and effect brings me to the formative period of our organization. It was when the rivers of the Mississippi Valley were submerging homes and property that a waterway convention was being held in June, 1908, in the city of Shreveport, La. Then it was our loyal President, Hon. Joseph E. Ransdell, invited the women, who had been in daily attendance, to organize "for permanent national welfare."

For the first time in the history of the country women took up the subject of water as a national issue. It did not take them long to learn two important facts. First, That our beloved land was richer by far in water advantages than any in existence. Second, That we were not keeping pace with other lands in the development of this vast natural resource. Then the value of systematic expenditure was made a prominent feature— since women are studying monetary values. We noted, too, how critical analysis sometimes followed certain waterway expenditures. As we had no hand in parceling out these allowances we could easily throw our banner to the breeze and stand for a just disbursement fair to all parts of the country.

Transportation, sanitation, beautification are three important words used in women's work for waterways.

We strongly urge sanitation, because nature's laws cannot be violated with impunity. We believe that, if the pollution of streams is allowed to continue, it will become a menace with our increasing population and that nothing will improve conditions like arousing public sentiment to the existing state of affairs. When municipalities and large manufacturing concerns will not of their own accord cease polluting interstate waters then, we claim, some federal regulation should compel them to exercise greater care.

Since a clean drinking water is one of the essentials of life, the problem of stream pollution becomes one of the utmost importance, and women find in the question a live issue where no cupidity of man should be permitted to set it aside. Do you know the authorities of the city of Cleveland used so much chemical, not so very long ago, to counteract the impurities in the water supply that the women called on the court for an injunction to stop its use? However, it is reported that· the city is installing an improved system of filtration, and let us trust other communities will follow their lead.

Certainly the subject of waterways has taken a firm hold on the subconscious minds of the women and they point with pride to our wonderful water advantages and their vast promise for the future, bringing a healthy and vigorous growth to our land. In thus creating an enlarged interest in waterways we are forging a link with all mankind.

To be sure, we women cannot point to any great concrete example of work accomplished, but rather our province has been of the inspirational and educational nature Yet, with fidelity to the interests of our great republic, we are reaching out to women everywhere—home women, women of industrial life, women of leisure, women of organizations—urging one and all to listen to the needs of the waterways and to note how they are creators of health and prosperity, and if properly manipulated will lower the cost of living

Oh, no, we cannot help this activity now we have learned the need, and since the woman is said to be the conservor of the race this interest is only a part of the "woman spirit," which, as Goethe says. "is ever urging us upward and on "

One more reason why women are interested in waterways. (Applause)

Mrs. Strout (In the chair)—From the beginning of our work other organizations have cooperated with us, and one of the first to come forward and help was the Daughters of the American Revolution We are pleased to have with us the President-General of that organization. I am happy to present Mrs William Cumming Story, of New York (Applause).

(Mrs. Story delivered an able and interesting address, but, unfortunately, the manuscript did not come to hand in time to be included in these proceedings.)

Mrs. Strout—We are pleased to state that we have had another acquisition to our ranks, another organization that is cooperating with the National Rivers and Harbors Congress, and which includes some 7,000 women, the National Housewives' League. We are very sorry that the National President, Mrs. Julian Heath, could not be with us, but I wish to announce that there is one more organization working with us.

The greatest woman's organization in the world, numbering, as it does, a million or more members, is the General Federation of Women's Clubs. The President of this great organization, Mrs. Percy V. Pennybacker, was unable to be present, but she has sent us an excellent representative to assist us in our work for waterways and to bring to us a message from that magnificent body of womanhood. I am pleased to introduce the Chairman of their Conservation Department, Mrs. John Dickinson Sherman, of Chicago. (Applause.)

UTILITY AND BEAUTY OF WATERWAYS
Address—Mrs. John Dickinson Sherman, Chicago, Ill.
Chairman Conservation Department General Federation of Women's Clubs

Deep waterways is one of the problems in which the General Federation of Women's Clubs is vitally concerned. We appreciate the need for adequate river and harbor development and regulation, and to this end we have directed our forces. We know that the rivers and river systems in the United States are the finest in the world and we want these rivers and streams developed to their utmost for every beneficial use. This is the aim of our Conservation Committees, working in every State in the Union.

In the early days our great rivers were the highways of exploration; later the highways of travel and commerce. Now they are neither. Their future is one of the great problems of the day. They contain infinite possibilities of good and evil, benefit and damage

This subject of Waterways is but *one* of the several divisions of work of the Conservation Department of the General Federation. If there is any phase of the whole water and waterway question that we haven't tried to incorporate in our general plan of work, I don't know what it is. There may possibly be a limit to what may be accomplished by our splendid clubwomen, but I am sure that there is no limit to their willingness to undertake big propositions when they see a need for the work to be done. (Applause)

Waterways is next to the oldest division of work of the Conservation Department. The general subject is so closely related to the other divisions of Forestry, Civics, Household Economics and Public Health that, either directly or indirectly, the conservation of water has been studied by nearly every Club in the Federation. Each State Federation has a Conservation Department and all State Federation conventions give it a place on their programme

We realize that water in its various uses is one of the important factors in our modern life. We agree with the French physician, who, in making his will, requested his children to remember that for health, long life and happiness they must use water externally, internally and eternally. (Laughter.)

It is our endeavor to bring to the people, through the one million clubwomen of the General Federation, a greater knowledge of water conditions, to show the important part that water plays in the lives of civilized people, and why it should be conserved and how.

The women of the Federation are learning that upon water for irrigation purposes depends the success of a large part of our agricultural operations; that the floods which destroy millions of dollars' worth of property every year can be checked; that the problem of drainage of swamp land, which is so important in many parts of our country, is being solved, and that there are still millions of acres which, if drained, would support thousands of people.

We have also learned that most of the drinking water in city and country is still polluted with filth and disease and our campaign for pure water never ceases.

We are, in addition, giving our attention to the preservation of the banks of streams, when these banks possess natural scenic beauty, and of natural conditions which make the water itself scenically attractive. To consider water as scenery, whether in lake, stream or waterfall, is not always popular, but it is a viewpoint for which there is great need and one that is coming to be better understood. It is significant of our awakening appreciation of this side of the question that the courts are beginning to hold that water and water power are not wasted when used as scenery. But will the American people wake up to the wonder of Niagara Falls as a National asset? The water of Niagara River, when permitted to flow over the Falls, possesses great economic and æsthetic value. But when these waters are diverted to hydraulic canals they are shorn of their full power and are limited to the purely economic.

It has been repeatedly shown that Niagara Falls would pay as large returns if kept for a scenic spectacle as it would pay as a power proposition. And if preserved for its refreshing beauty it would, each year, be a public recreation place where tens of thousands of people would be refreshed and inspired.

Water scenery, as well as scenery of natural beauty, has enormous economic value, but its highest value lies in the great ethical influence on our lives. The use of scenic areas for recreation places is putting them to their highest possible use. It is here that the physical, mental and moral health of the people is strengthened. It is here that we gather courage, grow more hopeful and gain a broader vision on life's problems.

The General Federation has undertaken the roadside planting of the Lincoln Highway, from the Atlantic to the Pacific. (Applause.) Traffic along this great thoroughfare will roll between two unbroken belts of beauty. Scores of beautiful bridges will span scores of streams. Every water highway crossed by this great ocean-to-ocean memorial to Abraham Lincoln should be even more beautiful than the road highway itself. Every stream that flows through the land should have the beauty of its banks preserved There should be many public places of recreation along these streams. Places of natural scenic beauty should be preserved and mutilated places should be restored

The growing demand for amusement and recreation in beautiful out-of-door places must be met. A nation progresses largely according to the use it makes of the leisure time of the people Nature is one of the strongest of the forces that control the people during their leisure hours It is a splendid antidote for the conditions growing out of a civilization that has become too complex to be wholly sane and wholly sober. To bring into every life some of the ennobling influences of our world of natural beauty and grandeur will, in time, stir us to a mental change of base and go a long way toward establishing the Brotherhood of Man.

When our navigable streams are developed, they will be used for passenger travel as well as for the transportation of products. Would you not be glad if the stream that passes through your locality had clear water and beautiful banks? Speed the day when we shall be able to speak of every river in the United States as the Indians spoke of the Ohio when they called it the "Beautiful River."

When the Mississippi Valley comes into its own, the people will need all the beauty of its waters and bordering lands as well as the benefits of transportation to round out their lives A running stream of clear water, bordered by banks of scenic beauty, is one of the most attractive objects of nature Disfigure the banks and the charm is gone Change this stream to a sewer, and it disgusts. Every stream, from source to sea, should have a primeval charm. The brook should have all the romance of the trail, and the river all the dignity and beauty of the highway

First-class waterway transportation, for which we are all working, would reduce all transportation costs and thus benefit all business and reach all interests But, as beauty goes so far toward satisfying the world's great longing, would not river development go forward more rapidly if beauty and utility were developed together? (Applause)

MRS. STROUT—We women certainly cannot get along without the men We are always dependent upon them, and even on "Ladies' Night" we want to give them a place on our programme The closing address of the evening will be one on the "Improvement of the Ohio River," by Capt. Harold C. Fiske, of the United States Engineer Corps. This address will be illustrated by moving pictures It is with great pleasure that I present Captain Fiske. (Applause)

IMPROVEMENT OF THE OHIO RIVER
Address—Capt. Harold C. Fiske
U. S. Engineer Corps

MADAM PRESIDENT, LADIES AND GENTLEMEN:

Despite the remarks of the presiding officer, and despite the printed programme which states that I am to deliver an address, I will not attempt to make a speech tonight, or an address. I have here some reels which have been taken of the locks and dams on the Ohio River, showing their construction and operation My part in the evening's entertainment will be simply to furnish a little additional information, specifying more particularly the different items which are being shown in the moving pictures.

Before the pictures are shown, however, there are two points which it might be well to mention: first, as to how the pictures came to be taken The War Department directed the Pittsburgh office to prepare a set of models to be shown at the Exposition in San Francisco next summer. We were allowed a certain amount of space. When we came to design the models we found that the space allotted us was so small that a wicket, for instance, which stands eighteen feet high, reduced in size to the extent that it would have to be in order that the space given would accommodate it, the entire exhibit would become so diminutive that its construction would not be clearly observable, and that the entire set of models would not convey to the public as a whole a correct impression of the relative size and importance of these locks and dams.

Not only that, but it is a fact that a large part of the most interesting things connected with these structures is their operation. I am referring to the movable dams and the locks, as well as the coal fleets which pass through these locks. We, therefore, asked for permission to have a set of moving pictures taken, through which we hoped all of these things could be more effectively and clearly shown. Permission was granted to have the pictures taken, which was done.

The other point that naturally comes up is that you be made acquainted with a few of the technical terms which are used in connection with these locks and dams. It is probable that many of the gentlemen are familiar with these terms, and so I will only mention a few.

These dams, as you know, are movable dams of the wicket type. They are made movable so that the wickets may be kept in an upright position during the summer and fall months of low water, and kept in their lowered position during the winter months of high water. When they are lowered traffic passes over the dam.

A lock and dam consists of about five different parts. The lock proper is 600 feet long by 110 feet wide It has a water chamber inside. The lock is always located on one bank of a river Next to it in the river comes the pass, which is so called because it is over this section of the dam that traffic passes when the dam is down A pass is from 600 to 800 feet long, or wide, measuring outward into the river. The next structure is what is called the bear trap. This consists of two leaves, which are about twenty feet long when of standard type. They have been built of varying lengths at different times from 50 to 120 feet long We will show you in one of the pictures tonight one that has 120-foot leaves. It is interesting to an engineer to see a leaf of that type move These leaves are horizontal, one overlapping the other, the upper one being on the up-stream side. They are hinged at the bottom. When they are upright they look like this, and when they are lowered they fall over each other in this way. (Illustrating.) They rise and fall in this manner. There are usually two bear traps in the dam which are separated from each other and from the sections on either side by piers.

Beyond the bear traps comes what is called a "weir." It is similar in a general way to the pass, except that navigation is not expected to go over it. It presents a slightly different type of construction which is less expensive. Then, at the farther bank of the river, the bank opposite the lock, is what is called the abutment. These terms will all be used in explaining the pictures later.

I may say that the navigation which you will see on the river is only a sample and that there is a great deal more that we have not shown. The first set of pictures which comes through is intended to show the Ohio River "before and after taking." Below the lock and the dam you will see the Ohio River in its normal low-water condition. At the time this picture was taken it is probable that a boat drawing eighteen inches of water would have run aground. As the camera swings above the dam you will see Pool No. 8, in which the minimum depth is nine feet.

The Ohio River, in its natural state, is navigable for about three months a year during high water. To make it navigable during the summer and fall, or low-water months, fifty-three locks and movable dams are being built by the United States Government. When the improvement is completed there will be pool, or slackwater, navigation from Pittsburgh to Cairo, 967 miles. Fifteen of the dams are in operation and sixteen are now under construction. It is still impossible to navigate the sections of the river where dams are not in operation except at high water. This almost prohibits local freight traffic on the river.

About seventy-five per cent of the traffic on the Upper Ohio consists of coal shipped in large tows from the vicinity of Pittsburgh to various points down stream. For more than six months there has been no opportunity for these fleets to leave the pools. This causes a heavy loss due to idle plant, idle crews, pumping charges and accidents.

One of the pictures will show fleets carrying about 160,000 tons of coal. If this were shipped by rail in modern, standard fifty-ton gondolas, it would make a train of 3,200 cars nearly twenty-eight miles long. The total amount of coal in this vicinity waiting for high water is about 325,000 tons, besides about 7,000 tons of manufactured products On several occasions the total has been as high as 600,000 tons, which would fill a train 100 miles in length

On the Allegheny and Monongahela Rivers, and on the Ohio River just below Pittsburgh, there is now a total of 210 miles of river which has been made continuously navigable by Government improvements. Manufacturing plants valued at billions of dollars have located along these rivers, water transportation being often an important factor in deciding the location. A single plant, which will be shown in one of the pictures, represents an investment of $50,000,000 The plant was built in this location solely because the Ohio River had been made navigable, and the 4,000 tons of coal needed every day could be shipped by water (Applause.)

The lights having been turned off, a most interesting series of moving pictures was shown, illustrating the construction and operation of the locks and dams and the methods used for transporting coal on the Ohio River. The pictures were frequently applauded, and at the close of the lecture Captain Fiske was given a vote of thanks, after which the Convention adjourned until ten o'clock on the following morning.

SEVENTH SESSION
Friday Morning, December 11

The Convention met pursuant to adjournment, President Ransdell in the chair.

Secretary Thompson read the following telegram:

"ASTORIA, OREGON, Dec 8, 1914

"NATIONAL RIVERS AND HARBORS CONGRESS,

    "New Willard Hotel, Washington, D. C

"We extend greeting and God-speed to you in your policy of insisting on not less than an annual appropriation of $50,000,000 by the National Government for the improvement of American rivers and harbors.

"We deprecate the vicious attack on this policy made by United States Senators during the last session of the Sixty-Third Congress, resulting in the defeat of many worthy measures recommended by the United States Engineers Though the Columbia River was well taken care of in the emergency bill following the defeat of the regular bill, we nevertheless feel that other sections of the United States are entitled to, and should receive, just recognition

"We voice our confidence in the ability and integrity of the United States Engineers, and feel that their recommendations should receive the respectful consideration of both branches of Congress

"We deprecate the cry of 'pork' in connection with measures calculated to provide competitive transportation for the relief of commerce as begging the real question, which is, Shall the producers and consumers and the Nation have the benefit of water transportation as a means of cheapening the haul to market, and the benefit of fully improved waterways as factors in agricultural and manufacturing developments?

"PORT OF COLUMBIA COMMERCIAL CLUB.

"By FRED J. JOHNSON, Vice-President,

"COLUMBIA AND SNAKE RIVER WATERWAYS ASSOCIATION,

"By WALLACE R STRUBLE, Secretary"

PRESIDENT RANSDELL—Next in order is the annual report of our Secretary and Treasurer, Mr S. A Thompson.

Annual Report—S. A. Thompson, Secretary-Treasurer

MR. PRESIDENT, LADIES AND GENTLEMEN:

It is not my intention to weary you with an extended report, but I shall be glad to answer any questions which you may wish to ask.

During the early portion of the year we were engaged in settling up the magazine matter. Besides our members, to whom the magazine, while published, was sent without extra charge, there was a considerable number of persons who were subscribers to the magazine only, and to these we were under both a legal and moral obligation for the unearned portions of their subscriptions. Every one of these—with the exception of a few who have not replied to our letters—has received a full settlement of his claim   (Applause.)

Later, we used every legitimate means at our command to offset the vicious attacks made upon the Rivers and Harbors Bill. Letters, literally by the thousand, were sent out to our members, to the press, to mayors of cities, and to commercial organizations throughout the country. One of these letters was read to you in the course of my remarks on yesterday. As you know, however, conditions were such that a lump-sum appropriation of $20,000,000, to be expended at the discretion of the Army Engineers on projects already begun, was substituted for a bill which, as reported to the Senate, carried, in cash appropriations and contract authorizations, a total of more than $53,000,000.

Our work might properly be described as consisting simply of a continuous, nation-wide campaign of publicity. Everything we do consists either of things relating directly to that end, or of things that are incidental and necessary thereto. The work done by our Field Secretaries in securing new members and subscriptions for our work is important because the amount of work that we can do is determined by the funds placed at our disposal   But the publicity work they do—in public addresses, private interviews and articles in the newspapers—is of at least equal, perhaps even greater, importance than the financial results they secure.

That the office force has not been idle is shown by the fact that we have sent out no less than 386,999 sheets of publicity material in the fiscal year just closed. And this, you understand, does not include the thousands of letters sent out in our regular correspondence. (Applause)

Turning now to my report as Treasurer, you will note that the total receipts for the fiscal year were $31,169.44. Of this total, more than half, or $16,330.00, was received through the work of our efficient Field Secretaries, while almost $10,000.00 was received in response to renewal letters sent out from the office. We had on hand at the beginning of the fiscal year $1,342.92, making a total cash available during the year of $32,512 41

For general publicity, which includes the salaries and expenses of the Field Secretaries, we paid out $11,101 81, while we expended for the Washington Publicity Department $5,194.71. Those who care to go more into detail can find additional items of expenditure in the detailed report which is before you, and which will be embodied in the proceedings of this Convention. The total expenditures for the year for all purposes were $32,287.98, leaving a balance in bank December 1st of $224.43. As is always the case, considerable amounts have been handed in by the delegates to the Convention, so that our cash balance today is very much larger than it was on the first of the month, but it would only be confusing to give any figures except those pertaining to the fiscal year for which this report is made.

Because of the widespread attacks which have been made during recent months upon the whole policy of improving our rivers and harbors, it is important that our campaign of education should be pushed more vigorously than ever before. This can only be done, however, if additional funds are provided. We need more funds, but most of all we need more members As between a contribution of $5,000 00 from some wealthy friend of waterways and a thousand members at $5 00 apiece, I would vastly prefer the latter, because this would mean so many more people to whom literature can be sent, who can urge their Senators and Representatives to support properly prepared Rivers and Harbors Bills, and who, as they become informed upon and enthusiastic about the waterway movement, can bring others into line. I hope that every delegate present who is not already a member of the NATIONAL RIVERS AND HARBORS CONGRESS will put in his application before he leaves the city, and I wish that every one who is a member now would secure at least one new member. That would be a small thing for each one to do, but the result would be to add greatly to the strength of the organization

As was to be expected, the serious disturbance in business conditions resulting from the outbreak of the war in Europe caused a decrease in our revenues during the latter part of the fiscal year just closed. This made it necessary that every one should work even harder than before, so that every dollar spent would accomplish the greatest possible results. Even under these difficulties we have done a greater amount of publicity work than in any previous year and have maintained the credit of the organization unimpaired.' (Applause.)

ANNUAL FINANCIAL STATEMENT

Fiscal Year, December 1, 1913, to November 30, 1914, inclusive

RECEIPTS

ALABAMA—

Birmingham	$ 5.00	
Gadsden	25 00	
Mobile	20 00	
Selma	10 00	
		$ 60 00

ARKANSAS—

Butler	$ 5.00	
Ft. Smith	10 00	
Little Rock	20 00	
Pine Bluff	15 00	
		50 00

Amount carried forward		$ 110 00

Amount brought forward	$ 110 00	
CALIFORNIA—		
Arcata	$ 140 00	
Bulwinkle	5 00	
Colusa	45.00	
Eureka	280 00	
Fruitvale	50 00	
Long Beach	100 00	
Los Angeles	1,360 00	
Marysville	205 00	
Oakland	400 00	
Red Bluff	70 00	
Sacramento	597 00	
San Diego	100 00	
San Francisco	2,070 00	
Scotia	100 00	
Stockton	55 00	
Yuba City	25 00	
		5,602 00
CONNECTICUT—		
Ansonia	$ 5 00	
Bridgeport	870.00	
Derby	35 00	
Groton	10 00	
Hartford	5 00	
Middletown	5.00	
Milford	45 00	
Milldale	10 00	
New Britain	15 00	
New Haven	45 00	
New London	15 00	
Shelton	40 00	
Windsor	5.00	
		1,105.00
COSTA RICA—		
San Jose	$ 200 00	
		200 00
DELAWARE—		
Edgemoor	$ 100 00	
Wilmington	375 00	
		475.00
DISTRICT OF COLUMBIA—		
Washington	$ 770 07	
		770 07
FLORIDA—		
Apalachicola	$ 5 00	
Daytona	5 00	
Amount carried forward	$8,262 07	

Amount brought forward. $8,262 07

Jacksonville	$ 90 00	
Miami	5 00	
Pensacola	5 00	
St Andrews	15 00	
St Augustine	5 00	
St Petersburg	125 00	
Santa Rosa	5 00	
Tampa	40 00	
		300 00
Augusta	$ 25 00	
Brunswick	5 00	
Columbus	185 00	
Rome	5 00	
Savannah	197 50	
		417 50

IDAHO—

Lewiston	$ 75 00	
		75 00

ILLINOIS—

Aurora	$ 10 00	
Berwyn	5 00	
Cairo	120 00	
Charleston	1 87	
Chicago	2 071 50	
Joliet	5 00	
Moline	175.00	
Oak Park	5 00	
Peoria	5.00	
Rock Island	135 00	
Warsaw	5 00	
		2,538.37

INDIANA—

Evansville	$ 260 00	
Ft. Wayne	700 00	
Goshen	10 00	
Huntington	200 00	
Indiana Harbor	10 00	
Madison	10 00	
Rochester	5.00	
		1,195 00

IOWA—

Burlington	$ 140 00	
Clinton	45 00	
Davenport	55 00	
Des Moines	10 00	

Amount carried forward $12,787 94

Amount brought forward		$12,787 94
Dubuque	$ 140 00	
Keokuk	5 00	
Sioux City	5 00	
		400 00
KANSAS—		
Clay Center	$ 1 25	
Kansas City	10 00	
		11 25
KENTUCKY—		
Burnside	$ 5 00	
Louisville	155 00	
Newport	5 00	
Owensboro	20 00	
		185.00
LOUISIANA—		
Crowley	$ 5 00	
Franklin	5 00	
Holly Ridge	5 00	
Lake Charles	25 00	
New Orleans	255 00	
Raceland	5 00	
		300 00
MARYLAND—		
Baltimore	$ 100 00	
Fallston	2 50	
Pocomoke City	5.00	
		107 50
MASSACHUSETTS—		
Arlington	$ 5 00	
Boston	388 75	
Cambridge	1 87	
Chelsea	5 00	
Fall River	5 00	
Haverhill	100 00	
Lawrence	5 00	
Malden	5 00	
Milton	1 87	
Newton	25	
Springfield	15 00	
		532 74
MINNESOTA		
Little Falls	$ 5 00	
Minneapolis	1,140 00	
Red Wing	10 00	
Amount carried forward		$14,324 43

Amount brought forward		... $14,324 43
St. Paul	$ 51 88	
Winona	35 00	
		1,241 88

MISSISSIPPI—

Glen Allen	$ 5.00	
Greenville	122 50	
Pascagoula	10 00	
Rosedale	205 00	
Shelby	5 00	
Vicksburg	10 00	
		357 50

MISSOURI—

Augusta	$ 74.00	
Boonville	100 00	
Caruthersville	5 00	
Dutzow	20.00	
Glasgow	45 00	
Hannibal	60 00	
Jefferson	109 50	
Kansas City	696 85	
Shelbyville	5 00	
St Joseph	200 00	
St Louis	235 00	
Washington	89 50	
		1,639.85

NEW JERSEY—

Atlantic City	$ 5 00	
Belleville	10 00	
Bordentown	5.00	
Camden	· 10 00	
Cranford	5 00	
Elizabeth	5 00	
Jersey City	5 00	
Newark	223 00	
Trenton	140 00	
		408.00

NEW YORK—

Albany	$2,107 00	
Beacon	5 00	
Brooklyn	42 00	
Buffalo	446 00	
New York	1,127.43	
Nyack	5.00	
Oswego	30 00	
Patchogue	5 00	
Poughkeepsie	435 00	
Rensselaer	5 00	

Amount carried forward	.... $17,971 66

Amount brought forward		$17,971 66
Rochester	$ 95 00	
Rockaway Beach	5 00	
Syracuse	5.00	
Tonawanda	10 00	
Troy	275 00	
Watertown	5 00	
Youngstown	50	
		4,602 93

NORTH CAROLINA—

Durham	$ 5 00	
Edenton	30.00	
Flat Rock	5 00	
Kinston	10 00	
Newbern	25 00	
Washington	40 00	
Williamston	10 00	
Wilmington	135 00	
		260.00

NORTH DAKOTA—

Bismarck	$ 50 00	
		50 00

OHIO—

Akron	$ 10 00	
Ashtabula Harbor	10 00	
Cincinnati	770 00	
Cleveland	10 00	
Columbus	101 50	
Conneaut	10 00	
Dayton	5 00	
Glendale	5 00	
Hamilton	5 00	
Lockland	5 00	
Morrow	1 00	
Norwood	5 00	
Steubenville	5 00	
Toledo	185 00	
		1,127 50

OKLAHOMA—

Tulsa	$ 15.00	
		15 00

OREGON—

Astoria	$ 60 00	
Athena	15 00	
Coquille	100 00	
Eugene	115 00	
Freewater	10 00	

Amount carried forward		$24,027 09

Amount brought forward   . . $24,027 09

Marshfield	$ 260 00	
Milton	5 00	
Newport	20 00	
Oregon City	10 00	
Pendleton	60.00	
Portland	625 00	
Salem	50 00	
		1,330 00
PENNSYLVANIA—		
Ambler	$ 5 00	
Beaver Falls	10.00	
Bryn Mawr	5.00	
Edgewood Park	10 00	
Endeavor	5.00	
Philadelphia	816 00	
Pittsburgh	981.50	
		1,832 50
RUSSIA—		
Blagovestchensk	$ 3 00	
		3 00
SOUTH CAROLINA—		
Charleston	$ 10 00	
Columbia	115 00	
Georgetown	10 00	
		135 00
TENNESSEE—		
Chattanooga	$ 120 00	
Harriman	5 00	
Memphis	25 00	
Nashville	222 00	
		372 00
TEXAS—		
Beaumont	$ 55 00	
Brownsville	35 00	
Corpus Christi	70 00	
Freeport	100 00	
Galveston	265.00	
Houston	300 00	
Port Arthur	36 50	
Riviera	15 00	
San Antonio	5 00	
Texas City	5 00	
Victoria	25.00	
Waco	35 00	
Wharton	5 00	
		951 50
VIRGINIA—		
Mosley's Junction	$ 5.00	
Norfolk	510 00	

Amount carried forward...... ...   .$28,651 09

Amount brought forward $28,651.09

Petersburg .... $ 20 00
Richmond 250 00
—————— 785 00

WASHINGTON—
Aberdeen . .   .   . $ 110 00
Bellingham 1 00
Chehalis 5 00
Clarkston 10.00
Colfax 25.00
Covada 5 00
Dayton 20.00
Everett 50 00
Garfield 5 00
Hoquiam 135 00
Huntsville 5 00
Kelso 5 00
Kennewick 40 00
Montesano 5 00
North Yakima 10 00
Ostrander 5 00
Pasco 15 00
Prescott 20 00
Pullman 25.00
Raymond 85 00
Rosalia 10 00
Seattle 236 85
South Bend 30 00
Spokane 190 00
Tacoma 2 00
Vancouver 20 00
Waitsburg 75 00
Walla Walla 145 00
—————— 1,289 85

WEST VIRGINIA—
Fayetteville ..   . . $ 2 50
Huntington 5 00
Moundsville 5 00
Wheeling 10 00
—————— 22.50

WISCONSIN—
De Pere   . .   . . $ 35 00
Green Bay 65 00
La Crosse 35 00
Milwaukee 76 00
Sheboygan 205 00
Superior 5.00
—————— 421 00

TOTAL RECEIPTS FROM 37 STATES AND 263 CITIES. $31,169 44

ANALYSIS OF RECEIPTS AND EXPENDITURES
RECEIPTS

Work of Field Secretaries	$16,330 00
Renewals	9,775 00
Special contribution for deficit.	2,525 00
Sundries	1,839 10
Magazine	700.34
TOTAL	**$31,169 44**

EXPENDITURES

General Publicity, including Field Secretaries and Special Agents	$11,101 81
Washington Publicity Department	5,194 71
Secretary's Salary	3,000 00
Secretary's Traveling Expense	88 15
Office Salaries	3,485 00
Office Expenses (Rent, Printing, etc)	2,326 64
Office Equipment	458 53
Magazine (Refunds, Commissions, etc.)	2,594 00
Convention (1913, $1,452 52, 1914, $225.54)	1,678 06
Payment on Note, including Interest	1,161 08
President's Office Expense	1,200 00
TOTAL	**$32,287 98**

CASH BALANCE

Cash on hand December 1, 1913	$ 1,342 97
Receipts to November 30, 1914	31,169 44
TOTAL CASH	**$32,512.41**
Total Expenditures	32,287 98
BALANCE ON HAND DECEMBER 1, 1914	**$ 224 43**

COMPARATIVE STATEMENT

		Receipts	*Expenses*
Fiscal year	1906	$13,540 00	$11,283 63
"	" 1907	22,315 75	22,499 81
"	" 1908	31,486 87	25,825.50
"	" 1909	28,143 83	26,845.43
"	" 1910	25,256 19	28,572 84
"	" 1911	35,648 26	28,546 41
"	" 1912	18,774 93	29,734 79
"	" 1913	56,781 34	57,295 79
"	" 1914	31,169 44	32,287.98
TOTALS		**$263,116 61**	**$262,892 18**

Respectfully submitted,

S A. THOMPSON, *Secretary and Treasurer*

NOTE—Treasurer's books audited by Expert Public Accountant and found correct

PRESIDENT RANSDELL—Is there any action in regard to this report? If there are no objections, it will be accepted.

Next in order is the report of the Field Secretary.

COMMODORE FRANK FESSENDEN CRANE, Quincy, Mass —I move a rising vote of thanks to our Secretary, Mr S A. Thompson, for his more than strenuous efforts during the last year   .

The motion was carried by rising and unanimous vote

PRESIDENT RANSDELL—Captain Davenny, one of our Field Secretaries, will now present his report.   I believe that Captain Davenny is known to all of us and needs no introduction at my hands—Captain Davenny.

Report—Capt. Wilson I. Davenny, Field Secretary

MR PRESIDENT AND MEMBERS OF THE CONVENTION.

Both tradition and precedent seem to have determined that if the Field Secretaries are heard in the Convention at all they must be brief.

However, I have some satisfaction in an item in the report of your Secretary to the Congress which indicates that something more than half of the funds that have been necessary to carry on the work of the Congress has been secured through the activities of the Field Secretary.   I am pleased to have this opportunity to acknowledge my obligation to the Directors of the Congress, in various parts of the country that I have visited, for their cordial cooperation. It is certainly a very great aid to a Field Secretary to find, when he arrives at a point at which a Director is located, that his interest in the work of the Congress is demonstrated by his cooperation with the efforts of the Field Secretary.

The fact is that the Convention, Mr President, is simply the expression of the interest that has been aroused throughout the country in rational development of worthy waterways.

I sympathize most heartily with the suggestion of the Secretary, who said that rather than have a single subscription of $5,000 00 from some one interested particularly in a particular project, he would rather have 1,000 members, each of whom contributed $5.00. I think you will agree with me in that, and it at least has the approval of some of those who are employed in securing the money. I am not content merely, Mr. President, to secure a check that may be transmitted to the Treasurer   I do not want support of this Congress, through my efforts, unless such support is predicated upon an intelligent conception of the work of the Congress and a genuine interest in what it is doing. (Applause.)

So I fall into the habit very frequently of saying to a man who has been kind enough finally to give me a check as a contribution to the Congress, that, while I appreciate his contribution, and while such contributions are necessary in order to carry on the operations of the Congress, when I transmit that check at the end of the week, frankly speaking, my interest in that particular check is ended, because I am out after another check   But I have a continuing interest, as I have a right to have, in the fact that I have, through that contribution, enlisted the representative of important interests to cooperate in the activities of the Congress

As you know, most every phase of the matters that concern this organization has been traversed in the course of this Convention; and I want to testify, Mr. Chairman, that the spirit of this Convention has armed the Field Secretaries anew for their campaign in behalf of the Congress. (Applause)

It is to be deplored that men in both branches of Congress will stultify themselves and defy their own knowledge of the facts in an assault upon one of the great movements for the development of our most important national resources, our waterways.

It is deplorable, Mr. Chairman, that great newspapers in some parts of the country have assumed to antagonize river and harbor improvements by their assaults upon the rivers and harbors bill and their malignant attacks upon the National Rivers and Harbors Congress, and that this charge of "pork barrel" by them must, in my judgment, in some cases at least, come under the head of ignorance of the conditions

I just have this word to say about "pork barrel" A short time ago I saw a street car advertisement deprecating the fact that substitutes were offered for every article of real merit, and the statement in the advertisement was that "just as good" was a term that a parrot might employ, not knowing what it was saying. I want to say to you that I know a vast number of the people who roll that term sibillantly under their tongues do not know what they are talking about. And so it is that by the use of the term "pork barrel" they betray an apparent erudition which would be completely punctured if they were asked to define what they actually meant by "pork barrel." (Applause.)

One further and final word. It has been my privilege during the past year to travel twelve thousand miles in the interest of the Congress During that time, as a coincidence, I made forty addresses, and secured eighty columns of newspaper publicity, which is exactly what I did last year in travelling eight thousand miles; so that in the two years I have travelled twenty thousand miles in the interest of this Congress.

Now, if a Field Secretary should be brief, I feel I have talked longer than I intended, but there is a compensation in the fact that the distinguished gentlemen who have addressed this Convention only have an audience once a year, whereas the Field Secretary goes up and down the land and speaks on all possible occasions I thank you for your courtesy. (Applause.)

President Ransdell—Let me present our other Field Secretary, Mr. Roy

Report—Sydney J. Roy, Field Secretary

Mr. President and Gentlemen:

I do not just exactly like that introduction that your President gave me—your "other Field Secretary"—because the real Field Secretary is Mrs. Henry, one of the most delightful women that ever went out in the interest of the Congress She is the "other" and only real Field Secretary.

I am delighted to be here, Mr President, because this is an aggregation of men who are making the greatest fight for the supremacy of this country in the commerce of the world. (Applause.)

It is delightful to go about over this country and to meet the business men who are busy, and find that they give so much of their time to studying how to make their cities and their communities of vital force in the life and supremacy of this Nation.

I have been working mostly in the granary of the United States, between Pittsburgh and Denver. I go out to Kansas City, where they have put a million and a half dollars of capital into a barge line to carry the grain of Kansas out to the ports of the world I go into the office of the Commercial Club, and it was a pleasure to meet those gentlemen and to have them say to me, "The National Rivers and Harbors Congress is not required to keep a Field Secretary in Kansas City; we will raise the funds and send them to you." (Applause.)

Secretary Thompson—And they did it, too

Mr. Roy—And they did it And then they sent a good big strong delegation down here. I went over to the delightful city of Peoria, Ill., where they collect more internal revenue on the spirit of American life than in any other city in the country (Applause.) They said, "We know you. We have not been contributing very much to the National Rivers and Harbors Congress, but we are going to open up the Illinois River and the canal into the Illinois and send the commerce of Illinois out to the world through the Mississippi River. We are going to send delegates to the Convention." Mr. Morgan is here. And they said, "We will raise a fund and send it to you;" and they are doing it.

Up in Minneapolis I met Mr. Decker. At Cincinnati I met Mr. Culkins, of the Chamber of Commerce over there At Louisville I met Mr. Murray   Then I went to Evansville, Ind , and.they said that they would send us a contribution (Applause.)

So you see what delightful privileges are enjoyed by the Field Secretary of the NATIONAL RIVERS AND HARBORS CONGRESS. Why, a President or a Senator here is not in it with the Field Secretary. It is so delightful to go around and meet these fellows that are building up this great country.

I want to say just another word. It is one thing to be a delegate to the NATIONAL RIVERS AND HARBORS CONGRESS— it is a delightful pleasure to come down to Washington— but it is another thing to meet the Field Secretary at the other end of the line and hear him say, "I do not believe you have raised your quota of money " A lot of fellows come down here—I know how it is, because I have done it myself—at the expense of the city council or some commercial body, and they find that the trip here is a great deal easier than to go home and raise money for the support of this movement   But I want to tell you something   This great Congress has just about half as much funds this year as it had last year, and the Field Secretaries are only poor weak instruments in the hands of these splendid men who are here at the head, and unless you can take care of us with your personal influence when we come to your communities, we cannot do much   The whole question is, gentlemen, how much are you going to give when you get back home to prepare public sentiment to overcome the attack which has been made on a just rivers and harbors bill by calling it a "pork barrel" measure?

If the other sections of the country have as .many good men in them as there are in the Mississippi Valley—and I guess they have—I have never travelled very much in the New England States, but they tell me they are a fine bunch of fellows up there, just as they are down South But, some way or other, the Mississippi Valley is so big, so rich, and there are so many empire builders in it, that I have never been able to get out of it to solicit funds anywhere else. I am going to try to get out of it next year and come down to New England and tackle the "hub" I would like to tackle the fellow that thinks he is right. I am going to come down there and get some more money at the "hub."

Now, Mr. President, I have nothing more to say I am delighted to be here and to see this great work going on and feel that you men are going to stay at it and stand by one of the greatest empire builders the world has ever seen, the Senator from Louisiana. (Applause.) And also to stand by that other splendid organizer and director, Mr. Thompson, your Secretary. (Applause)

But you have got to do it when you get back home as well as here I would like to see this Convention invite the real Field Secretary of the National Rivers and Harbors Congress, Mrs Henry, to talk to you. I thank you (Applause)

President Ransdell—The request of our "Other Field Secretary" is certainly going to be granted. We did not intend to overlook Mrs Henry. We knew what we were saying when we called Mr. Roy our "Other Field Secretary," because the real Field Secretary is undoubtedly Mrs Henry. Mrs Henry, however, has requested that she be not called upon to make an address this morning, so—unless she has changed her mind—I am going to ask that she be excused by this Convention. Is Mrs. Henry present? If she is present and has changed her mind, I would like to have her come up here. She has done such magnificent work for us (A Voice· "Let us see her!") If she is still of the same mind, she can at least let us look at her. (A Voice: "She is not in the hall ")

I will now introduce to you, gentlemen, the Chairman of the Resolutions Committee, Capt William B Rodgers, of Pittsburgh, who will read the resolutions to the Convention. (Applause.)

CAPT. W. B RODGERS—MR PRESIDENT, LADIES AND GENTLEMEN: At the command of this Convention, through our worthy President, some forty odd of us were selected to prepare a platform. I am not going to attempt to defend this platform in advance I do not think it needs any defense.

It was my privilege to be Chairman, and it is my privilege to submit to you now the work of that Committee, consisting of some forty odd members from every section of this country.

The Committee recommend the following for your approval and adoption·

Report of the Committee on Resolutions

The National Rivers and Harbors Congress now assembled in its Eleventh Annual Convention, representing by its delegates all sections of the country, hereby makes the following declaration of its policies and purposes

First, Experience has shown the wisdom of a strict adherence to the principle, adopted at the formation of this Association, that we should confine our activities to the advocacy of a waterway policy for navigation purposes and not to the advancement of any particular project, and therefore we declare again our motto to be "A Policy, Not a Project"

Second, We regard the policy of annual river and harbor bills as most essential to the economical prosecution and preservation of river and harbor improvements and commend Congress for its continued adherence to this policy since its establishment several years ago. But we firmly aver that real progress in the building up of a comprehensive plan of water transportation, as supplementary of transportation by rail. to meet the ever-increasing demands of commerce requires that such appropriations should be for not less than fifty million dollars per annum

Third. We would urge upon Congress the employment of the continuing contract system, wherever practicable, as the best means of securing that economy, efficiency and speed in the construction of Government work which is manifest in private enterprises

Fourth, We note with much satisfaction the provisions in the Panama Canal Act, of 1912, for the separate ownership of rail and steamship lines; for cooperation between rail and water routes in the issuance of through bills of lading and equitable pro-rating and for the physical connection of such routes wherever possible, and we urge upon the proper authorities enforcement of these provisions

Fifth, We commend the good progress that has already been made in the establishment of suitable terminals along the waterways now under improvement, and we strongly urge upon States, municipalities and all other interests a continuance of such work as the only means of securing the full benefit and advantage of dependable channels.

Sixth, We declare our unqualified confidence in the ability and integrity of the United States Corps of Engineers and believe it to be the safest reliance for recommendations as to the economy and feasibility of river and harbor improvements, as well as to actual construction of the same

Respectfully submitted,

WM B RODGERS,
Chairman.

Following the reading of the report Captain Rodgers moved its adoption.

PRESIDENT RANSDELL—Does the motion to adopt the report of the Committee meet with a second?

Remarks—William S. Bennett, New York City

MR. PRESIDENT I do not know whether what I am about to say is strictly in discussion of the resolutions. They have my hearty approval But this seems to be about the only place where some one from New York City can offer a brief expression. I happen to be one of the delegates appointed by His Honor, the Mayor of New York City, to represent the Harlem Board of Commerce, and I am also a member of the Atlantic Deeper Waterways Association I have not heard or read the exact terms of the letter of our Mayor; but if the synopsis that has been presented to me is correct, I do not entirely agree with him I have a very deep sympathy with what the Mayor is attempting to do in New York City. He is the first Mayor that we have had who has had the courage to tackle in all its completeness our port problem.

When a man is trying to do a big work, obstructions are irritating; but as a former Member of Congress, I do not want this organization to get the idea that we in New York City have all got a perpetual grouch on. We have not As a matter of fact, the Mayor's statistics, as far as I know, are absolutely correct Figures from official sources usually are; but that is no proof that New York City has been discriminated against.

We must not overlook the fact that in New York we have a magnificent national harbor and until about fifteen years ago, when we needed to improve our channel, we did not need very much in New York. When we needed to improve our channel, we came down to Congress and got it When we needed forty feet alongside of the Brooklyn shore, we came down to Congress and got it. And when we needed recently, as we need now very much, the improvement of the East River, we came down to Congress, Mr Chairman, to one of those committees of which you are a member, and they gave us every dollar in the bill that the U S Army

Engineers recommended.   Now we did not get it, but nobody else got anything this last time.   We are part of the United States, and we ought to take pot-luck with our neighbors.   It was an off day   (Laughter)

Now when that bill is up again our project will be in there   I know, and everybody that has ever served in Congress knows, that if it is not in the bill, we have forty-three Congressmen from the State of New York and we will attempt to mention it to them   But I have no doubt it will be in the bill.   We cannot get our project through before other people's projects go through

I want to say just one more word   We have not been badly used in New York   That might be an unpopular thing to say   It is always popular to get up when you come from your home town and say you have been badly used. But we have not   In the six years that I was in Congress, in addition to giving us what we asked for Harlem, which was the only thing which we were asking for then, they gave us $8,000,000 for public buildings, all that we asked, and $850,000 that they put in the bill without our asking it—we did not know anything about it

I am not criticising the Mayor   His figures are correct, as he can demonstrate, and I can demonstrate and you can demonstrate, Mr Chairman   Any man can take a piece of paper and pencil and prove that, we have not received as much money as some ports that have smaller commerce; but, thank the good Lord, we started with better harbors than those people did and we didn't need so much   I take pleasure, Mr Chairman, in offering these few brief remarks in seconding the motion to adopt the resolutions

The chair now put the motion to adopt the resolutions, and the same carried, and the resolutions were unanimously adopted

President Ransdell—I will now present to you Mr Olin J Stephens, of New York, Chairman of the Committee on Nominations.   (Applause.)

Report of Committee on Nominations

MR. PRESIDENT AND GENTLEMEN:

Your Committee on Nominations beg to present the following nominations for officers for the ensuing year:

President—Hon. Joseph E. Ransdell

Secretary-Treasurer—S. A. Thompson.

DIRECTORS

HONORARY FOR LIFE—

J F. Ellison . . . . .Cincinnati, Ohio

NORTH ATLANTIC SEABOARD—

Olin J. Stephens . . . . .New York City

William C. Sproul . . . . .Chester. Pa.

Theodore Justice . . . . .Philadelphia, Pa.

E W Douglas . . . . .Troy, N. Y.

Willard Thompson .Baltimore, Md.

Frank Fessenden Crane . . . . .Quincy, Mass

A V Hamburg .Newark, N. J.

Charles R. Miller . . . . Wilmington, Del.

Rollin S. Woodruff . . . . New Haven, Conn

George L Whitford . . . . .Warner, N. H.

George F. Washburn . . . . .Boston, Mass.

HUDSON, CHAMPLAIN AND GENESEE VALLEYS DISTRICT—

Lewis Nixon . . . . .New York City

F. W. Joslin . . . . .Troy, N. Y

John R. Myers . . . . .Rouses Point, N Y

Edward N. McKinney . . . . .Albany, N. Y.

James T. Hutchings . . . . Rochester, N. Y

SOUTH ATLANTIC SEABOARD—

Walter Clark . . . . .Raleigh. N. C.

M. I. Weller . . . . .Washington D C.

John C Freeman . . . .Richmond. Va

D. U. Fletcher . . , ...Jacksonville. Fla.

F. Horton Colcock . . . . Columbia. S. C

L. R. Aiken .   . . . .Brunswick. Ga.
Howell M Miller . . . . Washington, Va.
S. P. Gilbert   . . . .Columbus. Ga
Reid Whitford   . . . . Charleston, S. C.

Gulf Seaboard—
    Martin Behrman . . . . New Orleans, La.
    W. W Brandon . . . . .Tuscaloosa, Ala
    Thomas P. Hale .. . . Gulfport. Miss
    J W Worthington . . . . Sheffield, Ala
    T. Cheney Lawless . . . .Garden City, La
    J S Cullinan . . . . '   . . . . Houston, Texas
    Frank P. Holland . . . . .Dallas, Texas
    Roy Miller . . . . Corpus Christi, Texas

Mississippi Valley District—
    W. K Kavanaugh   . . . . St Louis, Mo.
    J. L Messmore . . . . .St Louis, Mo
    John A. Fox   . . . . .Memphis, Tenn.
    Charles Scott . . . . .Rosedale, Miss.
    Thomas Wilkinson .Burlington, Iowa
    M J Roach . . . . Memphis, Tenn
    J W Cooper   . . . .St Paul, Minn
    W G Streett   . . . . Lake Village, Ark
    A L Shapleigh . .   . . St. Louis, Mo.
    W F. Decker   .   . . . Minneapolis, Minn

Great Lakes District—
    James H Davidson   . . . . Oshkosh, Wis.
    Henry W Hill .   . .   .Buffalo, N. Y.
    T Edward Wilder   . . . . .Chicago, Ill
    Julius H Barnes . .   . .   Duluth, Minn.
    E. L. Southworth . . . . Toledo, Ohio
    P. W. Cullinan . . . . Oswego. N Y.
    Perry A. Randall . . . . Ft. Wayne, Ind.
    William A. Meese   . . . . .Moline. Ill.
    A. G. Wells . . . . .DePere Wis.
    J. W. Caswell   . . . . .Huntington, Ind.

OHIO VALLEY DISTRICT—
    Albert Bettinger ... ...Cincinnati, Ohio
    John L. Vance .... Columbus, Ohio
    William B Rodgers .. ..Pittsburgh, Pa
    George Parsons .. .. .Cairo, Ill.
    Pinkney Varble   . .. .Louisville, Ky
    M C Garber ... . Madison, Ind
    J. H Rohsenberger . ...Evansville, Ind
    R. F. Somerville .... Dayton, Ohio
    George M. Verity   . . . .Middletown, Ohio
    C. D. Dotson ....Parkersburg, W. Va.

TENNESSEE AND CUMBERLAND DISTRICT—
    M T. Bryan .... Nashville, Tenn
    J. A. Patten   . ... .Chattanooga, Tenn.
    E. C. Camp ....Knoxville, Tenn.

ARKANSAS VALLEY DISTRICT—
    George Sengel .... .Ft. Smith, Ark
    R T. Daniel ....Tulsa, Okla.
    W. M. Kavanaugh   . .. .Little Rock, Ark.

MISSOURI VALLEY DISTRICT—
    W T Bland ....Kansas City, Mo
    I. P. Baker . . .. Bismarck, N. D.
    Harry L George ....St. Joseph, Mo.
    W. B Wait   ... .Chamberlain, S. D.

PACIFIC COAST DISTRICT—
    A. H Devers .... Portland, Ore.
    Joseph R. Knowland . . .. Alameda, Cal
    W D Lyman .... Walla Walla, Wash.
    R. C Beach   .... Lewiston, Idaho
    J R McLaughlin .. . .Seattle, Wash

Respectfully submitted,

OLIN J. STEPHENS. *Chairman*

Mr Stephens thereupon moved the adoption of the report, which motion was duly seconded The question being put by Mr. Stephens, the motion carried unanimously and the respective nominees were declared duly elected to the offices named

Response by President-elect Ransdell

Gentlemen, I appreciate very highly and thank you sincerely for this renewed expression of your approval of my efforts as President of this organization You have had enough speeches from me and I do not intend to bore you with anything further There are a number of gentlemen here who have something to say in regard to their respective localities, and they are entitled to say it.

I can only promise you, gentlemen, that I shall work just as hard for this organization in the future as I have in the past (Applause).

Mr. Albert Bettinger, Cincinnati, Ohio

Mr President, Ladies and Gentlemen

May I be allowed to make a motion at this juncture? I am called away, which is my excuse for this interruption. I would like to move a vote of thanks to our very affable and capable Sergeant-at-Arms, Colonel John I. Martin, who has served this Convention not only on this occasion, but from the beginning; and also to his able assistant, Mr. J. J. Printup

The motion was seconded, and carried unanimously

President Ransdell—There are necessarily no Noes Colonel Martin, we are sincerely thankful to you, sir, for your splendid services

Mr Olin J. Stephens, Chairman, Committee on Nominations—Mr President, the Committee on Nominations have selected Mr Martin to act in the same capacity for the coming year. I am sorry that I did not include that in the report (Applause)

President Ransdell—We will have it included (Applause).

SECRETARY THOMPSON—The newly-elected Officers, Directors and State Vice-Presidents, who are present, are notified that we will have a meeting of the Board at two o'clock this afternoon.

While I am on my feet I will read the following telegram:

CORPUS CHRISTI, TEXAS, December 8, 1914.

HON JOSEPH E. RANSDELL,
PRESIDENT, NATIONAL RIVERS AND HARBORS CONGRESS, Washington, D. C

Regret exceedingly that my official and personal business prevents me, for the first time in eight years, from attending the National Convention of the National Rivers and Harbors Congress, especially since I regard this meeting as the most important in the history of our organization. Every true friend of waterway improvement should rally to the support of the Congress, in order that the splendid achievements of the past shall not have been in vain The great policy of the Congress, a comprehensive annual rivers and harbors bill based upon the country's need, is approved by the people, and will triumph in the end. We shall not fail if the splendid work of the Congress is continued with unrelenting vigor and determination.

ROY MILLER, *Mayor*

PRESIDENT RANSDELL—Under the rules of our organization, the various officers and the regular committees having reported, the Convention is now open for general discussion and brief addresses by delegates appointed to represent their respective States. If any member has anything special on his mind that he would like to present to this Convention, The Chair will recognize him for that purpose. We will be glad to hear from members from any State who would like to say anything to the Convention.

The Chair recognizes Mr Theodore Justice, of Pennsylvania.

Remarks—Theodore Justice, Philadelphia, Pa.

Mr Chairman and Gentlemen

I would like to have the attention of the Convention for a few minutes to enlarge on the question of intracoastal waterways as a means of national defense.

The President of the Atlantic Deeper Waterways Association touched upon that subject, but his time expired before he had an opportunity to fully develop his impressions.

The Senator from Massachusetts also briefly touched on that subject, and used these words: "The development in modern war of high explosives may relegate the battleship to the scrap heap." While I am not prepared to agree with him in that, at the same time the use of high explosives as a means of warfare in the future is a matter that should receive the profound consideration of the nation. Heretofore it has been considered that this was a matter affecting only the localities on the seaboard, but I wish to call the attention of the Convention to the fact that the interior of the country is in as much danger, and in as much need of protection, as the seaboard.

I have prepared a few remarks on that subject which I desire may go into the records of this Convention. These remarks have not been prepared so much for your entertainment as for the information of those who are to come after us, and who are to act on this question of the development of a belt line, as it were, of intracoastal waterways, as a means of national defense, in addition to their commercial benefits.

Waterways for National Defense

The United States Navy possesses 134 armed vessels, consisting of 21 torpedo boats, 62 destroyers, 20 revenue cutters, and 31 gunboats, all of which, with drawbridges, could pass through the locks of the new Erie Barge Canal, but since these bridges are fixed, none of them can now go through. On the other hand, similar craft in the hands of

Germany or any other enemy could enter our great lakes via the canals of Canada.

The Middle West has never realized that all of the lake cities of the Middle West could easily be destroyed, or held for a ransom equal to the whole cost of our Civil War, by an enemy approaching through the Canadian canals, while the United States, owing to the need of dredging a few feet out of the Hudson River and of converting the 198 fixed, low bridges over the Erie Barge Canal into drawbridges, is now totally unable to defend the lake cities of the Middle West against possible destruction from a fleet that may reach the Great Lakes via the Canadian canals

We do not require the huge armament of Europe We have in the Atlantic and Pacific Oceans allies which outweigh thousands of guns and hundreds of thousands of men We do need, however, to supplement these natural defenses by a military and naval establishment that will guarantee our shores from invasion. This may be supplied in part by an intracoastal belt line of waterways.

Europe will have been consumed in vain, as far as we are concerned, if we do not realize from the terrible conflict now going on that only by being prepared to defend ourselves can we ever be assured of lasting independence and security. Yet every attempt to provide against the ravages of war when it is brought to our shores, as any day it may be, is howled down by those in whose hands we have placed the keeping of the nation—and the loudest by those highest in office.

The man who sits on his roof while the property of his neighbor is going up in flames and the burning embers are falling all about him, is a subject for pity rather than admiration But the hour of universal peace has not yet struck. The lesson of these recent months is that war lurks in the dark corners of the world.

HISTORY BELIES PROPHECY

Two generations and more have passed since Victor Hugo presented to the International Peace Congress of 1849

his conception of a United States of Europe and prophesied
its early consummation—yet what a caricature has history
made of these prophecies! While our voice should never be
raised except in tones of peace, we cannot, until those who
surround us have struck the same note, afford to ground our
arms and turn our cannon into plowshares

The experience of the present European war will revolutionize naval warfare. High explosives utilized by submarines or torpedo boats may send the dreadnaught to the
scrap heap. Small craft that cannot carry sufficient supplies to remain long at sea may constitute the most effective
portion of the navies of the future. For this reason the
development of inland waterways becomes of the greatest
importance as a means for national defense

By connecting Massachusetts Bay, by canal through the
Taunton River, with Narragansett Bay, Narragansett Bay,
by canal inside of Point Judith, with Long Island Sound;
Newark Bay by canal with Delaware Bay, Delaware Bay
with the Chesapeake Bay, and the Albemarle and Pamlico
Sounds by canal with the Gulf; by connecting Lake Erie
through a canal to the Ohio River, or Lake Michigan by
canal to the Mississippi, and thence by both routes through
the latter river to the Gulf, we may, in the next generation,
develop the most complete and effective method for inland
defense ever possessed by any country in the world   Many
forms of naval craft that cannot voyage around the world
would be eminently practicable for national defense through
such of our inland waterways as are connected with our
great seaports.

It is being widely said by a certain class of thinkers that
"There is no surer way of provoking war than by being prepared for it"   And they point to the great war now being
waged in proof of this assertion   Much as we deplore war,
much as we desire peace, much as we may earnestly work
and pray for peace, based upon the experience of the past,
there is no ground whatever to justify us in looking confi-
dently for universal peace in the future.

Kipling says· "There are no ten commandments east of
Suez." What we may expect from the Orient is shown in

what Germany has experienced in China. Does not this warn us, when treaties are regarded as mere scraps of paper, to be prepared for defense, not only against the Far East but the West as well? There is a sharp distinction between aggressive and defensive power. There is nothing wrong or immoral in naval power as such. It is justified by the use that is made of it There is nothing to provoke war in the United States arming for defense Indeed, the surest way of preserving peace for the United States is to be adequately prepared. And there is no such easy and peaceful way of securing that strength as by making full use of the inland waterways for purposes of defense.

Indeed, it is manifest that inland waterways in no way lend themselves to aggression upon distant nations, but, on the other hand, are purely for self defense. Moreover, defensive waterways lessen the likelihood of aggression, inasmuch as they lessen the need of numbers of warships.

A large part of the coastwise commerce may pass through inland waterways Therefore such vessels of commerce as do not require to pass along the coast outside may dispense with naval convoy in time of war, and fewer warships of the aggressive battle class are required in proportion as inland waterways are developed and become the ideal channels for submarines and destroyers which may freely pass from one port to another, issuing forth when required for defense Amply protected by coast fortifications and inland waterways, and with a sufficient number of submarines and destroyers, the United States, secure in herself, depending upon the outside world practically only for luxuries, and sufficient to herself for all the necessities of life, may bid defiance to the world.

Due to Sinking of "Maine"

How many of us realize that, but for the incident of the sinking of the battleship "Maine," the Panama Canal today would not have been begun? When we were suddenly facing war, we found our fleet divided, part of it being in the Pacific

Ocean Each division then was liable to the hazard of being
defeated in detail. The long, hazardous trip of the "Oregon"
around the southern end of the South American continent
was a matter of intense daily anxiety to the whole Nation
and aroused the sense of the need of the Panama Canal as
a matter of importance in national defense. The Nation
was thus aroused to the necessity of extending our coast
line so that instead of having two small fleets, we could,
in case of need, unite both sections in one mighty fleet in
either ocean.

There are many international questions which are charged
with danger and at any moment may lead to conflict with
the whole world united against us, and this may come upon
us as suddenly as the sinking of the "Maine "

Then our greatest cities of New York, Philadelphia,
Baltimore, and the Capital City, Washington, may be at
the mercy of the united European fleets—a danger that
may be averted if the links that now connect New York Bay
with the Delaware and Chesapeake are deepened to torpedo
fleet requirements, which will be safe from attack from
battleships, but so protected by our coast line as to have
all the advantages of a short inside line or segment of a
circle for retreat, and from which offensive warfare may
also be made.

The broad, national value of such an expansion of our
waterways will be of far more value to the people of the
United States than even that of the Panama Canal, conceding as I do quite as much for the national value of the latter
as its most sanguine advocate.

It is quite within the range of possibilities that by the
time the Atlantic deeper waterways can be developed, if
begun immediately, hydroplane squadrons, in addition to
the foregoing torpedo fleet requirements, may be available.

The immediate expansion of the short connecting links,
that lack only fifteen per cent to unite the eighty-five per cent
of deep water already provided by nature, is the most imperative call upon Congress at this moment. Therefore, I
submit the question as to whether it is not incumbent upon

the United States to immediately prepare, in advance of all other projects, this greatest of them all, ample facilities for national defense.

Will any broad-minded and patriotic citizen of the United States not concede that matters for national defense should have precedence at all times over the many other meritorious projects that have been proposed? All of the latter contain great commercial value to the Nation, and I hope that within the course of reasonable time all of them will be developed. But, in the interest of the whole Nation, the greatest project of them all is the immediate preparation for national defense contained within the plans of the Atlantic Deeper Waterways Association, extending all the way from Maine to Florida.

Volunteer Call—Mayor Benjamin Bosse, Evansville, Ind.

Mr. Chairman and Gentlemen:

The State of Indiana is represented in this Convention by delegates from its various cities. We come to this Convention to urge all those in authority to continue the good work they have begun in the past years of the improvement of our rivers and harbors.

I cannot quite understand, after having attended these meetings for the past ten years, why the man who urged us to do the work is now the man that we have got to convince that the work ought to go on. (Applause.)

I received my instruction under Senator Burton. I would like for Senator Burton to know that the people down in Indiana, and especially those of us on the Ohio, have nothing in mind other than that this work is going to continue, and that it should continue. In fact, we understood it and took it that this policy has been determined on and fixed by the Government, and especially that the plan was that the improvement of the Ohio River was to be continued, and gentlemen, there is no question but what it should be continued, nor do I doubt that it will be.

Down in Indiana—to show you the interest we have taken in this matter—in our city a week ago, when a meeting was called to take up the question of improving our harbor, I was amazed to see the largest number assembled that had ever gathered in our city at any one time. The support for that movement was unanimous, and we were urged to go on to this Congress and say to you that nothing should be left undone, that everything possible should be done to urge upon those in authority in Congress that this work must and should continue The conviction is general among our people that the vast amount of money already invested justifies our asking that the work be continued in order to give us an opportunity of doing business over the great waterway that runs by our shores. I refer to the Ohio River and its tributaries.

Gentlemen, I congratulate you upon your work and I hope you will continue to meet in this Congress until all shall see the light

Gentlemen, I thank you for your attention (Applause)

PRESIDENT RANSDELL—I see in front of me the Mayor of that city which the people of Louisiana are proud to call the greatest city in the South. Will not Mayor Behrman give us a few words? Come to the rostrum, will you not, Mr. Mayor, or at least come to the front so that people can see what you look like? (Applause.)

Volunteer Call—Mayor Martin Behrman, New Orleans, La.

MR. PRESIDENT AND GENTLEMEN OF THE CONGRESS.

The thought came to my mind when the distinguished gentleman from New York was addressing the Convention that we down South might ask our representatives to ask the rulers of the Nation if they could not cast their eyes southward once in a while instead of eastward, as they are wont to do I can say to you, gentlemen of the Convention, that down where I live we never have had any appropriations forced on us by the Government of this country. (Applause.) And those that we have gotten we have gotten by tremendous hard work by those who represent us in Congress.

Now, my friends, we are here from Louisiana, a large delegation of representative men, who have not come, as the "other Field Secretary" said, at the expense of city councils or other crganized branches of the Government, but at their own expense, because they believe that the work of this Congress ought to be helped along, because this National Congress of Rivers and Harbors is doing a great work in educating the country as to the need for waterways   Down where we live, my friends, we are badly in need of waterway improvement; we have been doing tremendous things in that way ourselves.   The Chief of our State Board of Engineers, who is in attendance at this Convention, advises me that on the first of November we had over $3,000,000 of contracts for the levee work in our State at the expense of the people of the State.   We have been doing that for years and years!   We have been taking care of the water that comes to us from all of the States east of the Rockies   The water from all sections of the country has come down to us, and we have had to take care of it, which we do not think is exactly fair.   We are glad to do it, however, but we think that where a community like ours has done so much to help itself that the great arm of the Government ought to reach out to help that great Mississippi Valley.

The city of New Orleans, down South where I live, with due apologies to the city of New York, will yet be the greatest city in the country.   (Applause)   We have been doing things there, my friends, things which in a certain sense have been forced upon us.   Nature has been very kind to us, it is true.   The great Government of this country saw fit to begin the construction of the Panama Canal, and my city of New Orleans is the nearest large seaport to the canal, and must be in condition to handle the merchandise that will come in there, a great deal of it from the Mississippi Valley to find an outlet to the sea   So down there we have assumed the responsibility of taking care of that condition, and at a tremendous expense to our people, who are already overburdened with taxation, they have met that situation and have made that as fine a seaport as any in the country. (Applause.)

As you may perhaps know, we at New Orleans own our own river front. It belongs to the people, we have never parted with it. We have magnificent steel sheds, about eight miles of them—mammoth warehouses as they are, to receive the cargoes that come there, and for the use of outgoing vessels. You are all interested in that because you want what you raise in your section of the country, when it comes down to our section to find an outlet to the sea, to be handled not only carefully but at minimum cost Our facilities for loading and unloading cargoes are unexcelled, and we are held up as an example to the rest of the country in that we occupy the unique position of having the only publicly-owned-and-controlled municipal belt road in this country.

We own our own road connecting with every wharf and every industry on the river front. If you have a car of merchandise consigned to a ship side or to an industry on the water front, that car does not remain blockaded in some railway yard subject to charges, but we handle the cars of all the roads over that belt line road at $2 00 per car That is practically all the charges to which it is subjected. . When I tell you that, will you not believe that we have been doing something down our way and that the eyes of the Nation ought to look southward and not force appropriations on the people of the East who do not ask for them? (Applause.) We are asking for them, and we think we are justified in asking for them since we deserve them.

Down where we live, my friends, especially in the great city that I have the honor to represent here today, no people have suffered more than we have. Of course, we do not talk about the war any more, we have forgotten it. This great country is all one now. But we passed through the war, and through the reconstruction period that came after that and which was worse than the war We have suffered also with disease, pestilence and flood Every one of those situations were bravely met by the people down there, and met successfully. I tell you, it took a brave people to meet crises of that kind.

Do not believe it when they tell you that our people down there are a slow, easy-going people, satisfied to "let well enough alone." They are not. They may have been in the olden days, but the new generation are not satisfied with things as they were We want things that are up to date, and we are striving and working hard to build up our community When they tell you that our city is a good place to have a good time, and praise our cocktails and gin fizzes, that is true, we have them all; but we do not want them for ourselves. Our people have grown accustomed to them. There is so much dry territory in this country now—theoretically dry I mean—that we want to have something for all of you when you come down to visit us (Laughter.)

New Orleans is a charming city to visit, and it is a splendid place, my friends, to do business in. Let me tell you in all seriousness, my friends, that we are doing wonderful things down there, and we have a wonderful future in store not only for the city of New Orleans but for the entire State of Louisiana.

Do you know that our State has produced more lumber than any State in the Union except the State of Washington? The largest sulphur mine in the world is located there. We have the greatest salt mines in this country there. Of course you know about our rice, corn and cotton We have a great oil and natural gas field also in Louisiana Above all, we have got the finest and best people on earth down in Louisiana All we want is to be treated fairly, not any better, but just as good as any other section of the country

I thank you (Applause).

Volunteer Call—M. C. Thornton, New Albany, Ind.

Mr President and Gentlemen:

I am here from New Albany, Ind . I just want to inform the Mayor of New Orleans that we sent the steamer "Sprague" to New Orleans the other day with five acres of coal so that they can keep things warm in New Orleans.

Volunteer Call—Harry E. Cook, Lake Village, Ark.

Mʀ Pʀᴇsɪᴅᴇɴᴛ ᴀɴᴅ Gᴇɴᴛʟᴇᴍᴇɴ:

No single feature has contributed more to the splendid success of this Convention than the magnificent labors of the Woman's National Rivers and Harbors Congress I believe that the Committee on Resolutions, of which I was a member, was derelict in their duty in not recommending that that splendid organization have a representative upon our list of Directors We should authorize them to select their own representative upon our Board of Directors; and to that end I move that we request the Woman's National Rivers and Harbors Congress to select some representative from their number and that we add that name to our official list of Directors and incorporate the same upon our minutes

The motion being seconded was stated by The Chair, carried unanimously and so ordered

Pʀᴇsɪᴅᴇɴᴛ Rᴀɴsᴅᴇʟʟ—I desire to state that the Chairman is highly pleased that that suggestion was made. The Chair will be glad to hear any further suggestions for the good of the order

Volunteer Call—Clarence E. Wood, Eustis, Fla.

Mʀ. Pʀᴇsɪᴅᴇɴᴛ ᴀɴᴅ Gᴇɴᴛʟᴇᴍᴇɴ ·

I feel very much impressed with the magnificent speeches that we have heard here and am ready now to enlist in the war for this great cause (Applause). I come from the oldest State in the Union, if you gentlemen of Boston will permit me to say it—one that Columbus discovered—the second largest State east of the Mississippi River in our Union I come from a State which has increased more largely in population in 1910 than any other State except Oklahoma. I come from the State which has the largest water front in the Union, and the largest and longest line of navigable waters I suppose Florida has ten thousand lakes My county has thirteen hundred, and not one of them is less in size than the District of Columbia (Applause). We are nearest to the Panama Canal. Our ports are ample, and New Orleans is not in it as compared with Key West, Tampa and St. Petersburg

We are the sun parlor of the United States. You come down there to warm your feet in winter and you get at breakfast bananas and all those tropical fruits. You up here know nothing of the beauties of Florida. I will merely say to you,

> "Come in the evening, or come in the morning;
> Come when you're looked for, or come without warning;
> Come if you must without others before you,
> The oftener you come, the more we'll adore you!"

(Applause)

Volunteer Call—Frank Fessenden Crane, Quincy, Mass.

Mr. Chairman and Gentlemen:

It is with a great deal of diffidence that I speak for so small and retiring a State at this time as the State of Massachusetts (Applause). After hearing from these large and glorious States of Louisiana, Arkansas and Florida I really feel extremely delicate about saying anything with reference to so small a State as Massachusetts; yet I have been selected by my delegation to represent them in this matter, and they have told me, "Do not sit still and let those Western fellows entirely down you; get up and say something for the good old State of Massachusetts." So I feel that it is only my duty to say a little something for the State of Massachusetts

My remarks will be very brief I wish to tell you why Massachusetts is interested in water transportation. It is true that we have a large ocean frontage there, but we are paying the highest freight rates of any State in the Union. We have shipped around Cape Cod annually 25,000,000 tons of freight during the last 10 years That trip around Cape Cod during that period has cost this country 2,176 vessels, 700 lives, and $40,000,000. Therefore, we are intensely interested in the intracoastal waterway which is included in the Atlantic Deeper Waterways proposition

We have in our State various things of which we are as proud, perhaps, as the gentleman from the preceding State We have a banking system in our State of which we are proud, in view of the fact that it is popular. One-fifth of the savings of the whole American people is in the savings banks of Greater Boston. (Applause.)

We have mechanics in Massachusetts of whom we are justly proud, by reason of their superior skill. We are proud of the superb organization of our factories, because of which these mechanics have a greater producing power by eighty per cent than any other mechanics in the known world We have more men in Greater Boston earning $2 50 per day, and less men earning $1 50 per day, than any other portion of the known world We have other things of which we are not so proud. We have an annual coal bill of $100,000,000 We pay out $70,000,000 a year for freight We are not so proud of that

Massachusetts contributes annually to the United States Government $35,000,000. Massachusetts has herself contributed to the rivers and harbors of that State $26,000,000; and we have received from the United States Government, from the very beginning, appropriations aggregating $21,000,000. It has taken us so long and we have been so busy in expending the $26,000,000 that we have ourselves appropriated in our State, that we have not given the time, we have not put in the effort, to have the United States Government do for us all that we expect to have it do in the future I thank you (Applause)

PRESIDENT RANSDELL—Are there some other patriots here who are willing to defend their Commonwealth?

Volunteer Call—Ernest H. Rowe, Jersey City, N. J.
Executive Secretary Chamber of Commerce

MR. CHAIRMAN AND GENTLEMEN·
I speak largely because we are the baby or infant of this Congress. On the stroke of midnight, at the end of the

last fiscal year, November 30, 1914, we joined the Congress —the Jersey City Chamber of Commerce. We appreciated your remarks regarding Mrs Henry, because Mrs. Henry got that membership, and I was in hopes that she would make a report of that colossal achievement, because it. has taken that organization ten years to come to that point. Some years ago the opportunity was offered our organization, but it was then declined. But Mrs. Henry secured the membership (Applause.)

Another excuse for my speaking is the fact that New Jersey is about ninety per cent of the Port of New York, and the port development work which the Chamber of Commerce, of which I am Executive Secretary, has now undertaken, is so serious that it is necessary for the engineering staff to make a special study of the problem, and it is devoting more money to the solution of that problem than it had two years ago for the prosecution of all of its work. This proves that at least our city has awakened to the vastness of the difficulties which are commensurate with the possibilities of the work

Eight of the transcontinental trunk lines are obliged to reach the city of New York through our territory, and the problem of the Port of New York is equally the problem of Jersey City, which is contiguous to it Eighty-seven per cent of the commerce of the country passes through the Port of New York. We are the spout of the funnel and we are within a distance of less than five miles from the termini of the railroads which handle all the goods that you send across the Atlantic and which Europe and South America send to this country.

From the bottom of our hearts we envy New Orleans because we are today where Mayor Behrman says they used to be With all of those railroads there. it costs you anywhere from $5 00 to $18.00 to get a car from your siding to another railroad which may be within gunshot of your factory door. we are striving or hoping that some day we can give our manufacturers and shippers, as well as shippers all over the United States. similar advantages to those provided by New Orleans. With so many railroads in close proximity a great problem arises because of the fact that the shipping lines, coming across the Atlantic and receiving and discharging cargoes from and to the railroads, are isolated from the railroads by a water barrier a mile wide. That is to say, those railroads are on our side of the North River, whereas sixty-eight of the seventy-five steamship lines that make the Port of New York regularly dock on the New York side; and countless millions of tons of freight have to be interchanged between those carriers over that water at a cost the amount of which nobody knows The railroads charge three cents per 100 pounds, and they load the freight with that charge for lighterage We have estimated that it costs as high as $2.00 per ton to move that freight across that mile of water, counting in the cost of equipment, maintenance, and operation; and nobody can tell what it costs in the way of inconvenience and lost time The problem is appalling in its dimensions It is absolutely one of the great national problems that we are attempting to solve. (Applause)

THEODORE JUSTICE, Philadelphia, Pa —Gentlemen: The delegate has stated that about eighty-seven per cent of the tonnage in the country comes in at New York harbor. I would like to ask him to elaborate that thought for our information.

PRESIDENT RANSDELL—I would be glad to call upon others here who represent their sections, I want to give them a chance to be heard. The United Commercial Travelers are so proverbially retiring, that they never offer to speak unless called upon. So if there be a representative of that great organization here, I am going to ask him to say a word or two to us in its behalf for the general cause Is Mr. C. C Taylor here? Will you not kindly say something, if you please? Let us hear from you.

Volunteer Call—C. C. Taylor, Greensboro, N. C.

Mr. Chairman and Gentlemen of the Congress

This is the first time that I have had the privilege of attending this great Convention; therefore, quietness and modesty was the keynote with me. I have the honor to represent a great organization known as the United Commercial Travelers of America at this Convention.

I have the pleasure of living in a Southern State—North Carolina. I have not heard much said about the great State of North Carolina and its great ports of entry as compared with statements made concerning great ports of entry on other coasts. Wilmington, the second largest port of entry on the Atlantic Coast, stands second in the exportation of cotton and other southern commodities. The inland waterway connecting Chesapeake Bay with Albemarle Sound will avoid the hazardous point of Hatteras, the most fatal on the coast of North Carolina, and the Government of the United States, in making provisions for that waterway improvement, can expend money nowhere else to such advantage. (Applause.)

There are more lives lost off the coast of North Carolina because of the dangerous surroundings of Cape Hatteras than at any other one point of the Atlantic seaboard. I feel that the President and other members of the United States Senate and House of Representatives realize the great importance of connecting up the Atlantic Coast canals that have been talked about in order that vessels can be gotten through to Baltimore, Philadelphia and New York from Chesapeake Bay, and further south connecting with Albemarle Sound, in order that this great transportation of commerce may be carried safely through inland waterways. I feel sure that there will be no criticism whatever of such investments. They will serve the commercial interests of the people of this great country, and are badly needed.

I must confess to you, gentlemen, that I have never made a study of this proposition before and that I have been ignorant concerning it, or practically so, until after I happened to be sent as a delegate to this Congress, but I have

been surprised to hear the statements of our Secretary and
the statements of our President, as to the severe criticisms
that have been made of this organization and the decrying
of its purposes Gentlemen, you are enlisted in a great and
noble work You are serving not only the interests of your
individual States, but also the interests of this great country
of which we are all a part (Applause)

It is said, you know, when a man opposes a railroad
scheme that he is destructive and not at all constructive—
that his acts are confiscatory. Why, gentlemen, the premier
carrier road of the South passes through the heart of the
State of North Carolina, and after they have squeezed the
water out of the stock the Southern Railroad can pay upon
its present dividend basis about nineteen per cent on the
actual amount of money invested. (Applause)

Now we have had in the State of North Carolina, and
on the river particularly, a man who has recently received an
appointment at the hands of this Government, Mr E J.
Justice, who has been said to be so radical in his views that,
in trying to bankrupt the Southern Railroad by reducing its
railroad rates, he would throw the State of North Carolina
into bankruptcy as well.

Mr Chairman, I do not want to exceed my time limit,
but I am so enthusiastic on this proposition that I hope you
will bear with me

President Ransdell—One minute more, then

Mr Taylor—What was the result? The Legislature,
through the efforts of Mr Justice, passed what they called
an intrastate freight rate bill, and the railroad company said
that if they would not put that into force they would hold an
investigation at the courthouse in the city of Greenville,
N C, and would reduce rates that they had been charging,
and save to the State of North Carolina $2,000,000 a year
on interstate freight rates. They practically volunteered
that proposition; but it was due to the fact that intrastate
freight rates were going to be fixed, and we were going to
require also overhead bridges to protect the people at dangerous places, and rather than be put to that expense they

said, "We will give you a decrease in the freight rates amounting to $2,000,000 a year."

We have two great rivers in our State The Neuse is one and the Cape Fear is the other Wilmington is on the Cape Fear River, about thirty miles from the mouth of the river, or from the ocean. Right at the dock in the city of Wilmington there is about thirty-four feet of water. (Time was here called.) I am through my speech anyway! (Laughter and applause.)

President Ransdell.—We will now hear from any volunteers Do not all speak at once, gentlemen! Representative Collier, of Mississippi, has been asked to say a few words for that great Commonwealth—Mr Collier!

Volunteer Call—J. W. Collier, M. C., Vicksburg, Miss.

Mr President, Ladies and Gentlemen:

In the brief time allotted me on this occasion I want to assure you that it gives me great pleasure to represent the State of Mississippi at a meeting where each and every one is actuated by the high sentiment of improving the rivers and harbors of our country, which means so much to the material development of my Commonwealth. (Applause.)

My time, as I understand it, is extremely limited. I thank you for giving me this opportunity to speak in behalf of a State whose shores on one side are washed by the mighty "Father of Waters," while within that State there are many streams now navigable, and many which in the future will be navigable, and also to give you the assurance that, humble as my cooperation may be, yet that cooperation in this most vital question is with you as to all the purposes of this Convention (Applause.)

My friends, during the last twelve or fifteen months there has been much adverse criticism indulged in at the expense of rivers and harbors improvements Some of the criticism has been actuated by honest motives and with an honest endeavor to get the best which can be gotten along these

lines; but I say to you that the greater part of this criticism
comes from those who know little or absolutely nothing
about river and harbor development, and who, by reason of
their ignorance, have made the wildest and most extravagant
statements   (Applause)

Another source of criticism, and one by far the most dangerous, comes from those who are familiar with the work of
river and harbor improvement, and by reason of their famil-
iarity, by reason of their knowledge of details, have selected
some small and perhaps unimportant item which may be
an unfortunate one, an item, perhaps, which might not or
ought not to have been in the bill, and holding that item up
to public scorn and public ridicule, have attempted either
by insinuation or innuendo to make it appear that the great
national improvements which are so necessary for the commercial development of our country are on all fours with
non-meritorious improvements.

My friends, you can talk about the Interstate Commerce
Commission regulating rates throughout the United States
—and far be it from me to disparage in any degree the
splendid work of that Commission; but I say to you that
unless we have these great natural highways of competition,
the rivers of our country, developed so that our commodities
may be cheaply transported, you will never have that free
and easy and perfect competition which is desired, and
which we ought to have, no matter how many Interstate
Commerce Commissions we may have   (Applause)

I say that the Interstate Commerce Commission is doing
good work; but we cannot do without these great natural
highways of transportation; and if the programme that we
have mapped out for river and harbor development is hindered, obstructed and stopped, the American people will find
to their cost that they have made an economic error disastrous in its consequences and almost overwhelming in its
paralyzing results.

Statesmen in countries across the sea have had the constructive genius and the prescience to prepare for their
countries' needs, and it seems to me as though most of our

people here are familiar with our country's wants and our country's needs, and that that fact was never so well emphasized as by this splendid gathering, this meeting we have held in Washington for the last three days, where are gathered representative men from every State in this Union, all animated by a common interest and a common purpose—the development of our waterway system   (Applause)

Why, my friends, the merchant at the crossroad store, the farmer whose farm lies on the bank of a river, the artisan in his shop, the business man in the city, the lawyer at the bar, the physician pursuing his practice, all know that unless our rivers, those great arteries of transportation, shall be so improved that they will be kept open to carry our products and commodities from one point to another, and unless our harbors, those other great and essential instrumentalities of commerce, shall be preserved and kept open to the entry of ships of the largest tonnage so that our agricultural products and our manufactured articles may be transported at minimum cost to the markets of the world, they all know that unless this can be done. unless that work be not hindered, our great country, despite the fact of its greatness, despite its wonderful resources, despite its wonderful commercial development, will be destined to play but a restricted part in the great drama of commercial history.

Therefore, from every section of our country there is in the hearts and minds of the great masses of our people a conviction, which is given utterance by these delegates sent from every State in this Union to this Convention, that when the material prosperity of our country is considered, the upbuilding and the preservation and the taking care of our navigable streams and the preserving of our harbors, so that they will be free to the commerce of the world, must be kept up to the fullest extent commensurate with the means and ability of the American people   (Applause.)

Volunteer Call—Dr. T. E. Baird, Norfolk, Va.

We have waited long and patiently for our State Vice-President, Captain Dobie, my distinguished friend and attorney. We have waited for him, but he has not arrived, and so I, who am merely an ordinary pill-roller, will endeavor to take his place.

I have listened with a great deal of pleasure and a great deal of profit, and have been much informed by the eloquent speakers who have appeared representing their respective States. I shall not try in any way to measure up to the Congressmen or the Senators that have spoken, or to our President.

I simply want to say to you, in a few words, that we are on the map, and we believe that the birds sing nowhere so sweetly, the flowers bloom nowhere so beautifully, the sun nowhere shines half so brightly, as down in old Virginia.

We are from the President's home, as you all know, and are proud of the fact that we are first, as the Irishman said when he waked up after a debauch in the cemetery and found himself surrounded by tombstones, "Well, I am the first man to wake up!" And so I say, I am not the representative, but I am the first man to wake up. (Applause) Our present President, who sits in the executive chair of the White House, was formed from the soil of Virginia, and we are still ahead.

This is the first Convention of the National Rivers and Harbors Congress that it has been my privilege to attend. I have received much inspiration. I have heard a great deal about the Mississippi River and the Ohio River, something also of the Merrimac and some other rivers; but we have one little river down our way, a very short one, upon which is situated Norfolk. You cannot go from Maine to Florida, or to California, by boat without stopping at Norfolk and getting some coal to help you along. (Applause.) We have there the greatest coal depot, I think, in the United States, millions and millions and millions of tons of coal, to stow away in ships and help them on their way. It happens to be my fortunate privilege to be State Health Officer of

Virginia, and I know whereof I speak when I tell you of the great numbers of vessels that come into that port from your different ports

But I will not prolong these remarks I have listened with a great deal of pleasure to the gentleman who has told us how New York State was developing its canals and its water fronts. As I looked upon the lantern slides with my wife, who sat beside me, I said to her, "That is wonderful, that is amazing, but God in His infinite wisdom and goodness has smiled upon Virginia and we do not have to make our channels down there, we get them naturally" (Applause.)

President Ransdell—Will some one else volunteer? Mr McKinney, of Albany, can you say something for the Hudson? We have not had anything here about the Hudson as yet. Gentlemen, I present Mr McKinney, of Albany, N Y

Volunteer Call—Edward N. McKinney, Albany, N. Y.

Mr. Chairman and Gentlemen:

I rather hesitate to talk, because the last time I addressed a gathering I got myself in trouble

President Ransdell—We will promise not to put you in trouble this time.

Mr. McKinney—I was on a committee that gave me a little work to do and therefore I just had the opportunity to come up here and was immediately called upon.

I am very much interested in the Congress and its policy —"A Policy, Not a Project;" although I think that every individual delegate comes here with a policy as well as a project. We are all here to talk our projects, and I rather think that if you were to take away all the delegates with projects you would not have a corporal's guard attending this Convention. (Applause)

I am willing to come a long distance to hear Senator Ransdell and these other distinguished gentlemen talk, but in reality I am down here in the interest of the Hudson River and my native town of Albany Albany has a very large interest in a certain project, as well as the whole State of New York; and I rather think we have the largest number of delegates of any city in the country We have about eighty of them attending this Convention from the city of Albany. In looking over the report of the finances of this organization, I find that Albany has been interested enough in this Congress and its policy to have contributed between one-sixth and one-seventh of the entire amount brought in by the Field Secretaries. (Applause)

We have also made the largest contribution of any single city in the country. Mind you, we are a city of only from one hundred to one hundred and twenty-five thousand inhabitants, and we have paid into your treasury about $2,500 this year.

Albany is a city, as I would like to tell my friend Secretary Bryan, that is doing nothing but talk water, and more water, all the time (Applause.)

I want to tell you what we are doing in our State, and how we feel about this waterway matter You know we are not narrow up there. We send lots of people down here from New York State, but New York is a large State and Albany is a large city, and while we believe that New York State and the Hudson River do not deserve all the recognition to the exclusion of the Western States, which should have their proportion according to their needs, we are just as ready to work for all parts of the country as we are for our own individual locality ((Applause) And I want to tell you that New York State is doing that for the rest of the country. I hope I have not exceeded my limit.

President Ransdell—You have still a half minute

Mr. McKinney—Is that all?

President Ransdell—Well, one minute.

MR. MCKINNEY—Of course this is one of the principal things that we are interested in. We figure that the work we are doing in New York State for our Barge Canal is going to favor at least one-third of the people of this country in reducing freight rates. We believe that it will affect favorably 16,000,000 people in the great West and Northwest. We further are figuring on making our Barge Canal more effective by deepening the Hudson up to Troy so that ocean-going vessels may go up to that point. It will cost $16,000,000, but we believe it will benefit at least 16,000,000 people, and therefore we say that for $1 00 per capita tax at least one-half of the Nation will be benefited when we make this great improvement, because the whole country can freely use our big Barge Canal at a tax of not to exceed $1.00 each for 16,000,000 people

The State of New York has spent approximately $16.00 per capita for every one of its inhabitants for building this Barge Canal which the people of the western and northwestern country have had the use of. Now that is a 16 to 1 proposition which should appeal to you, we think, more than the one that was enunciated eighteen years ago. Now that is what we are asking the Federal Government to do for us in New York State. If we are satisfied to pay $16 00 per capita for your benefit, we think that you should be willing to spend $1 00 per capita for us. (Here time was called.) Very well, that is all I wanted to say.

PRESIDENT RANSDELL—And you said it well

Volunteer Call—James R. Yerger, Lake Village, Ark.

MR. PRESIDENT AND GENTLEMEN

I cannot sit tamely in my seat and hear the praises of other States sung without saying something for Arkansas. I do not know whether it is generally known in the United States, or not, but Arkansas could build a brick wall around her boundary lines and live without the rest of this Union We have everything in Arkansas that is necessary for human existence and human pleasure.

We have iron and coal, we have oil, we have diamonds and we raise everything on our soil that can be raised anywhere else in the United States, except bananas, lemons and oranges—and we can do without them, because we have steamboats to New Orleans, Mayor Behrman's town.

Arkansas opals are found in New York, and also Arkansas diamonds While the people of the United States seem to think that the only thing they can find in Arkansas is the Hot Springs, I want to say to you that while we are very proud of Hot Springs, in Arkansas Hot Springs is very much like Vicksburg, Miss Hot Springs does not think it is part of Arkansas and neither does Vicksburg think it is part of Mississippi I would not make that statement except for the fact that my friend from Vicksburg is here (Laughter)

I am from that section of the State, southeastern Arkansas, which is deeply interested in the purposes of this organization I come from that section where, when the Mississippi River rises to the top of the levees, we people have to get out and fight it; and I have done that night after night myself, stood guard alongside of those levees to see that we were not swept away by the mighty floods of that stream I have planted my crops and stood on my front porch and seen the waters roll over them. So I say that we people down there are heartily in sympathy with this great movement, and there is nothing on earth that we would not do to assist it. (Applause.)

President Ransdell—We had some very interesting statements a day or two ago in regard to the obsolete character of the navigation on some of our rivers. I see a great navigator in front of me I wonder if he would not like to say something on that subject—Captain Barrett, of the Ohio River (Applause). Maybe you would like to talk on some other subject, Captain? Gentlemen. Captain Barrett, of Ohio!

Volunteer Call—Captain Oscar F. Barrett, Cincinnati, Ohio

Mr President, Ladies and Gentlemen:

I would like to talk to you about the Ohio River I would like to have some of those people, especially some of the Senate and perhaps a few in the House, that do not believe in waterway improvement, come down and see what the Ohio has looked like for the past year or two. We have had a lower river than I have seen for a long while. In fact there was not a boat stage anywhere on the Ohio River except where the Government had improved it by locks. On the greater portion of the river from Pittsburgh to Cairo, during a great part of the time, only a few little gasoline boats were plying, because they were the only craft that could get over the bars. You have heard about the difficulties of navigating on the Mississippi River; but I want to tell you that we are worse off than they are on either the Mississippi or the Missouri

I thank you .

PRESIDENT RANSDELL—I see a gentleman from the city of Houston, Texas, which has done a great deal to improve its own waterway. I call upon Mr Boldt to say something to us— just a few words of encouragement.

Volunteer Call—Adolph Boldt, Houston, Texas
Secretary Chamber of Commerce

MR. CHAIRMAN, GENTLEMEN OF THE NATIONAL RIVERS AND HARBORS CONGRESS, AND LADIES.

I like to talk to the ladies, but I would rather talk to them one at a time! (Applause.)

Now you are going to hear from a real State. Texas has 248 large counties, while poor old Delaware has but three counties at low tide, and only two at high tide

PRESIDENT RANSDELL—You will get the Delaware man after you next

MR BOLDT—I never realized how large our State was until I crossed it on a slow train. Recently we have completed the Houston Ship Canal and have divided expenses with the Government. We have very recently in addition issued bonds in the amount of $5,500,000, part of which is for wharf facilities.

Houston has a wonderful strategic location in relation to the geographical center of the United States   Smith County, Kan , is the geographical center of our country   It is 1,300 miles from there to New York and an equal number of miles to San Francisco, but only 720 miles to Houston.

Houston as a port is 500 miles nearer geographically than any Atlantic or Pacific port, with down grade freight haul   In other words, every great freight-producing section seeks tidewater with the least mileage and the least resistance, and the ports of Houston and Galveston are the logical routes   All of the great trunk lines, most of them operating in the Trans-Mississippi country, point their noses toward Houston   Hence Houston is a city with seventeen railroads running to the sea

Naturally we are proud of our city   As the Irishman said, "Every man should be proud of the land of his nativity whether he was born there or not." (Laughter)

We have more home-owning persons perhaps than any city in the United States for our population; and I assure you there is something in those homes to spank   In fact, for every car load of coffins there are six car loads of baby carriages

Around Houston there is some of the richest land in the world   I understand that in some of the New England States the soil is so poor that the natives are compelled to fertilize the cemeteries to ensure the resurrection of the dead

I will not talk to you at greater length about our State as it is too large a subject, and I know the program is long and other speakers desire the floor

Gentlemen, I thank you for your kind and considerate attention (Applause)

Mr Olin J Stephens, New York City—There are a number of us here who would like to hear from our Congressman-elect, Hon Murray Hulbert, of New York City

President Ransdell—The Chair would be glad to recognize him

Volunteer Call—Murray Hulbert, M. C., New York

Mr. Chairman and Gentlemen of the Congress, and Ladies:

It is rather false modesty which has constrained me from addressing you before this time As one of the previous speakers said of the Irishman, I am one of those native New Yorkers who is proud of his nativity, having been born and brought up upon a farm in an agricultural district, so that I early learned to appreciate the necessity for the waterways of New York, and also by reason of my being selected from the upper part of the great metropolitan city of New York as its Representative in Congress from a district bounded on the west by the Hudson River and on the east by the East River, and intersected by the Harlem River. (Applause) So you will see that during the next two years that I shall hope to represent that district in Congress I will have occasion to well remember the interests of that district so far as the development of its resources are concerned

Now, as the Mayor of our city said earlier in the session, the harbor of New York, despite the fact that it has furnished fifty per cent of the commerce of the country, has received only two per cent of the total appropriations which have been made by the Federal Government for rivers and harbors throughout its entire history

As Congressman Bennett said this afternoon, we have not needed appropriations for a greater amount, because New York harbor is a great natural waterway; but I want to call your attention to the fact now that from henceforth New York, as well as all other parts of the country, will demand its allotment of the expenditure of the public funds, because in the development of our country we have reached a point where we think it necessary to obtain for New York harbor more than has up to this time seemed reasonably sufficient.

You have been told that the State of New York had under construction waterway improvements for which it has expended up to this time the enormous sum of $140,000,000 in order to work beneficial results to at least 16,000,000 people in the West and in the Northwest.

I ask you to consider what that will mean to the future development of the harbor of New York. It will be absolutely essential to take care of this enormous traffic which will come down through the Barge Canal to New York, and a considerable part of it will be diverted from the Hudson River through the Harlem River into the East River channel. In order that that may be done and every necessary improvement may be carried out, namely, the straightening of the bend in the Harlem River, there must be mutual legislation on the part of the Federal Government and the State of New York and an assessment on that part of the land adjacent to the present ship canal, in order that that bend may be straightened out and admit of the passage of the boats that will come down the Barge Canal from the upper Hudson.

The State of New York has done its share in that respect. A law has been passed making the necessary assessment on the land and the bill has likewise passed the Senate and is now up for passage in the House of Representatives. That bill, when it goes through Congress will carry with it an expenditure on the part of the Federal Government of $1,000,000; but we have that confidence in Congress and in the forty-three Members from the State of New York, that we believe Congress will appreciate the wisdom of the enactment of that measure in the Lower House, and give to the city of New York the necessary financial assistance to carry out that improvement, and thus give to New York harbor another great outlet for the commerce that will come to us from our internal sources of the Hudson, through the Barge Canal and from the Great Lakes on the north   (Applause.) There is another matter ————

President Ransdell—Your time is up, I am sorry to say.

Mr Hulbert—Very well, I thank you, Mr President.

PRESIDENT RANSDELL—Can we hear from any other volunteer? It would be impossible to hold a RIVERS AND HARBORS CONGRESS without hearing from a man who was in it at its birth, and has been constantly one of its best friends and workers. He does not live anywhere, but his home is the United States—Mr. John A. Fox. Will you not say just a few words? We cannot excuse you, come forward and say a few words to us

Remarks—John A. Fox, Memphis, Tenn.
Secretary The Mississippi River Levee Association

MR PRESIDENT AND GENTLEMEN:

It has afforded me the greatest pleasure to watch the success of this movement which was started under such good auspices back in 1905. While, as the President states, I have not been able to participate actively in it for the past two years, it is with the greatest sense of gratification that I notice that the magazines are publishing accounts of renewed activity in transportation matters, and that the farmers are taking action with reference to terminal facilities, to see that all the good work that we have done is going to bear fruit.

Many of the people did not understand at the beginning that the movement on the part of our organization was not simply to force great appropriations from Congress. It has been the greatest gratification to all of us to know that we have planted the seed to prepare for an appreciation of the advantages of the waterways in every section of the United States.

As I meet men from the different parts of the country they tell me of the great interest that is being taken in their section in this work   One man said to me, "Fox, we date the activity in our State in the interest of waterways from the time that you were with us and awakened our vision to its possibilities. Since then we have been making great strides, not only in our own State, but for the general improvement in carrying out the policy of promoting navigation."

I think that is one of the greatest things that has grown out of the National Rivers and Harbors Congress I do not care where you go, whether passing down the Ohio, whether on the Atlantic Seaboard, or in New York, or down in Georgia, you will find that the agitation that was started by the National Rivers and Harbors Congress to call the attention of the people to the value of their waterways, has been taken up and is rapidly growing stronger and stronger I think that that is perhaps one of the reasons why it is so difficult now to get funds for the great parent organization —so many organizations have sprung up, all of which have to be taken care of, and there is so much local interest in projects of importance.   But I think that, as time goes on, this apparent lack of appreciation of the parent organization will be overcome, and work will go on nationally just as in the past.

Down in Georgia, on the Ocmulgee River, the city of Macon, when I visited there in 1906, a great many of them began to take an interest, and I noticed the other day that that city had built in Philadelphia ten 1,000-ton steel barges, and are now carrying their cotton on four feet of water from Macon to Brunswick, Ga   That is one of the finest illustrations of the usefulness of the National Rivers and Harbors Congress education campaign in calling attention to the value of waterways transportation, and I think that that field is going to be more and more exploited by the work of the Association

Out in that little city of Davenport, Iowa, they have made most marvelous strides in showing what can be accomplished in the way of terminals.   That is another illustration of the value of the work of the National Rivers and Harbors Congress

Wherever you go throughout the United States you will find the business men more inclined to encourage the utilization of the waterways as they are now, even without waiting for improvement   There is a useful field in this way for

present development, and it ought to be started and kept
going until the great ideals that all of us have cherished
shall be realized. I hope to see the time when all of these
dreams, as they have been sometimes termed, will be carried out.

I thank you for your attention. (Applause)

PRESIDENT RANSDELL—Is there any one else who has something that he would like to tell us? If not, a motion to adjourn
is in order. I want to say, before we adjourn, that the
officers, the Directors and Vice-Presidents are earnestly requested to attend a very important business meeting of the
Board of Directors in the committee room at the north end
of this hall at two o'clock sharp. We hope that all will be
present.

On motion, the Convention then adjourned without day.

Constitution and Rules
Governing the National Rivers and Harbors Congress

ARTICLE I—*Name*

This organization shall be known as the NATIONAL RIVERS AND HARBORS CONGRESS

ARTICLE II—*Objects*

(a)—The objects of this Congress shall be the collection and preparation of all obtainable data touching the scientific improvement,.development and uses of the rivers and harbors of the nation; these data to include findings of the Board of United States Engineers and other scientific facts dealing with questions of waterway transportation and allied subjects;

(b)—To disseminate to as many of the people of the United States as possible the scientific knowledge collected and prepared, through the publications of this Association, its news bureau and its field representatives—to the end that the people may be educated to the importance of waterway development, and that the greatest good to the greatest number may be had through the scientific improvement and maintenance of our lakes, rivers, harbors and canals for navigation and commerce

ARTICLE III—*Membership*

The membership of this Congress shall consist of commercial, manufacturing, and kindred organizations, waterway improvement associations, corporations, companies, and individual citizens engaged or interested in commercial or industrial enterprises, who may subscribe to this Constitution and contribute to the support and prosecution of the objects of the Congress

ARTICLE IV—*Officers*

The officers of this Congress shall be a President, and one Vice-President from each State or Territory having membership in this organization; Directors not less than twenty in number, selected from the different important geographical sections of the United States; a Secretary and a Treasurer. The offices of Secretary and Treasurer may be filled by the same person. The officers shall be elected at any regularly called meeting of the Congress, and shall continue in office until their successors are chosen.

ARTICLE V—*Conduct of Business*

The business of the Congress shall be conducted, and its objects pursued, in the interim between meetings, by the President, Secretary and Treasurer, and the Directors of the Congress, such officers to be known and designated as the "Board of Directors of the National Rivers and Harbors Congress," and to whom full power is given as to the manner in which the affairs of the Congress shall be administered.

ARTICLE VI—*Meetings*

The Congress shall meet in convention at such time and place as may be designated by the Board of Directors. The Convention shall consist of all the duly accredited members of the Congress, and others invited by authority of the Board of Directors.

ARTICLE VII—*General Duties of Board of Directors*

The Board of Directors shall designate the place where its general offices shall be located, and said Board of Directors shall keep the records of the Congress, conduct its correspondence, fix salaries of officers and employees, arrange for meetings of the Congress, and, in general, exercise all powers, as ordered in Article V, to promote and advance the objects of the Congress.

ARTICLE VIII—*Miscellaneous*

The President shall have the power to fill all the vacancies that may occur, by resignation or otherwise, in the offices of the Congress, and shall also have the power to appoint such person or persons as may be necessary to properly carry forward and prosecute the work of the Congress, reporting his action in all cases to the Board of Directors

All meetings of the Board of Directors shall be by call of the President, countersigned by the Secretary

Article IX—*Quorum*

A quorum of the Board of Directors shall consist of the members present at a meeting held in pursuance of call by the President.

Article X—*Dues*

Individuals	$ '5 00	per annum
Firms or Corporations	10 00 "	"
Organizations of 400 and less.	25 00 "	"
Organizations over 400 and less than 600	50 00 "	"
Organizations over 600 and less than 1,000	75.00 "	"
Organizations of 1,000 and more . . .	100 00 "	"
Waterway associations	100 00 "	"
Municipalities, 2,500 or less . . . . . : .	50 00 "	"
Municipalities, 2,500 to 5,000.. . . .	75 00 "	"
Municipalities, 5,000 and less than 10,000.	100 00 "	"
Municipalities, 10,000 and more	200 00 "	"

Article XI—*Votes*

All duly enrolled members shall be entitled to vote as the membership dues paid indicate—one vote for each $5 00 subscription, or the multiple thereof

TABLE OF CONTENTS

PAGE

www.ingramcontent.com/pod-product-compliance
Lightning Source LLC
Chambersburg PA
CBHW051314060726
PP18533700001B/17